LAST
CALL

LAST CALL

10 COMMONSENSE SOLUTIONS TO AMERICA'S BIGGEST PROBLEMS

ROB NELSON

Delacorte Press

dedication copy to come

ACKNOWLEDGMENTS

CONTENTS

1.

The Twilight's Last Gleaming

I WAS BORN AT THE beginning of the end of the American dream. Depending on how you see the world, I am either the tail end of the Baby Boom or the leading edge of Generation X. The bookends of two different eras, I'm either the last of the big winners in this country or the first of the big losers. Losers in an unconventional sense. Over the course of my lifetime, I've seen America grow to a level of economic success unmatched by any nation at any time in world history. Computer hackers and stoner skateboarders become multimillionaires overnight. Everybody's famous. People get their fifteen minutes today the way a generation before used to get a vaccination. We can do anything, go anywhere, become anyone. It is as if there are no longer any limits. We watch babies born on-line and see people having sex on the Internet. We can know the gender of an unborn child or cosmetically alter the size, shape, even the sex, of our bodies— overnight. We can take a cell phone to the top of Mount Everest or put a camera on Mars. We've got airbags, e-mail, ATM cards, portable computers, cell phones, hand-held global positioning systems, digital television, and remote controls. Yet despite the stunning economic and technological gains over the past three and a half decades, despite the promise, the potential, and the possibility, America began to come apart in a way that no amount of money, material achievement, or superficial prosperity could fix.

It doesn't show up in unemployment and inflation statistics, rising stock prices or a 10,000-point Dow. But as I grew up, America fell down. Beneath the blue skies and nicely manicured lawns, something wasn't right. On the surface things kept getting better, but beneath the façade of supreme world power and a thriving economy, the heart and soul of America went sour. As we became materially richer, we grew spiritually poorer, and the more we made the less we actually seemed to have, until nothing could be enough. In the process we lost our national ideals, our compassion for those with less or nothing at all, the notion of individual responsibility for the collective whole, and—perhaps worst of all— our sense of possibility, our belief in what could be, and our expectation that our leaders, our friends and neighbors and even we ourselves could be the best people we can be.

During my lifetime, America dug itself into almost $6 trillion of national debt, placing a devastating fiscal ball and chain around my future and that of my children. I watched the core, the urban center, of every major American city turn into a hell hole, wracked by violence, drugs, pollution, and rundown housing projects. I was given my most basic and critical schooling in a public school system that lacked money, talented teachers, and any real idea how to educate my generation. I saw millions of kids get lost to violence, poverty, poor education, and moral decay while the generation before me—the Baby Boomers—looked away, living with a degree of self-interest that was shocking both for its callousness and hypocrisy.

In 1994 I met with Jann Wenner, the fiftysomething founder of *Rolling Stone* magazine, to seek financial support for a political crusade I had helped begin. The organization was called Lead . . . or Leave, and its radical call for every member of Congress to pledge to quit office unless the federal deficit was chopped in half by 1996 already had attracted an enormous amount of national media attention, tens of thousands of members, the backing of Hollywood movies stars Val Kilmer and Christian Slater, and the support of national political leaders Senator Bill Bradley and presidential candidate Paul Tsongas and businessmen Ross Perot and Peter Peterson.

Wenner—a self-proclaimed liberal and unabashed Democrat—understood Lead . . . or Leave's mission and said he strongly supported it, although he wanted to be sure we weren't seeking deficit reduction at the expense of the poor. His magazine had even considered naming Lead . . . or Leave the hottest political group of the year. He was friendly, even inviting me to come up to his country house to go motorcycle riding. But when I pressed him for financial support, he looked at me rather quizzically and asked why. It seemed to me that the goal of our initiative—to demand accountability from a Washington power establishment that was out of control and recklessly mortgaging the economic future of the nation—was reason enough. Still, I suggested to him that if that alone didn't do it for him, there was another more self-interested reason—to protect and improve his children's future. I'll never forget Wenner's laugh. His children? He looked at me and smiled. His children would never need anything, he assured me. They would always be protected. The millions Wenner had made from *Rolling Stone* had made sure of that.

That's great, I thought. But what about the rest of his kids' generation? The ones who weren't lucky enough to have the founder of *Rolling Stone* magazine for a father? Even more troubling, what had happened to those ideals that Wenner and his friends made such a big deal about in the 1960s? Had he lost them or conveniently forgotten them in favor of financial security? Sure he was a "liberal" when it came to taking a position on abstract policies, but, like so many of his peers, the compassion and the sense of responsibility didn't seem to reach his own doorstep. Talk is cheap—as long as you aren't the one who has to pay for it. After all, Jann Wenner would be dead by the time the bills came due. In the meantime, he'd lead a great life, go to all the right parties, and never want for anything. And, as he pointed out to me, his kids would inherit a multi-million-dollar trust fund.

If I sound a little bitter, I guess it's because the mess that many in Wenner's generation want to avoid seeing is something my generation will spend the rest of our lives trying to repair and to pay for. Trillions of dollars in unfunded liabilities like Social Security and Medicare, a massive national debt, skyrocketing living costs, medical inflation and rising numbers of—mostly younger—uninsured people, deteriorating public schools, growing racial tensions, the highest rate of incarceration in the world, an environmental sustainability crisis, and global economic and political climate that poses multiple risks to American prosperity and security.

Meanwhile, our so-called political leaders are all talk and

no action. They're so vested in partisan politics that they'll disregard the national good for political gain—as in the 1994 congressional election, when the Democrats trashed the Republican's moderate and necessary reforms of Medicare; or in 1993 when Republicans pounced on President Clinton's much-needed attempt to revamp our healthcare system. Both sides are so determined to destroy each other that they can barely agree on what the problems are. Neither party accepts responsibility for the nation's problems; few, if any, nationally elected officials accept personal responsibility (if you're not part of the solution you are part of the problem) or will admit that there is so much more they could do both individually and collectively. No one wants to risk his or her political future to achieve solutions. And you wonder why we're all so apathetic.

In 1996, my role as a twentysomething political activist in the previous election earned me an offer to join the national youth steering committee for President Clinton's reelection campaign. Despite my independent status and my hatred of the two-party lockup on politics, I accepted the role—hoping that in exchange for my help in bringing the president more votes, I could get him to do more to reach out to younger voters and begin to reinvest them in the political process. Not an easy thing to do, convincing the cynics in my generation to get involved, but I had a plan: a Kennedy-like challenge from the president to younger Americans, combined with a first-of-its-kind real admission by a president that he understood young America's political apathy and accepted partial responsiblility—along with his party—for the disconnect and would promise to do more to combat it. It wouldn't end apathy overnight, but it would be a great start. OK, I was going to sell my soul a little bit to support an "insider" about whom I had mixed feelings, but it would be worth it, I reasoned, if I actually got the president to do what I was proposing.

It was the beginning of my second year at law school, so I decided to split my time between California and Washington for the months of September and October, and I jumped on board the reelection campaign with all my energy. But getting the campaign to support my idea proved difficult. I soon discovered that some people didn't really want this event to take place and, after a series of setbacks that threatened the whole endeavor, I knew the only way it would happen was if I could get a shot at selling the president on my idea face to face. Presidential campaigns are full of back doors as well as trapdoors, and through a mutual friend I was able to arrange a meeting with Mr. Clinton. This was my chance. In some ways it was one of the most unique opportunities I'd ever had—an informal, private meeting with the President of the United States.

The meeting took place late one October night in the Solarium—kind of like the president's living room—on the second floor of the private residence in the East Wing of the White House. The room was warm and comfortable, so lived in that Mr. Clinton's nephew's toys were scattered across the floor. On the wall, amid pictures of the president and his family with all kinds of famous people, were pictures of one of Mr. Clinton's political heroes, John F. Kennedy. It was impressive, I had to admit. Unlike JFK, this guy had gotten himself here on his own drive. No one gave this to Bill Clinton, and I admired that.

I walked onto the balcony overlooking the South Lawn and the Rose Garden. What a view. From the balcony you could see straight out to the Jefferson Memorial, and there was Thomas Jefferson staring straight at you—the only place in the world you could get that perspective. I climbed up on the wide ledge and started pacing, a Diet Coke in my hand. Not bad, I thought. Then I heard a woman's voice behind me, and I turned to see a darkly clad Secret Service agent patrolling the roof and manning an anti-aircraft gun. You surprised me, she said—much to my relief, with a smile. Don't worry. I figured if you'd gotten this far you must be OK. I laughed but was also dramatically aware at that moment of the immense power of the presidency. I hurried back inside, stoked for the meeting I was about to have.

A few minutes later the president walked in, smiled, and said hello. He was dressed casually in jeans and a Polo shirt, and he looked fit and rested. I had to give it to Clinton; he wore the presidency well. As I shook his hand, I couldn't help thinking of the image of a young Clinton shaking John F. Kennedy's hand thirty years earlier right below the window I now stood in front of. What did Bill Clinton feel on that day? Was it more than the thrill of coming to face to face with power? Did he feel what I did now—an intangible, almost spiritual sense of the meaning of America, of what it stood for, what made it work, and the awesome opportunity and responsibility we the people shared in making it work?

The pictures of JFK reminded me that the reason the martyred president had left such a deep mark on Clinton and others in his generation was because they were so inspired by him. Whatever else he was, whatever his other faults, Kennedy had the ability and the willingness to get out front and lead. We'd been talking for a few minutes when I took a deep breath, looked right at the president, and told him what was on my mind. I said that I thought most people in America, and particularly those in my generation, were longing for someone today to lead in the way Kennedy did thirty-five years ago. Clinton could do that, I suggested. He had that kind of energy. But so far he hadn't done it, at least not in the eyes of most people I knew.

Until that moment, the president had seemed more interested in the TV to his right, which was playing CNN Headline Sports. Now he was looking me straight in the eyes, his stare sharp and intense. He didn't disagree. In fact, the president actually acknowledged the problem to a degree but said he didn't think it was entirely his fault. People were apathetic, there was anti-Clinton bias in much of the media, and his own political handlers often held him back. The president said he wanted to do more to reach out to younger voters. Exactly what did I have in mind?

Things are different for us than they were for you, I said. You don't need to set up any more governmental programs or offer any new entitlements for younger voters. We don't need to be bribed, we need to be inspired. This is your chance to do something truly historic. At the pinnacle of your presidency—at the height of your power—you rise above partisan politics, call on younger Americans to plug back into the political process and forge a cross-generational alliance to tackle the problems facing America. Then to the surprise of everyone, in the middle of a reelection campaign, you accept responsibility on behalf of the entire political power structure for the problems that have led so many younger Americans to disconnect—and you promise to meet us halfway. You make us a generational challenge. This, I told the president, could be his legacy. This could be his JFK.

I know it sounds a little like a movie script, but at that moment, the president agreed with me. He even asked me to write a draft speech and set up an event where he could issue such a challenge. He'd be there, he promised. Idealistic—or maybe naive—but I believed him. So I suspended any fears that I was just getting the famous "presidential treatment" and set out to get it done, convinced that the only thing that stood between me and seeing the president begin something that could really make a difference for my generation was a couple of weeks of time and some logistical concerns.

A few weeks later when the president stepped off of *Air Force One* in Atlanta, I was there on the tarmac and in the receiving line to shake his hand. I rode in the motorcade to the event, wide-eyed as traffic on the main freeway into Atlanta was stopped to let us pass.

It was noon, and 15,000 people were gathered in Woodruff Park in downtown Atlanta for what was a dedicated campaign event for younger voters. I couldn't believe it. Cracker, a southern band I've always loved, opened the event. Michael Stipe was on the dais with the president; along with the governor of Georgia; the mayor of Atlanta; John Lewis, a well-known congressman and former civil rights activist; and a handful of random VIPs. MTV came with cameras, along with the usual network news people, the national press, and some big daily newspapers. It wasn't Woodstock, but it was a start.

I was offstage, about twenty feet from the microphones, and I felt a shake go through my body as the president approached the podium, speech in hand. His speechwriters had rewritten my draft the night before, and while the rewrite wasn't everything I had hoped for, it came close to the mark—close enough anyway. Besides, the president is famous for his improvisational skills. He'll take the spirit of it and make it even better, I thought.

Sadly, he didn't make it better. He didn't even read it. The president tucked the prepared text into his suit pocket and gave a slightly modified version of the same old campaign speech that he had given a hundred times before in the last two months and would give three more times before the end of the day—all about building a bridge to the twenty-first century and how he and the Democrats were going to do it. There was no inspiring call to action, no admission of responsibility for the generational disconnect, and no non-partisanship.

My speech had the president admitting that partisanship and finger-pointing between Democrats and Republicans was a major reason for the political disconnect among younger Americans and promising to begin to change that. The president's speech bashed the Republicans, blamed them for most of America's problems, and praised Democrats—all of them—arguing that theirs was the right path for America. My speech asked younger Americans to vote—regardless of whom they voted for, even Bob Dole—but to vote. The president's speech made clear that voting for anyone but him and the Democrats was a big mistake. My speech issued a clear challenge to younger Americans, promising to meet them in the middle if they would give the political process a second chance. The president's speech criticized our apathy and warned that it would lead to the kind of bad policies the Republicans and particularly Newt Gingrich proposed. The president's solution, of course, was voting for Clinton-Gore and electing more Democrats to Congress—and he urged everyone to go out and encourage their friends to go to the polls to do just that. What the president said that day in Atlanta didn't really make things any worse. It just didn't do a thing to make them any better.

I was shocked. I was angry. My knees felt weak and I had a knot in my stomach. I wanted to run up and take the microphone away from him and tell everyone listening that this wasn't what the president had said he would say; that he really believed something else but was just afraid to go out on a limb and say it. But of course I didn't. Instead, I stood silently, my heart in my stomach, feeling another layer of my idealism peel away, to be replaced by a veneer of apathy and discouragement, the very thing the president's speech was supposed to counter.

As Mr. Clinton walked toward his limousine, he came up to me and placed his big hand on my shoulder. "How'd we do?" he asked me. We—how did *we* do? Because, after all, I was now part of it. And I am ashamed to this day to admit that I looked the president straight in the eyes and said: "Fine. You were great." What was the point of saying what I really thought? I argued to myself. I'd already done that. He wasn't going to listen. He couldn't hear. What would my honesty accomplish, I rationalized, other than to make certain that I never had another conversation with the president? So I remained silent. And the frustration at feeling unheard, the fury at a leadership that doesn't get it, and the disgust of having watched the president give younger Americans a Hallmark card invitation to vote all went unspoken.

I'd truly compromised myself and felt betrayed by my decision. Talk about losing your ideals. Just a few years before I had written an article in the *New York Times* that called Clinton a coward for refusing to take a principled stand on Social Security reform, a generational economic issue I knew had critical implications for the future of the country. I'd felt fearless then, that anything was possible, and that if enough of us refused to sit by quietly swallowing the status quo, we could redefine it. Standing with the president in Georgia that day, I couldn't have felt farther away from those convictions and the events that inspired them.

JANUARY 1992: UPSTATE NEW YORK

I climbed out of my tent and looked at the thermometer: −25 degrees. It was so cold I wondered if maybe I should just forget about the ice climb I was planning to do. But after a warm breakfast I felt better. The sun would warm things up, I figured. Besides, I'd recently come back from summiting Mount Chimborazo, a nearly 21,000-foot peak in Ecuador, and I really wanted to do as much ice climbing as possible before the winter was over. Resolved, I put on my climbing boots and headed out to the site.

After walking up a steep pathway to the base of the climb, I decided to see how well my new boot crampons held to the face. Testing the ice, I hacked up a couple of feet on the short wall in front of me. I skipped the usual protection to avoid falls as the whole thing seemed harmless enough. I figured the worst that could happen is I'd fall a couple of feet onto my ass. As I kicked a couple quick steps up, I felt the steel points of the crampons dig into the wall. But as I planted my axes, the thin crust of ice covering the rock crumbled, and I found myself holding to the wall by only my toes. As I reached to replant an ax, the ice at my feet broke free, sending me crashing onto the ledge four feet below.

A wave of shame rushed over me. I was an idiot to have been playing around without protection on an exposed wall of ice. I knew better. In fact, it was exactly the kind of thing that I would have been quick to point out to someone else. Still, other than embarrassment, it wasn't really much to worry about—that is, until I realized I was sliding upside down and backward toward the edge of the cliff. I had just enough time to roll over onto my stomach and see the rock-strewn, ice-covered field below me. In a desperate last-minute attempt to avert disaster, I swung my axes toward the ground, a maneuver called a self-arrest. But it was too late. I was already halfway into the void, falling headfirst toward a hillside of frozen ice and snow nearly thirty feet below. I landed flat on my back, the reflex action of the fall driving an ice ax into the right side of my climbing helmet, shattering the helmet and missing my temple by three inches. The impact of the fall broke my leg, severely sprained my ankle, bruised several of my ribs, and gave me a minor concussion. I should have died. In fact, as I tumbled over the edge, there wasn't a doubt in my mind.

As I slid face first over that ledge, my initial thoughts of defiance—that death is a roll of the dice, that nothing in life is preordained, that other people have fallen farther than this and lived—were quickly covered by an overpowering feeling that came from somewhere deep inside myself. It was a quiet, unassuming, and certain sensation of my own death. "You are about to die," I heard my inner voice say. "You are about to die."

So with my body hanging between two worlds, the past where my feet and legs remained and the future toward which my upper body had begun to fall, I did the only thing left to do. I gave in to fate. As I plummeted toward the ice below, I closed my eyes, put down all resistance, and was, as I had never been before and have never been since, completely and totally present.

It saved my life. Accepting the inevitable end that was to come, I completely relaxed. Like a drunk going through a windshield, my body offered no resistance to the severe impact it was about to absorb. Time slowed down, the chaos replaced by calm. Even the ice field looming below seemed to change, my mind's eye replacing the hard sharp surface with pictures of the giant snowdrifts I remember from my childhood in Wisconsin.

As I somersaulted toward the ground, episodes of my life flashed through my mind—sort of a best-of rerun. I saw everything from my first Christmas tree to the day my little brother died. Nearly three decades of life rushed across my brain—right up to that morning when I lay huddled in a tent, the temperature outside 25 below zero, almost deciding it was just too cold to get up.

Then I saw myself lying in a bed, surrounded by four men and a woman—the Technicolor flashbacks of a moment before replaced with stark black and white. The woman keeps asking me to tell her what happened, but I can't seem to remember. I don't understand why she won't just tell me. Finally she gets up and turns toward the men. They nod their heads slowly and in unison. The woman smiles at me. "You were all right," she says quietly.

The room vanished, and I suddenly felt my will begin fighting against the cocoon of the out-of-body experience. I'm not ready to go yet, I thought. It's not my time. Not now. Not yet. For the first time, I felt my body rushing toward the ground and then there was a terrific thud, as I slammed flat on my back into the ice.

Back in Washington, D.C., as I lay in my bed recovering, I couldn't shake the feeling of that fall, the haunting images. It awoke in me a sense of my own incompleteness. What had I done in my life that really mattered? How had I really made a difference? Sure, I had thought about it plenty. My own idealism had led me to Washington, but five years later I was more disillusioned than ever. Politics in America was a sham. Despite an electoral system that promised citizen control at the ballot box every two and four years, politicians were completely unaccountable. Their shortsighted thinking, and

our willingness to go along, had put at risk an entire generation of Americans.

From environmental standards to fiscal and budgetary
policy, Washington was mortgaging the future to finance the
present—and the consequences were growing more severe.
Our schools were in disrepair; 20 percent of our kids lived in
poverty; the environment was deteriorating; and, worst of all,
massive increases in military and entitlement spending had
saddled America with a $4 trillion debt, a deficit rising at the
rate of $200-plus billion a year—and no one in Washington
appeared willing to do what was necessary to plug this leak
in America's fiscal dam and begin to revitalize the country.

I was right about Washington, right about the deteriora-
tion of American democracy and the loss of accountability
from our leaders. And I was right that most people, just like
me, had lost their faith in politics. But I couldn't shake that
nagging question: What had I done to try and change it?

Ten weeks later, my leg and ankle tightly wrapped, I returned to the Adirondacks, hired a guide, and climbed
Chouinard's Folly, a 250-foot vertical wall of frozen water.
This time I was scared. The truth is, I have always been
afraid of heights, and although I managed not to let it bother
me for most of the climb, as I neared the top, the overhang
jutting out above me became terrifying. It was only about
twelve vertical feet of ice, but it bulged out two and half feet
behind my head like a massive breast. Once over it, it was an
easy twenty-five feet to the top, but to get there first I had to
maneuver out and over the lip of the overhang, an endeavor
that meant climbing sort of upside down, with my back and
head hanging out into thin air.

I drove my ax into a solid-looking spot on the ice as high
up as I could reach, planted a boot at about knee level, and
started to pull my body up. Suddenly my hold gave and the

ax broke off the ice, sending me toppling down six feet to the end of my safety line. As I felt the line jerk tight I let out my breath. My heart was in my throat. I hung there—cold, tired, and frustrated. I couldn't go down, and I didn't feel like I would ever get over that bulge. My ankle was throbbing, my hands were numb, and as I looked down at the Jeep Cherokee parked 200 feet below me, I wondered what I was trying to prove.

"I'm stuck," I yelled up to the top of the ridge where my guide sat waiting. "I don't think I can make it."

There was a moment of silence and then my guide's distinctive New Hampshire accent. "You don't really have any other choice, now, do you?" Ten hard minutes later, as I scrambled up the scree at the top of ridge, I realized my guide's wisdom applied to more than just this ice flow.

When I looked out over the rest of my life, I realized that I had been avoiding all kinds of tough choices. I'd arrived in Washington a believer, convinced that real change in politics was possible and that I could help make it happen. Yet, as the wear and tear of daily life in the Capitol set in, I started to become like everyone else—immune to the problems, convinced that real change was impossible—or at best could happen only gradually—and resigned myself to the fact that the notion of a nation governed by the people and for the people existed just in textbooks. Sitting on top of that mountain that day, I knew that didn't have to be true.

Within five weeks I had quit my job, deferred law school at Stanford, and teamed up with Jon Cowan, a frustrated young aide to a mediocre California congressman, to launch Lead . . . or Leave, a grass-roots citizen movement with a simple but huge mission: Call the political system to accountability. Our plan was straightforward and, depending on how you choose to look at it, either brilliant or stupid. At the time, most people we knew thought Jon and I were nuts. Those unfamiliar with the inner workings of the national government thought the system was so massive and well guarded that average citizens couldn't possibly have an impact. Friends on the Hill warned that we would never succeed and that we'd piss off so many powerful people in the process that neither of us would work again in Washington or national politics—a prospect that seemed much worse to them than to either of us.

The cynics were right about how much our actions would agitate people. Our tactics, our brashness, and our undiluted conviction threatened Washington, from the ultra-insider members of Congress and the White House, to staffers on Capitol Hill, national news reporters, special interest lobbyists, heads of think tanks, traditional political activists, and even those in the Washington-based national nonprofit community. When you rock the boat hard enough, it pisses off everyone on board.

Lead . . . or Leave's opening salvo was a deficit pledge. Cut the deficit in half—or quit. The pledge warned that the national debt and rapidly rising federal deficit were putting at risk the future of an entire generation of Americans; that Congress had tried and failed for over a decade to fix the problem—in our view not very sincerely; and that the only solution left was for individual members of Congress to take personal responsibility for the problem by promising to leave office in 1996 if the deficit wasn't cut in half. We reasoned that if every single member of Congress (or even a substantial majority) put his or her job on the line for deficit reduction, the deficit would get cut. Otherwise, they'd all just keep pointing fingers at one another and the problem would continue to worsen.

We were right—and they were scared. Because when you

came right down to it, most members of Congress didn't really want to be accountable to the voters; they preferred to hide behind the constitutional façade of biannual elections to argue that they were. Convinced that a stronger form of accountability was needed, and determined to be heard—even if we failed—we sent all 535 of them a copy of the pledge. We were ignored. Staffers on Capitol Hill refused our calls. Reporters laughed at us and hung up. Our friends said I told you so. Then something serendipitous happened. A very rare and convicted politician took notice of what we were doing. Former U.S. Senator Paul Tsongas (D.Mass.) had just withdrawn from the presidential race. A straight talker and a deficit hawk with years of experience in the national government, Tsongas realized that conventional methods were failing. "I guess it's come to this," he told us one day after agreeing to support our effort.

A month later, in early August, Tsongas and Republican heavyweight Warren Rudman, a former Senator from New Hompshire, stood beside Jon and me at the National Press Club and endorsed the Lead . . . or Leave pledge. "What these young people are asking for . . . is imminently doable," Senator Rudman boomed. "The plans exist to do it today, the political will does not. . . . These young people are simply saying stop killing off our future. They're right. We're going to help them in every way that we can." Tsongas issued a stern warning to the packed room of reporters: "It is my view that this country is heading towards generational warfare. . . . [T]hat is the legacy of the last decade, and both Democrats and Republicans are responsible for that."

The political establishment was shocked. Two of its own, caving to the little people—throwing their political capital behind two guys with a populist dream and a plan of action. Presidential candidate Clinton called the pledge a gimmick and refused to take it. The Bush White House lied outright and claimed they had already addressed the deficit problem. The leadership of both parties in Congress remained silent, trying to avoid the whole event. But the ball was already in motion. The Lead or Leave pledge was the top story on NBC news that night, with reporter Lisa Meyers calling it a politician's worst nightmare and labeling our fledging effort David against Goliath. National Public Radio warned politicians to watch their backs. The next day over 20,000 people called Lead . . . or Leave's makeshift headquarters. Almost overnight a political movement was born.

During the next two months, Lead . . . or Leave organized a national campaign that pressured over 100 candidates for Congress to "Take the Pledge." The ranking Republican in Congress, Illinois Congressman Bob Michael, took it. So did longshot Georgia senatorial candidate Paul Coverdell, who, after taking the pledge, won the support of both Lead . . . or Leave and Ross Perot's United We Stand party, helping him defeat incumbent Wyche Fowler, Jr., by only 7,000 votes. Ross Perot even took the pledge on national television during the third presidential debate.

People all over America joined our cause, creating the first-of-its-kind citizen accountability movement in American history—an outcome-based term limit, administered nationally, and enforced by a self-imposed pledge to leave office if the goal wasn't met. Mini–Lead . . . or Leave chapters sprang up all over the country creating pressure on their respective congressional candidates to take the pledge. Challengers often led the way, forcing incumbents to an uncomfortable place: Meet the bid or lose credibility. In Colorado this forced all three candidates for the U.S. Senate (the Republican, Democrat, and Independent) to take the pledge so as not to lose votes to the others. Talk radio boosted the effort and helped spread the word. At one point, albeit briefly, the leadership of both parties in Congress considered having their candidates take the pledge en masse to galvanize support and sweep their party into office. President George Bush even considered taking it. Maybe it would have helped him win.

By election day, only two months after we entered the public consciousness, our effort had shown that a broad-based citizen accountability movement was both feasible and appealing to a broad cross-section of the American people. And although pledge takers didn't win anything close to a majority of seats in Congress, Lead . . . or Leave had an impact that reverberated for over a year in the White House and kept pressure on Congress to deal with the deficit problem, which it finally started to do.

Over the next two years, Lead . . . or Leave became the most prominent "Generation X" political organization in the United States, with 30,000 official members, chapters in all 50 states, and a loosely affiliated college network spanning 150 universities. Lead . . . or Leave organized the biggest student voter registration campaign in U.S. history, held the only national youth summit in America since 1970, and made headline news by holding the first-ever rally in support of reforming Social Security. In just over two years we raised almost $2 million in contributions, generated a national public dialogue over Social Security reform, and distributed an economic curriculum to thousands of high schools across America.

Our bipartisan approach generated both support and opposition from every corner. Lead . . . or Leave's advisory board included people as different as Lee Iacocca, former Congresswoman Barbara Jordan, Paul Tsongas, governors Bill Weld and Ann Richards, and actors Val Kilmer and

Christian Slater. Lead . . . or Leave was profiled on all three network newscasts, CNN Headline News, and *60 Minutes,* and in the *New York Times, USA Today,* and *Time.* Jon or I appeared on *Nightline, Politically Incorrect, Talk Back Live, C-Span, The Today Show, Good Morning America, Crossfire,* and numerous other national news programs and talk shows, and were on the cover *U.S. News & World Report.* It was quite a ride.

Of course, success always looks easier—and more glamorous—in hindsight and from the outside. By the beginning of 1995, Lead . . . or Leave was running out of money and into an increasing number of seemingly insurmountable hurdles. We had too many people on staff for our budget, but still not enough to do all the work we had before us. Grassroots operations were costing far more than they were bringing in from new members. Our national phone network alone was costing us upward of $15,000 a month in long-distance bills, and our national high school education campaign, "Get Real!"—something both Jon and I were enormously proud of—wasn't designed to produce a cent, but it cost us thousands.

Having a mostly under–thirty-five constituency hurt us financially and hindered us inside the Washington Beltway, where constituencies made up of older voters carry the most clout. Thousands of people had joined Lead . . . or Leave, but the average donation was only about $5.00—barely enough to cover the cost of sending out information several times a year. And the big donors that every nonprofit political organization depends on to stay alive were harder to come by for a nonpartisan group like Lead . . . or Leave that wouldn't pick one political party or the other to support. Our diehard donors were getting tired of contributing. They wanted us to broaden the financial base. We wanted to as well, but to do so we needed more time and a different political climate.

The 1994 congressional election didn't give us either. It put in power a conservative Republican Congress, bringing partisanship in Washington to a new high. If remaining politically neutral was a challenge earlier, now it was nearly impossible. By 1995 almost no one in Washington wanted to help a nonpartisan accountability organization. Although we had 30,000 members, we were still way short of the critical mass necessary to force the kind of legislative changes we wanted, and since we had been pigeonholed as a "youth" organization, it was tough to attract significant support from the older generations—support that would be critical to winning reform of Social Security.

On top of the external problems, I was tired, burned out, and discouraged. I questioned whether Lead . . . or Leave was viable in its current form, whether we could remain independent, and, for the first time, I began to doubt whether I could continue to make a difference. I felt like I'd had the shit kicked out of me for two and half years and wasn't sure any longer how effective I or our organization was. Despite the leverage we had created, change in Washington seemed so elusive and even then possible only by compromising on core principles in order to garner support—something both Jon and I remained unwilling to do. Yet by refusing to compromise on our radical positions regarding Social Security and the deficit, we alienated both the huge special interest groups like the American Association of Retired Persons (AARP) (with 35 million members) and also large and influential advocacy organizations on both sides of the political aisle who feared our efforts would lead to cutbacks in their pet programs.

A good example of the way you can get shut out was our

experience trying to get corporate support for our efforts. As we neared completion of a deal to have an MCI/Lead . . . or Leave phone card (a great vehicle for fund raising since a portion of every cardholder's phone calls would go to our nonprofit organization), an MCI executive privately informed me that a top AARP lobbyist had just threatened to send out a national fund-raising letter telling all AARP members to switch to Sprint if MCI issued the phone card. He told me that even if 1 percent acted on it, it would be a serious dent in MCI's business. He was sorry, he said. MCI just couldn't take the chance.

At the same time, our refusal to side with either the Democrats or the Republicans cost us not only financial support but political backing. We had a growing list of powerful opponents in both the White House and on Capitol Hill. We were blocked from participation in the President's Special Commission on Entitlement Reform—something the president had agreed to attend and support in exchange for a critical democratic vote on the budget from Pennsylvania Congresswoman Marjorie Mezvinsky. Although the congresswoman had expressly asked that Lead . . . or Leave participate, and there was no other twentysomething group that was more deserving of a seat at the table, a top white House staffer told one of the congresswoman's senior aides in no uncertain terms that if Lead . . . or Leave was there, the president wouldn't be. A less controversial organization was chosen in our place.

So in early 1995, facing growing financial and logistical difficulties, Jon and I reluctantly closed the doors of Lead . . . or Leave and went on with our lives. I went off to law school, which I had already deferred for the past three years, and Jon took a job in the Clinton administration. It was one of the low points in my life. I had good reasons for leaving and knew that it was only temporary—that one day I'd be back again—and yet I always will believe that by going when I did, I let the bastards beat me down. Walking away was exactly what a lot of insiders and people in power wanted us to do. It played right into their hands—and into their ideas about citizen movements. And they wasted no time trashing us for leaving—attacking our character, commitment, and genuineness.

It was terribly hard to accept. After all, Jon and I had built a national political organization from scratch—starting with just the two of us in a tiny one room office and ultimately mobilizing tens of thousands of people and becoming a critical force in creating awareness about generational economic inequities. Lead . . . or Leave had helped Washington find the political will to take on the budget deficit. It had led a successful effort to show Americans that Social Security was heading for collapse and to force our national leaders to stop denying the problems, and begin to address it. And Jon and I had dedicated two and a half years of our lives, spent thousands of dollars from our own pockets, and fought tirelessly for our cause. But success breeds jealousy and contempt. There was a line of Judas' forming outside, and no matter what good we had done, we were going to get crucified.

We went from media darlings and political wonderkids to charlatans and pariahs. *Newsweek* ran a scathing article titled "Gen X's Dynamic Duo Burns Out." *U.S. News & World Report*, which had put us on their cover two years before, smugly noted that "the leaders of Lead . . . or Leave have decided to leave." It seemed that everyone in Washington who ever had a grudge—real or perceived, personal or professional—against us, who had ever been jealous of our success, who had ever said we would fail, took their shot. Jon and I had stormed into Washington with guns blazing and a take-no-prisoners approach and stirred up the dust. Now we were leaving—our work unfinished, our sprits broken, and our organization bankrupt.

Still, worse than all that, I felt I let a lot of people down—people who shared my desire for fundamental political change and who were emotionally invested in our cause. That fact will probably always hurt, although, looking back, I don't know if I could have done it differently. I felt defeated. Despite everything I had put in motion, I'd lost faith in my own ability to make change. I felt powerless, as if I were hurtling myself against a brick wall. That's how insidious and entrenched the system is and how hard it is to do anything transformative.

I was also beginning to feel sucked in, swallowed alive, like Captain Ahab in *Moby Dick*. And in a way, I had been. I left Washington, but that sense of powerlessness and futility moved with me across the country. I entered law school looking fine from the outside but feeling like a complete failure within. A cloud of shame hung over my head. No matter how I justified it, I was throwing in the towel on my own ideals—and that had consequences I had not prepared for. Leaving the East Coast for sunny California may have looked easy, but it came at a high price.

Standing with the president in Atlanta a year later, I realized how high that price was. I now doubted my once–rock-sure confidence that real change in America was possible—that enough of us united could make a difference, that America's biggest challenges could be met, and that America could again become the vibrant democracy it once was. I'd lost sight not only of my ideals but also of my faith in myself and of the power in standing for the truth whatever the cost. I'd started to sell out, to compromise, and to settle. Like almost everyone else I knew, I justified my feelings and my corresponding actions, but that didn't make them any more valid or any less disappointing.

I realized something else as well. The only way the system wins is if you let it declare victory. As long as you keep trying—as long as you are in there fighting—you are making progress. When the people who want something different—those who believe there can be something better—give up, stop trying, or, even worse, stop caring, that's when the status quo plants a flag and declares victory. That's what had started to happen to me. I'd begun to give up, and that's exactly what we cannot afford to let happen.

TODAY IN AMERICA

As we head into the twenty-first century, America faces the most serious dilemma in the 200-plus year history of our nation. Our democracy is in trouble. Despite a superficial gloss of good times, the social, economic, and moral foundations on which this country was built are cracking. For the first time in history, one generation of Americans is going to pass to another a nation worse off in so many critical respects than the nation they inherited from their parents. And the sad fact is that most people seem resigned to this fate.

Apathy, wide and deep, rushes through the veins of the American public. Less than half of all Americans vote, and of those who do many do so out of obligation—voting for the lesser of two evils. Despite an almost total absence of good leaders, few candidates step forward with a new vision or the promise of actually being different. Diversity in our political process is all but gone, leaving us with a homogeneity and mediocrity that is both boring and bad. Most people just tune out. Can you blame them? It's not that people don't care; rather they don't think there is anything they really can do to change the big problems affecting our nation. But we can.

There's an opportunity to change the course of America, to restore the economic, social, political, and moral foundations that brought us this far—but the window is closing. We stand at the crossroads of the most historic time in modern human history, the end of one millennium and the beginning of another. In the generation that I have been alive, America has reached the apex of its material orbit, becoming a nation of unsurpassed economic and technological development. At the same time, we've bottomed out politically, losing sight of our ideals, relinquishing our commitment to participation, and burying our sense of a greater national purpose. We have become a nation oblivious to the long-term consequences of our actions, arrogant in our economic and political security, and indifferent to the fate of those less fortunate. We have become, politically speaking, fat and lazy.

It's not that things, from a material standpoint, aren't good for most Americans. Nevertheless, an enormous number of people fall between the statistical cracks and are not riding the economic boom, and sooner or later in some form or another their failure to make it will affect us all. Besides, life is about so much more than making money, and when it comes to many of the things that a paycheck can't satisfy—from noneconomic quality-of-life issues, to emotional and spiritual satisfaction, to the world we will leave future generations and the nature and meaning of our national purpose—few people I know are truly satisfied with the course America is on.

"Things are good right now." I hear that comment so often it makes me wonder all the more what we're trying so hard to avoid seeing. If everything is so great, why does everyone feel the need to say it so much? Who are we trying to convince?

OK, the stock market is good, the subway is safe in New York City, and property values in a handful of places are rising. New technology is creating new jobs, and for the best and the brightest, the world has never looked better. But what about everyone else? How wide and how deep is the economic boom? And how much wider and deeper is the economic despair? Maybe you're all right today, but will you be in five years? What about your kids and their kids? And even if you and your family will stay on top, is "I'm OK, so screw everyone else" the kind of nation you want to live in, the kind of community you want to be a part of and the kind of values you want to practice? It's not the kind I want.

Idealism in America isn't dead, but it's being buried alive. There are millions of people out there who want a different kind of politics in America, who want to see things done differently, and who don't feel the current political system speaks for them, to them, or about the things that most concern them. Yet despite the massive disconnect, when you talk about making radical changes to the system, many people equivocate, defending the status quo and arguing against reform. They say America's political system has worked for more than 200 years; that it may not be perfect, but it's the best one ever designed; and that if we try to change the parts that are broken, it might only make the whole thing worse.

I don't buy any of it.

Just because the original plan worked for the first 200 years doesn't mean it's going to work for the next 200. American democracy may have done well for twelve generations of Americans, but I'm part of the thirteenth—and from where I sit, I see a system that is a real mess and only getting worse.

The establishment is bankrupt, and in the last thirty years American democracy has become a caricature of the powerful ideal the 1776 Revolution created. That doesn't diminish the greatness of the first two centuries of the American political experiment. It only highlights the need to put our democracy back on track. And now is the perfect time to do it.

Could repairing what's broken cause more damage? Possibly. But when something as vital as the operating system of a nation is damaged, the argument that trying to fix it might cause more damage is a bad reason to avoid the necessary repairs. In fact, it borders on irresponsible. Our democracy is in real jeopardy, and looking the other way while it completely disintegrates is stupid and unacceptable. The phrase "fiddling while Rome burns" is a metaphor based on historical fact.

Finally, to the argument that American democracy is the best political system in human history, I couldn't agree more. But that doesn't mean it can't be improved upon. The Founding Fathers did a good job, but they designed something that was suited for a world 300 years ago, before television, the Internet, and instant communication; before global finance, electronic surveillance, and metropolises; for a society that still thought of women and blacks as property. It might be possible for one system to go unchanged for a half a millennium, but holding to the past for the past's sake is naive and shortsighted. I'm not saying the basic premise of American democracy is bad. I think it's brilliant. But let's be honest: The Founding Fathers weren't gods. They couldn't see the future. And what made perfect sense in 1776 doesn't necessarily fit in the year 2000.

That the Founding Fathers and other heavyweights of American political history did or didn't think something doesn't make it automatically true or false. Just because they were very right about some things doesn't mean they weren't very wrong about others. And just because something worked for them in 1776 doesn't mean that it's still best for us today. The fact is some of the institutions they created need to be changed to fit the times we live in. And that's true whether you're talking about Thomas Jefferson, Alexander Hamilton, George Washington, or Franklin Roosevelt. It's about the right idea at the right time. It's about institutions that fit the needs of the people they are supposed to serve. We should ask the simplest, most pragmatic question: What works and what doesn't? Forget about what they did or didn't do before us. What is right for America today? What would make your life, my life—our children's lives—better?

Besides, no good institution is reform-proof, and no system, however well designed, can continue to operate effectively without being upgraded and adapted to the times. Even the VW Bug and the original Jeep were refitted for the '90s. So before anyone goes and calls me a Communist or anti–free market, or un-American, I want to be really clear. I believe in this country and what it stands for. That's why I'm so angry. In fact, I'm not arguing at all with the basic premise of American democracy, only with our national inaction in the face of the fact that this ideal is going unfulfilled and that the promise of a better America for generations to come is in serious jeopardy. The nation that Lincoln said was of the people, for the people, by the people has become anything but. The "people" are getting screwed. A small number of institutional insiders run the country, control the media, and manage and own most of the wealth. American democracy is running on autopilot.

Be patient, say the generations ahead of me. Fuck that. I've waited my whole life. Promise after promise. Lie after lie. Nothing ever changes. The basic premise of America was to leave things better for each generation to come. That's history. But worse is that no one even expects it anymore. Instead of outrage, there's resignation. Instead of anger, there's apathy, and that's terrifying.

Look at the impeachment hearings and the Senate trial. What little integrity there was in Washington disappeared and has shown no signs of returning. The Republicans and the Democrats in Congress all made up their minds before the thing even began. And just about every time anyone from either party spoke, it was simply to advance their own partisan spin and to finger-point at the opposing side. The whole thing was a mockery of justice and of the American political process. Right or wrong, whatever Clinton did or didn't do. Was that the best they could do? That circus! Is that the most I can expect from these guys?

Yet how many of us demanded or even expected our representatives to make a decision based on integrity—regardless of whether it helped their party? We did the same thing. Made up our minds. Bought the group-think, the media spin, whatever it was. How many of us actually read the depositions, looked at the evidence, and made an honest informed decision? How many of us just made a decision based on our political loyalties and from information based on what everyone around us was saying?

What about our "as long as the economy is good it doesn't matter what he did" attitude regarding the president's personal and political behavior? In mid-January 1999, as the Senate impeachment trial of President Bill Clinton dragged on, a USA Today poll showed that a majority of Americans believed the president was doing a good job despite the fact that nearly 80 percent of all Americans believed he was untrustworthy and a poor moral leader. That's refreshing. He's a skunk, but he's our skunk.

Everybody knew Bill Clinton was lying—but nobody cared. More outrageous, a Fox News poll in February showed that over 65 percent of the public believed Juanita Broderick's accusations that Bill Clinton sexually assaulted her twenty years ago to be most likely true, yet only 30 percent thought they should be investigated. What's wrong with us? Why have so many of us stopped caring about the behavior of our leaders? So what if Clinton's behavior is no different from that of others before him? Is the standard I'm supposed to use for judging my president? That he's no worse than anyone else is?

What happened to the Bill Clinton who in 1992 asked for the chance to be different—to show us a new kind of politics? Clinton played on our hopes and then he betrayed them. He made a mockery of the presidency. He made a farce out of his ideals. He lied about what he stood for. He lied about what he would or wouldn't do as president. And then he lied about what he did do. He put his own personal interests ahead of the nation's time and time again, all the while pretending he was doing the opposite.

It's the almost total lack of integrity that's so hard to swallow. As far as I'm concerned, the president could have just said it was nobody's business whom he slept with and left it at that. That would be true, honest, and fine with me. He could have refused to answer. He didn't. Instead, he lied repeatedly under oath and obstructed the legal process that sought to uncover those lies. Sure, everybody lies about sex. I have. But that's not the point. It's not OK to lie under oath, especially when you're the president. You and I are *expected* to uphold the laws. Our elected leaders are *sworn* to uphold them. I don't care who Clinton had sex with. When he's under oath, as president, he has to suck it up and tell the truth.

Even if it doesn't bother you that he lied to all of us and

then under oath, why aren't you furious that he would risk the credibility of the American presidency, gamble all his political capital, and jeopardize his entire agenda, all for a little intern action? Why doesn't it disgust you that on three different occasions he launched cruise missiles at foreign countries, always on the eve of major Monica bad news or votes on his impeachment, coldly sacrificing innocent lives to divert our attention from his personal political troubles? And where is the shame at our individual and collective willingness to drop the story and look the other way when, in each case, it became apparent after the fact that the timing of the attacks was beyond suspicious—and, in the case of the missiles fired at the El Shifa Pharmaceutical Industries Company, a *supposed* chemical weapons plant in Sudan, that the justification was all but fabricated, the decision rushed, top intelligence sources not consulted, and it turned out the target was in fact a completely harmless but essential medicine factory whose destruction cost untold lives to disease? Is there anything we won't tolerate from our political leaders as long as the economy is good and the stock market rising?

Why is it OK that they consistently act with so little decency, integrity, and honor? Why is it OK that they rarely stand for anything beyond the latest poll results? Why is it OK that they almost uniformly lack conviction, character, and personal accountability? Why is any of that acceptable, even tolerable, from our national political leaders—and especially from the president—the symbolic head of state of the United States of America?

Why can't I expect more from the president than I do from my neighbor—or even myself? Why shouldn't I hold him to a higher standard? Forget about being a good role model; why can't I at least expect him to get out in front and lead? We give the president an expensive house, an unlimited public platform, luxury jets, boats, cars, an entourage, a military guard, and a Secret Service that will die to protect him. We immunize him from traditional criminal prosecutions. We put at his disposal the military force of the most powerful nation in the world. We give him the singular authority to sign or veto any bill passed by Congress, our elected legislative representatives. All that we ask is that he honorably and effectively represent our country.

People say that our political leaders reflect our culture and values—they are who we are. It's a democracy, after all. Yes, and no. They're still supposed to be leaders. They're still supposed to be the ones who move us forward. It's probably more accurate to say that our political leaders match our expectations for our country and for ourselves. They reflect our ideals, our hopes, our dreams as a nation—and they, especially the president, embody a vital part of national character. Their job is representing us. Their job is to advance the national good. Yet day after day, their top priority is the next campaign, and the long-term interest of the nation takes a backseat to political ambition. They set their sights on the next election, not the next generation, and we continue to let them.

That's the problem. We've stopped expecting more than bearable behavior from our national leaders. We've given up on them—and on what politics in a democracy needs to be. What does it say about where we are as a nation when we no longer expect those given the sacred task of governing our country to have to meet a higher standard of integrity than the standard we impose on the guy who fixes our car? We've reached maximum dysfunction. We've become a nation of codependents. Tired of being let down, we expect little from our leaders, and they never disappoint us. Afraid of our own responsibility for the fate of our democracy, we elect leaders who ask little of us—and they in turn neither inspire nor challenge us.

We've crapped out, all of us. We've let our political system become a farce, a sitcom, a soap opera; we've let our political leaders become spineless cowards lacking character and vision; and we've let ourselves stop believing in a bigger dream for America. We've given up. Frustrated and intimidated by our relative powerlessness against the system, overwhelmed by the enormity of our underlying national problems and the seemingly irreversible nature of some of our worst social and economic trends, most Americans have chosen to opt for short-term gains, shortsighted leaders and immediate gratification over real solutions to many long-term, deeply rooted problems like crime, poverty, the disintegration of our inner cities and our public education system, the coming collapse of social security and the entitlement structure, and the insidious corruption of our political system.

Look at us. In a participatory democracy, with the highest potential participation ever (meaning more people with the right to vote), we have the lowest voter turnout ever. In an era where technology allows for the widest, fastest, and most complete information dissemination ever, we have the least informed and least interested electorate in the history of democracy. And at a time when our society is undergoing some of the most dramatic changes in world history (with possibilities both fantastic and catastrophic), we have the most apathetic and indifferent public mind-set in generations.

Too many of us have bought into the insidious belief that meaningful reform is unachievable, that our individual and collective power to effect change is minimal, and that it's not worth caring about things beyond our own immediate interests. We've become a nation that prizes cynicism and flips off idealism. Rather than risk disappointment, we lessen our expectations. As a result, less is exactly what we get.

Bill Clinton wanted a legacy. He got one. His tattered presidency came to represent the last blow to whatever idealism was left hanging out there in the American spirit, the last stake in the heart to the American dream. We became a nation too tired to care, too beaten down to believe, too desperate to ask for more, and too spiritually lost to know what to hold on to. Instead, we held on to ourselves, to our little piece of the rock, to our jobs, our portfolios, our shrinking relative wages and rising costs of living. We held on to what we had, and felt sorry for those who didn't do as well, until we couldn't feel sorry any more, and then we just looked away, reminding ourselves how good things were. We looked to the past for comfort and guidance—going retro in clothes, music, art, movies—and politics.

We stopped asking what could be and settled for what had been. In the 1960s people dreamed of ending racism, poverty, and crime. In the 1990s we scaled those dreams down. No more talk of wiping out poverty, just putting an end to welfare. No more talk of ending racism, just creating separate but equal. No more talk of eradicating the underlying causes of crime, just tougher laws, harsher sentences, more jails, and a frightening fiscal battle over how to house a prison population that had grown to its highest percentage of the population in the history of the free world.

How did political consciousness—the lifeblood of any democracy—in the most amazing nation on earth become so bankrupt, hollowed out, and meaningless? How did our indifference grow so strong? How and why did we let it happen? And what is it worth to us as a society to change course? For how long will we continue to settle for what has already been done rather than seek to do what has not yet been done? For how long will we leave things the way they are just because that's the way they have always been? For how long will we continue to pretend to ourselves that it doesn't matter?

It's time for an intervention. No more lying to ourselves. No more looking the other way. No more enabling behavior. It's time we collectively step back in and take control of our government, reclaim our political ideals, and rediscover our national destiny. As we enter the new millennium, what will we ask of ourselves as a nation, what will we expect from our leaders, and what, if anything, will we refuse to compromise? Will we settle for the same broken record that we seem to have gotten so comfortable with during the last 30 years? Or will we start setting our sights on something better—something new, visionary, and meaningful?

We are past the point of minor reforms. In fact, they might do more harm than good. Tinkering around the edges just allows opponents of real change to stall, essentially ensuring that no significant changes occur. If we want to put America back on track, we need something of a shakeup. I'm not talking about revolution, just some pretty significant changes in order to revitalize our democracy.

Throughout this book, I outline ten simple ideas that can change politics in America. They are not a comprehensive solution to America's political crisis, but they're more than the usual Band-Aids. They are bold, necessary, and transformative changes—the kind of changes we need to consider if we want to move American democracy successfully into the twenty-first century.

I'm aware that if you're determined to do so, you're going to be able to find something wrong with any one of these

proposals. Few people will like all of them, and, if the re-
sponses I got in talking about them is any indication, most
people will like a couple of them a lot and then find one or
more that they can't stand. That's because these ideas are not
the result of a particular ideology or partisan way of looking
at change. Instead, they flow from a single, pragmatic standard: They offer potentially transformative solutions to a
number of the fundamental long-term problems that have
crippled American democracy. They are not the be all and
end all but a series of ideas that would help us move forward.
As you come across them in the book, there are a couple of
big-picture things I hope you'll keep in mind.

None of these ideas is a cure-all.
The problem at the heart of our democracy is *us*. Too
many of us have stopped believing in our political system
and in our ability to affect it meaningfully. No single political, economic, or social initiative will be a cure-all for American democracy. It's the other way around. A revived
democracy will lead to the cure of countless national problems. For that reason, these proposals are all jump-starts of a
sort. In one way or another they're each designed to help
improve the process through which we participate, to eliminate a current or future crisis that could short-circuit our
democracy, or to shock the system into action.

Every one of these ideas is possible.
These proposals are not pipe dreams, no matter what the
status quo types will tell you. All of them could be accomplished over the next ten years. That isn't to say they won't
take a lot of work, challenge us morally and intellectually,
and require sustained effort. But that's been true of every
major national challenge, from freeing the slaves, to winning

World War II, to putting a man on the moon. It's not about what's possible but about what we're committed to. If we are committed to any of these proposals, and to the changes they seek, we can and will accomplish them.

Each one of these ideas would, if carried out to its full realization, make America a better place to live.

This is true even of the most radical of my proposals, since the effect would be to catalyze the participatory instincts in us and push us to take greater control of our nation. At the same time, as unconventional as some of these ideas might seem, they make total sense. Each one would improve the quality of a vital sphere of American life. These ten proposals are exactly what this country needs—commonsense solutions to some major problems that up until now have seemed intractable.

There is nothing un-American in any of these proposals.

Every one of these ten initiatives upholds the spirit of American democracy. There is nothing un-American, antidemocratic, or anticapitalist in any of the ideas I am proposing. Even the most revolutionary are in the spirit of a free people, committed to equality, opportunity, and self-governance—the basic premises that underlay the American constitutional ideal.

Some combination of these proposals is necessary to revive and sustain American democracy into the next century.

These ten initiatives take aim at a wide spectrum of economic, social, and political problems, and absent some combination of them we're completely screwed. No amount of wishful thinking is going to change that fact. We can't continue just to muddle through. That said, none of these ideas is foolproof, and if you try hard enough, you can find something not to like about all of them and probably a plausible reason why they might not work. But if you're going to do all that negative work, just consider that 30 years ago we sent a man to the moon—something most people thought couldn't be done. And in 1927 Charles Lindbergh flew across the Atlantic. Before that, the Wright brothers proved that man could fly. Think about these proposals intuitively rather than academically. Think about them from your gut. These are some hard choices, some radical steps. It's tough medicine for America, but it's better than the drugs we're on now.

Like the *Titanic* nearly a century ago, America is on a crash course with a dangerous destiny. Like the *Titanic*, the iceberg in our path can be avoided, but not by cruising obliviously ahead at full speed, arrogantly refusing to face the consequences of our choices, and unwilling to accept limits on our actions. Like the builders of the *Titanic*, America's political leadership has promised something they can't deliver—that America is an unsinkable ship. And like the ill-fated passengers on the *Titanic*'s maiden voyage, we, the American people, seem content to enjoy the ride, oblivious to the potential dangers and completely unprepared for the crisis that lies ahead.

But there is still something we can do.

It's not too late for us to take control of our national destiny, redirect the course of our country, and reaffirm our ideals and our faith in democracy. The results will be more than fiscal and social solvency well into the lives of the next generation but a powerful, spiritual reconnection with the part of each of us that believes in something bigger than our own self-interest, that has faith in something better than our individual best efforts, and that seeks something that will last beyond our own lives. America's millennial challenge is to rediscover our democracy, before the damage is too extensive, the wounds are too deep, and the costs are too high. It's a challenge to put America back on track—before it's too late.

The bottom line is this. There are no panaceas. We are the key to fixing America. And while future generations of Americans will benefit from the bold steps we take today, it is we who will be the real winners—victors over our own apathy and recipients of our own renewed ideals. The heart of the American dream is much more than an economic state of being—more than a good job, a booming stock market, a nice house, and a white picket fence. It's a moral and spiritual ideal. Whether that ideal lives or dies affects each of us individually and also shapes the collective course of our nation. Most of us want to believe in America. I know that. The point of this book is to convince you that you can.

You think your voice doesn't matter, your vote doesn't count? You think you can't make a difference? With that attitude nothing important or meaningful or fantastic would ever have been accomplished. There would be no Sistine Chapel, or *Starry Night*, no great novels, no 1924 Yankees' pennant or 1996 Packers' Super Bowl victory. Humans wouldn't fly and there would have been no reason for Tom Wolfe to have written *The Right Stuff*. There also wouldn't be racial equality under the law in America, women wouldn't vote, and we might be living under the Third Reich of Germany. Our actions matter, individually and collectively. And anything is possible if you believe in it enough. The great Irish revolutionary Michael Collins said that. But he was quoting Peter Pan, who, whether you believe in him or not, was telling the truth.

You *can* make a difference. Everybody can. How much is a matter of passion, commitment, and timing. Not everyone is going to change the world single-handedly, but the power of collective action for social good is something that the world really has just begun to explore in the last half century. And the jury's still out on what a collective recommitment to our ideals would create—on the possibilities that the most advanced and powerful democracy in the world would achieve if we wanted it to. No doubt there's a short-term cost to finding out. But the long-term price for waiting will be even higher. So the real question is not whether you are willing or ready to do this but when it becomes too costly not to.

For how long will you stand by as the power brokers in Washington sell out our nation and your children's future? How many millions of kids are you willing to watch get lost to poverty, malnutrition, bankrupt schools, and crime-infested streets before you demand an end to the ghettos in America? How many schoolyard shootings do you have to see on the news? How many "friend of a friend's" have to die? How many private security guards will we have to hire, and how many state prisons will we have to build before we realize that too many people are on the other side of the fence? How much smog will we have to breathe, how many forests will we tear down, how many dead fish will have to float up on shore before we realize that when we kill the planet we kill ourselves? How bankrupt does Social Security need to become, how many billions of dollars more debt will we run up on the backs of our children, for how many more generations of Americans will we mortgage their futures before we learn to live within our means?

We can each make whatever choices we want about how

we live our personal lives today, what actions we take and don't take, which issues we want to address and which we want to ignore. We can say that the black kid in the ghetto isn't our problem, or that the homeless man on the corner could get a job if he really wanted to, or that the pregnant teenager who drops out of school has only herself and her parents to blame. No one can make any of us take responsibility for problems beyond our own front doors. But whether it's our fault or not doesn't change whether we can be part of the solution—whether there is something more that each of us can do that will make a difference. The truth is that our actions today do jeopardize, possibly irreversibly, the future of those who come after us. The next generation of Americans is being sold down the river. And if we don't act soon, not a few of us here and there, but all of us, collectively and with a common purpose, then it may be too late.

America will become a second-rate nation, morally and fiscally bankrupt, split down the center by racial, economic, and generational differences. And your children and grandchildren will hate you for it. Because they will one day ask why, when you had the chance, you chose to ignore the warning signs, to close your eyes to the problems and to refuse to take responsibility for finding and carrying out solutions. And the worst part of it is, they will be right, and you will know it. We are not yet too far gone to put America back on the course it followed for most of the last 200 years. We still can restore national greatness, achieve fiscal balance, social stability, racial equality, and generational equity. It is not too late. But it will be soon. How many more excuses can you make before you decide to act? What are you waiting for? And what, if anything, would make you change your mind?

2.

The Year of the National Enema

A COUPLE YEARS AGO I was talking to Congressman Joe Kennedy, Robert Kennedy's oldest son. He had asked me to help him develop a campaign aimed at reengaging American voters. I'd help him develop it, but it would be his baby. Although his burst of civic-mindedness was motivated at least in part by an underlying presidential ambition, Joe had some really good ideas. What's more, on the surface at least, Joe appeared to believe that people wanted and deserved better than Washington was giving them. After traveling and meeting with lots of activists, experts, and thinkers I came to a fundamental conclusion about what was necessary for the campaign to work. To have the power to really make change, Joe needed to be an independent, not a Washington insider.

My advice to him was simple: Quit your seat in Congress

and start the campaign as a real citizen. When I told him this, he looked at me as if I had lost my mind. Are you fucking crazy? he practically shouted at me. Congress is my platform. Why would I want to give that up? He thought it was just about the most stupid idea he had ever heard.

That answer said a lot about Joe Kennedy, and it says everything about why leadership is in such short supply right now. There are plenty of candidates for public office but few if any who are willing to risk what they already have gained to make possible the kinds of changes most of us want to see. And the effect is trickle-down, with the rest of us following the actions of those in front. Which is understandable but ultimately shortsighted.

Less than half of all adult Americans vote. Talk about a show of no confidence. The sad fact is that despite the sorry state of political affairs, most of us don't think it's worth the time or trouble to try to change things. Instead, we are content to blame the politicians in Washington as if we can't do anything to stop them. But we can do something. After all, we put them there. We can send them home.

The problem is that we send one home and what difference does it make? Or, for that matter, if we kick out ten or even a hundred? There's always a majority left behind to hold down the fort. You throw out a few and a few more come in. They promise to be different, but sooner or later the institutional majority corrupts them. That, or they leave disgusted and frustrated. Like Tim Penny, a five-term member of Congress from Minnesota who resigned a safe seat in 1994 because, as he told me, he realized that one guy against the pack couldn't make a difference. As he saw it, staying in that situation just made him a part of the problem.

Tim Penny is a rare example of a man in Washington with integrity. The majority of our so-called leaders just follow the pack, becoming the same as those who came before them. Soon they become the incumbents, and so nothing ever really changes. As long as a majority of Congress is controlled by insiders, of either party, by people whose priority is the next election, not the next generation, I guarantee that nothing truly meaningful or substantial will happen in the political process.

Depending on which party is in power, we may get some policy shifts here and there, but if you look closely, the Democrat and Republican parties have become more alike than different. Think about it. What's the fundamental difference between the Reagan era and the Clinton era? There are a few more women and minority judges because of Clinton, a few more weapons and a little less red tape because of Reagan. Social Security was heading for collapse under Reagan. It has continued on that path under Clinton. We had a $5 trillion national debt under Reagan. With Clinton, despite the recently balanced budget, the debt is almost $6 trillion. We had a crisis in our inner cities under Reagan. With Clinton we still have one—only now we have swept the problem under the rug by throwing a record number of people in prison and enacting ill-conceived and superficial welfare reform.

Regardless of which party is in power, the fundamental problems remain because right now the whole system is so screwed up that it's almost impossible for any meaningful, systemic changes to occur. No matter how dedicated a handful of people in Washington may be to advancing a particular agenda, sooner or later they too get stuck in the virtual hamster wheel, driven by the inexorable momentum that the mundane majority creates.

The push-me-pull-you circus that goes on within Congress and between Congress and the president will continue unless and until we make some fundamental changes in the process. These changes—whether campaign finance reform, or term limits, or changes to the Constitution, or easier voting procedures, or limits on judicial power, or any—and I mean any—comprehensive social, educational, political, or economic reforms—will not happen as long as either party retains control, because neither the Democrats nor the Republicans are going to commandeer systemic change.

No matter the positive effects these changes might bring for the nation as a whole, broad-based institutional changes won't help either party retain control. And control, not national renewal, is what Washington, what Democrats and Republicans both, what Congress and the president and the nine life-tenured members of the Supreme Court are ultimately all about.

The kinds of changes that would liberate and empower millions of Americans, revitalize our democracy, and ensure a stronger nation for generations to come would in the process weaken the two main political parties, undercut the titans of the current political establishment, and hurt those who have made a comfortable home in positions of power, lessening their iron-clad grip on the system and exposing the self-interested finger-pointing hypocrites that so many of them are.

That kind of revelation is something that neither party will allow to happen. Because the truth is that the emperor has no clothes, and our national political leadership will do everything in their power to keep that truth from being discovered. They will lie, stall, obfuscate. They will say radical and innovative changes are naive and impractical. They will say they can't be done and that they won't work. They will warn of unseen dangers. And finally, if pushed hard enough, they will say they will make the changes themselves-gradually. But they won't. They never have and they never will.

So this then is what I propose—the opening salvo of the war to reclaim our democracy. We do it ourselves.

SOLUTION #1

- **In the next election, we throw *everybody* in national elected office out and start over again.**

We throw them all out at once—all 535 members of Congress. I'm talking a clean sweep. In this upcoming election we make a national citizen commitment not to reelect any incumbents to Congress—and we refuse to vote for any candidate for the presidency who runs on a Democratic or Republican ticket. Those congressional incumbents who are brave enough will step away on their own, voluntarily agreeing not to run for reelection. Those who resist get the electoral boot. If you want to be in Congress, you can't be there now. If you're already there, apply again in two years. Same thing is true for the Big House. If you want to be president, no more hiding behind the party apparatus. If you want the golden egg of American politics, run as an independent.

Why can't we have a Democrat or a Republican for president? Ultimately we can and we will again. Currently, however, both parties are politically and morally bankrupt, and that won't change without a cleansing process, which the clean sweep will begin. Until then party affiliation pretty much defeats any claim to genuine leadership legitimacy a presidential candidate might otherwise have. So right now coming into the presidency as a Democrat or a Republican is a deal-breaker for creating a new kind of politics in America. Party-backed candidates end up beholden to their party and not to the people. As a result, their ability to take the risks that would lead to real political, social, and economic improvements in America is undermined and, ultimately, becomes impossible.

Running as an independent is the only way I can think of for someone to break the deadlock, advance a meaningful agenda, and inspire the American people. I'm not saying it will be easy. To succeed against the opposition of both organized political parties and most of the traditional political establishment would require a citizen candidacy that reached the apathetic masses who have tuned out politics altogether. A tall order, but one that a true populist with a heart and vision probably could fill. Enough of us committing to elect someone who runs as an independent would help, giving qualified candidates the incentive to run and the possibility of winning without party machines backing them.

Republican or Democratic candidates who want the presidency badly enough can throw off their party affiliation and run as independents. This by itself would help destroy the vast party structures and the complex fund-raising machines. Sure, a partisan in independent's clothing will have a head start, but it will be different. For starters, that person will have already distinguished him- or herself by showing the courage to take such a bold step, in the way that Joe Kennedy wasn't willing to do. It sets the real leaders apart and becomes a test of who really can lead us.

Anyone who runs and wins without party backing, who actually does what it takes to win the hearts and votes of a majority of us—independent of a party, independent of a national political machine—deserves to win and will prove that he or she is a genuine citizen president. Think of it like Camelot. When Arthur drew the sword from the stone he not only became king, but demonstrated that he was the only one meant to be king.

Finally, as a safety measure, if no qualified independent candidate emerges—if no one can draw the sword from the stone—then we protest by refusing to vote for anyone at all. That's right—we refuse to vote for a candidate running as a Republican or Democrat. Write in "no one" if you feel the need to vote. By refusing to vote for anyone but an independent, we will ensure that whichever Democratic or Republican candidate does win (and someone will) wins with such a small percentage of the vote that he or she cannot claim a popular victory, only an institutional one, and for the next four years that person will not be able to take our support for granted emotionally or practically. Instead, he or she will have to earn it every day.

The bottom line is this: In the upcoming November election, we demand a new slate of national leaders. We demand it, and then we make it happen. We have the constitutional and moral authority to do it. We have the political and people power to do it. And we have every good reason to do it. We have waited long enough; it's time to take control.

The premise is simple: Washington has been screwing up everything from taxes to healthcare, from the budget to crime and drug policy, from fighting poverty and reforming education to defending civil liberties and securing privacy on the Internet. Yet when you try to affix responsibility, everybody ducks and points fingers. Republicans in Congress blame Democrats, and vice versa; they all blame the president, and the president blames Congress. Meanwhile, nearly every member—no matter how old, feeble, obnoxious, vile, and ineffective (Jessie Helms, Strom Thumond, Ted Kennedy, Phil Gramm) gets reelected. There's a 95 to 98 percent reelection rate in Congress. They get reelected because they have the resources of the office and the ability to promise and deliver to their constituents.

This I-can-deliver-the-goods approach has become part of the problem. It basically sets all of us against each other. No state or congressional district wants to lose the seniority their members have so carefully built up, but that makes us all into little special interest communities, more interested in getting our little slice of the pie than in making sure the country gets what is best for it. At the same time, the more seniority—the more power, special interests, and money our elected officials have in their pockets—the less representative and responsive they become to us, their constituents. And the less concerned they become with the greater public good. It's a vicious circle.

Longer stays in Washington have another adverse affect. The longer someone is in Washington, the more complicated he or she generally seems to think running the country is. Long-termers increasingly believe that many issues and decisions are just too complicated for the average American. Well, if that's true, it's only because of what incumbents do once they are in Washington. Bills become longer, policies needlessly complex, and legislative language virtually incomprehensible to the average person. Look at the IRS tax code as an example. I had to study it for a law school exam. As evidence of how convoluted the code was, the professor made the test closed book except for the actual 2,000-page statute. The tax code, he noted with amusement, was so complex that if we actually needed to use it during the exam, we probably would fail.

So let's just simplify things. Go to the source, and eliminate the problem. Unfortunately, a lot of the bureaucracy will have to stay just to keep the government operating. But the guys in the big chairs go. In their place come a whole new crop of ripe and ready citizen legislators—and one independent president—free and clear of the baggage of both parties.

Think of it like a national enema, cleaning out the colon of government. Sure, eventually it will clog up again, but this single cleaning will refresh our national government, invigorate the policymaking process, and rejuvenate politics in America. It also will set the stage for the kinds of changes we want and need to make, changes which can help make certain that the situation never gets so bottled up again.

I know people will say it can't be done—that it's hard just to get a neighborhood to agree on a date for a block party, so how can you get a country to agree not to reelect anyone in national office? But we can. We simply have to want to badly enough. It will require an expensive, but doable, national publicity campaign (which private donors can fund through a tax-exempt nonprofit organization), aggressive support from talk radio hosts, extensive organizing on-line, and a nationally coordinated effort to monitor and inform people in every state where their members and election races stand. Mostly, though, it will depend on a commitment on the part of millions of Americans to see this through—as a nation. It's an all-or-nothing proposition. The only way it can work is if everyone goes at once. There can be no holdouts—no states or districts clinging to the relative power or seniority that their representatives have over the others. If enough citizens get on board with the idea, and a few people with real money agree to provide launch funding, it can happen. It can be publicized, coordinated, and realized.

Lead . . . or Leave was a similarly outlandish and, what some at the time thought, preposterous proposal. But in just three months we pressured over 100 candidates for Congress to pledge to quit Congress if the deficit wasn't cut in half by

1996. That was 1992, before e-mail and a national on-line community and network that could facilitate the organization.

It's all about momentum. If enough of us in enough states and congressional districts start calling for it, pressure will build on incumbents to step down on their own. A few brave legislators will go first, helping to energize the process. Seeing the historic opportunity for change, qualified citizen legislators will emerge to offer their candidacies. Then, as the wave takes off, recalcitrant incumbents will lose support, credibility, and ultimately the power to win reelection. Those who refuse to step aside voluntarily will get swept away by the rising tide of popular opposition to any incumbent.

The only people we can't absolutely force out are the sixty-seven senators whose terms don't come up for reelection in 2000. (U.S. Senators are elected every six years, instead of every two as congresspersons are or four as the president is, so every two years one-third of the Senate is up for reelection.) However, with enough public pressure, a number of these not-up-for-reelection senators might be persuaded to step down voluntarily to support the larger campaign. Others, like Strom Thurmond, are so old they might just die in office, thereby creating open seats. What's more, given the current makeup of the Senate, if we tossed out the thirty-three who are up for reelection and replaced them only with independent candidates, neither the Democrat nor the Republican parties would have a majority in the Senate—and there would be enough independents to keep either traditional party from taking control of the Senate and to ensure that a new populist citizen agenda is pushed through.

Still, even with the Senate six-year split problem, even if none of the senators who were not up for reelection stepped down, and even if we didn't elect only independents to the Senate, on the whole, a throw-them-all-out strategy would put in office a Congress that for the first time in almost two centuries is comprised by a majority of new members. That outcome alone would stir the pot up enough so that whatever came out of this new Congress would be different and more productive than the stale results we have today.

The fearful will say the government will collapse. It won't. The government will continue to run just fine, infused now with vital citizen power necessary to take advantage of the next millennium.

First, imagine the quality and diversity of candidates that will emerge. A national call for the best and the brightest, for the most inventive and the most creative—for artists and scientists, businesspeople and teachers, healers and Hollywood producers, athletes and factory workers—to take a break from their jobs and careers and run for a single term in Congress. We will see a whole different type of politician: citizen legislators who want to come for a two- or four-year stint and then get back to their "real" lives.

Throwing out all the incumbents at once will set a whole new precedent for who holds high federal office and for how long elected officials stay once they're in. In a single blow it will bring down the concept of a permanent political class in America, giving us once again what this country was originally designed to have—a legislature of the people, from all walks of life, fit to serve and ready to lead, committed to creating legislative change rather than to a career in Washington.

Second, throwing out the current incumbent Congress will drive a wedge through the incestuous knot that the Democratic and Republican parties have created in Washington, breaking their chokehold on the policymaking process and infusing Washington with nonpartisan spirit, new ideas, and fresh energy. We will for the first time in decades be able to make real change through the government.

Think of the opportunity a completely new Congress will bring. It will open a window for change unknown since the founding of our country. We will be able actually to address and resolve some the foundational problems that hang over our future—things that our elected officials promise year after year to fix and never really do.

It also will give us the chance to repair or replace the institutions that are broken or no longer necessary, to strengthen the institutions that work but are in danger, and to bring American government into the twenty-first century as a vital, productive, and modern vehicle for national governance and policymaking. We will give American democracy a much-needed jump-start.

Once in place, the all-new and improved Congress would need to do a number of things immediately to make sure that this megashift in the makeup of the political establishment is more than merely a changing of the guard. The primary one is to pass term limits. Upon taking office, and within the first hundred days, the New American Congress should pass term limits on themselves and future incumbents—something most Americans say they want but Congress continues to avoid doing.

Term limits will ensure that the current problem of a clogged political system doesn't happen again. Elections themselves are supposed to be a check on an unwanted buildup of power, but we all know that this isn't working. Once someone gets in, it's nearly impossible to get that person out.

That's why so many people will say we won't succeed in making a clean sweep of Congress. Incumbency is built-in power. Once you are in office, you've got power, access to money, and a platform to reach the public through the media. You've also got carrots to buy off special interests and sticks to weaken your enemies. It's not a level playing field, and unless there is an imposed limit, a new Congress runs the risk of starting to become incumbent laden just like its predecessors.

So first order of business for the new Congress is to impose statutory limits on incumbency. In fact, to make sure they do this, we should ask all candidates running for the 2000 Congress to take a pledge to enact term limits, no matter what, if elected.

Beyond term limits, there's plenty more a new American Congress would, could, and should do in its first hundred days and then for the rest of its term. You'll see a number of these proposals throughout the rest of the book. The point is that a nearly incumbent-free Congress would create an opportunity for an aggressive and innovative legislative agenda.

A clean sweep in Congress will do more than make a practical difference. It will have an emotional and psychological effect on us as a nation as well. Even the most disenfranchised and disconnected will take notice. Millions more of us will get involved, and the apathy that has dominated America for as long as I have been alive will begin to recede. A majority of us actually might start to care about politics. Not because we are supposed to care. Not because we feel guilty or ashamed for not caring. But because we will want to care, because we will see a reason to care, and because for the first time we will see that caring about politics, speaking out and acting up, actually might make a difference.

In the fall of 1992, movie star Val Kilmer invited Jon and me to Hollywood to help generate support for our deficit-busting crusade. We met late one night at the Bel Air Hotel, where he had arranged a meeting for us to talk about our fledgling campaign. Among those attending the meeting were Sean Penn, Jackson Browne, Christian Slater, and rock legend David Crosby. It excited me that Val had invited David, because when I was a teenager I was inspired by Crosby's role in shaking up his generation. Now he was listening to what I was trying to do motivate my generation and bring some accountability to the American political system.

Among packs of Marlboro Lights and bottles of beer Jon and I explained our nascent effort to create a citizen accountability movement. Sean Penn seemed to get the energy of what we were doing and surprised me not only with his passion but with his rather detailed understanding of how the debt worked and how the government was deliberately keeping the public in the dark about the issue. Jackson Browne sat off a little from the rest of us, watching and taking in what others were saying.

As we started to explain the importance of celebrity support for our campaign, Crosby—the old activist with real roots in the idealism of the 1960s—came to life. He put his hand on my shoulder and told us that he'd been waiting twenty years for someone from our generation to wake up and do something about what had gone wrong in America. Someone to pick up where his generation had left off. If our generation led the way, he was convinced the Baby Boomers would follow. Otherwise, it wouldn't happen. It was a bit surreal. Here was David Crosby telling us that *we* inspired *him*.

Suddenly Crosby looked over at Christian Slater and practically leapt out of his chair. Don't you realize the power you have to affect people? Don't you realize what you alone could do? he said, leaning into Christian. I'll never forget Christian's stunned and genuine reaction. He looked down at his expensive new black Nikes and then back at Crosby. "Why would people listen to me?" he asked. "I'm just an actor."

It blew me away. If Christian Slater, one of the hottest young actors of his generation—a guy who had an audience of millions, could be on *Letterman* in a heartbeat or host the MTV Movie Awards—if he thought that no one would listen to what he had to say, then how is the guy waiting tables at Denny's supposed to feel that someone would listen to him? And yet Christian's reaction was authentic. He really believed he didn't have the power.

"What difference can I make?" It's a response I've heard from people all over the country: from movie stars and network television heads to CEOs of wildly successful companies and doctors and lawyers from the most prestigious universities in America; from farmers and teachers to students and strippers; from waitpersons and flight attendants to journalists and White House staffers. Few people in America, whatever their job, whatever their level of affluence, whatever their relative power to the rest of us feel they can make much of an impact.

It's true for almost all of us. We feel silenced, neutralized, disconnected. And we'll continue to feel that way until we all join together and do something about it. It can't happen one individual at a time, not any longer, not in this day and age.

It's just too hard to reach critical mass, too hard to break through the cultural sound barrier and be heard and listened to by the people in power.

Change is a numbers game, and believing that we can have an impact depends on enough of us seeing enough others doing the same thing. Maybe we're all just lemmings. Maybe it has to do with the complexity of our world and our need to feel safe before we act. Maybe it's just too hard to believe in radical possibility anymore. But whatever the reasons, the result is the same. Although we live in age when it is possible for a single person to be heard almost instantaneously all over the world—although it has never been so easy to reach and affect millions—we have never as individuals felt less empowered and more in need of collective action, unified direction, and common purpose.

We're not going to change the world one person at a time. We're not going to clean up our ghettos one block at a time or save the next generation one kid at time. We're not going to eliminate our national debt one dollar and one balanced budget at a time, or solve the crime problem in America one criminal at a time. And we're not going to change the malaise in our government one seat, one office, or one elected official at a time. It's a nice fantasy, but that's about all it is—a fantasy.

Economies of scale make a difference. We live in a mass media, mass market, mass culture age—and we need some mass solutions. We need some sweeping changes, some aggregate solutions, and some all-encompassing reforms. Base hits aren't going to do it. Not now. Not today. Not this late in the game. We need a couple of grand slams. And the first one, the most critical one, and the one that will pave the way for all the others is to remove all of our nationally elected officials from office, all at once in a single election, and replace them—with ourselves. It's the   ction of the new millennium. Nothing could be more appropriate, more timely, or more essential to revitalizing American democracy.

2000: the year of the national enema. It will give a whole new meaning to politics in America.

3.

Trouble in Paradise

I cried for me and you and all the world. Bobby would cling to life for another day, but the truth was already there. Camelot was lost.

—BORIS YARO, Los Angeles Times reporter

STEVE HARVIS CRIED WHEN BOBBY Kennedy was shot. He wasn't alone. Across America, thousands of people broke down in tears. In his second year at Georgetown Law School in Washington, D.C., Steve had seen the events of the late 1960s up close, including a frightening encounter with mounted police in 1967 during a "routine" antiwar protest. He'd faced bullets himself. And he'd had friends die in Vietnam. But Bobby Kennedy was different.

Bobby Kennedy's death did more than shock people, it broke their hearts. It was the fourth in a string of violent and horrifying assassinations of America's boldest and most prominent political leaders. First there was JFK in 1963, then Malcolm X in 1965, Martin Luther King, Jr., in April of 1968, and finally Bobby Kennedy in June of that year. Boris Yaro, who took the famous picture of RFK as he lay dying on the floor of the Ambassador Hotel in Los Angeles, would wait ten years before he could put the picture on his wall. He couldn't physically handle the negatives for six months. Thirty years later he still has nightmares. John F. Kennedy aide and Robert Kennedy speechwriter Richard Goodwin would go to New Hampshire and live in the woods for five years. He'd become a cynic with a drinking problem who would never really enter politics again. And Steve Harvis would never cry again. Even worse, he'd grow to regret that he ever had.

"I was naive," Steve told me three decades later. "We all were." Steve would never recover his faith in the dream of a new kind of politics. Now a successful lawyer and entrepreneur, today he looks back at those years with shame. "We didn't know what we were talking about. We thought we could change the world. We were wrong. This is the way the world is." When I protested, Steve got louder and even more insistent: "Every generation has its radical ideas. Ours was no different. Then you grow up."

Like so many in his generation, Steve lost his ideals that summer of 1968 the way most people I know lost their virginity—quickly, too young, and with a certain finality. And like so many in his generation, Steve would spend the rest of his adult life trying to escape his shattered dreams and rationalize the pragmatism he put in their place. Steve didn't become a bad person, just a disillusioned one. He's a good father, a solid member of his community, and a truly decent person. But that's the point. That's what happened to America during my lifetime. Lots of decent people let a lot of bad things happen to our country. An entire generation turned their backs on their own youthful convictions and on the social and political reforms they once dared to dream for.

It wasn't just the assassinations. The year 1968 was consisted of a string of events, from the Tet Offensive and the Mai Lai massacre to Prague Spring and the bloody police response at the Democratic National Convention in Chicago. It was the first time an incumbent president stepped down rather than run again and the first time there was a feminist protest at the Miss America Pageant. Primarily, however, it was the first time an entire generation watched their nascent ideals get steamrolled into the pavement. Bobby Kennedy's death was the final blow. It came with such force and brutality, such terrifying finality, that it took the spirit and hope out of an entire generation. And my generation has been paying for it ever since. A thirty-year meltdown in America.

From 1968 on, with too many heroes dead, too many dreams smashed, and too many problems still unsolved, America began a steady and painful political and spiritual decline. Most Americans lost sight of the core principles that made up this nation and forgot about the historic American compact of a better nation for every generation to come. From Vietnam to the Gulf War, from Watergate to Whitewater, from Richard Nixon to Bill Clinton—America's political leadership and political landscape soured.

Before that time things somehow seemed different. An era of activism and change redefined the American political landscape: Thurgood Marshall's meticulously crafted impact litigation project, which peaked in 1954 with the landmark Supreme Court case of *Brown v. Board of Education;* the freedom rides, lunch counter sit-ins, Birmingham–Montgomery marches and the march on Washington in 1963; James Meredith enrolling at Ole Miss; and legislation like the Civil Rights Act of 1964, the Voting Rights Act of 1965, and the Civil Rights Act of 1968—the last major piece of transformative social policy legislation of that era.

When you look at the past three decades, in contrast, the level of disengagement is alarming, and the near-universal apathy stunning. Sure, there has been some activism. The 1970s in particular saw major advances in the women's movement as well as the birth of organized environmentalism. Not to diminish the importance of these efforts, but that was pretty much it. On the whole, the slide toward national disconnect from 1968 on was fairly steady, with the 1980s becoming an era of materialism and self-absorption never before seen in America. Until the 1990s—which by the end of the decade had managed to make the excesses of the 1980s seem like nothing.

From 1968 to 1998, America would take an unprecedented thirty-year detour from idealism. Six months after RFK's death, America elected the least idealistic and possibly the most amoral president in the twentieth century. An angry, paranoid man with a small heart and a big ego, Richard Nixon would see America put a man on the moon and he would open the door to Communist China. He would also take the country to a new political low with Watergate, subverting the very institutions he was elected to uphold and doing irreparable damage to the presidency. But Nixon and Watergate were just a prelude.

In 1998 the man who sat around with his friends at Oxford and swore at Richard Nixon had by then eulogized him as a great American, followed his footsteps into China, and then one-upped Nixon's Watergate scandal by actually getting impeached and almost losing his presidency over a semen-stained coverup. The wheel had come full circle. The man we elected in 1992 as the most idealistic president in a generation, the first in his class and th. . . of his generation to assume power, had become a shadow of himself—defensive, paranoid, finger-pointing, and, most of all, standing for nothing but himself.

It was as if Clinton had waited his whole life to get to where he was, and now it was his turn at the trough—and he was going to get his, whatever the price to the rest of us. If 1968 was the beginning of the end of the American dream, 1998 was the year we watched American politics go down the drain. The film *Wag the Dog* became reality as a president who couldn't keep it zipped up lied, cheated, and bribed his way to political salvation, callously disregarding his oath of office; lying repeatedly and extensively under oath and to the American people; intimidating, bribing, and coercing witnesses; ruthlessly manipulating public opinion; and ultimately resorting to unnecessary, inconsistent, and poorly timed and planned military actions against foreign countries—with deadly consequences—in order to avoid being removed from office.

But the thirty-year span that began with the bullet that brought down Bobby Kennedy and ended with the girl who almost brought down Bill Clinton did a lot more than wreak havoc on our perceptions of politics and politicians. During those three decades we accumulated nearly $6 trillion of debt, mortgaging the future of tens of millions of younger Americans. We watched an entire new generation grow up in poverty, degradation, and seriously broken families. We witnessed the birth of the crack baby and the onslaught of AIDS. We saw the housing projects of the 1960s turn into the garbage dumps of the 1990s and watched a new underground economy emerge in the drug-ridden inner cities—where eleven-year-olds act as drug runners for their sixteen-year-old bosses. We watched our air turn toxic, our beaches become polluted, and our freeways and streets become so congested a new phenomenon called road rage was born. We endured a level of violent crime unheard of in the modern world that included a wave of murder sprees with teenage kids entering their schools and opening fire on their classmates and "postal worker" shootings at workplaces, the birth of a protracted violent drug war, the spread of gangs from big cities to small towns across America, the rise of a new class of serial rapists and murders, and even the emergence of domestic terrorism. We watched the prison population increase sixfold and the level of police brutality become so high that it triggered riots in Washington, D.C., and Los Angeles. Civil liberties receeded and the Bill of Rights was reduced to a token document, as the Supreme Court whittled away fundamental protections like the Fourth Amendment ban against unreasonable search and seizure and reduced privacy to a token right. We even saw America falter on some critical international commitments: stiffing the United Nations (which we helped found) of billions of dollars of dues and failing to provide the kind of support countries like Russia and other eastern European nations needed to make the transition to democracy. That, after we had spent trillions of dollars in military budgets for forty years to bring them to their knees. So much for follow-through. At least partly due to our relative indifference since the Cold War, today Russia stands on the verge of total economic collapse and the likely emergence of a fascist/nationalist anti-American regime.

Maybe most tragic of all, we witnessed the gradual death of the values and ethics that made America and drove the American dream. We lost our national ideals, our sense of national purpose and identity, and any belief in the efficacy of our government, the credibility of our leaders, and the morality of patriotism and democracy. We saw one president after another fail to meet our expectations until we stopped having any expectations. We watched and tolerated the profound failure of the American political establishment to keep the faith and secure the ideal of a better America for generations to come (my generation is the first since the Civil War to inherit a lower overall standard of living than the one preceding it), while all the time pretending—in fact, lying—that they were effectively caretaking the American dream.

America's fall from grace may have begun with the death of Robert Kennedy and then hit bottom with the Clinton sex scandal, but what happened in between is the real story. That's the tale of a thirty-year spiral of fiscal debt, social destruction, and political deception that left America a superpower on the outside but a lost soul on the inside; a democracy without its guiding light—lacking both a spiritual and moral compass, a shadow of what we could be—a nation with the true potential for greatness, instead weak at the knees and stuck in our ways.

Some landmarks on the way down:

- In the last thirty years, America has amassed a nearly $6 trillion buildup of the national debt— more than twenty times what we had accumulated in the entire history of the United States before 1960. Today almost 40 percent of every personal income tax dollar goes to paying interest on the gross national debt, an amount that will not decrease for years despite the marginal budget surpluses of 1998 and 1999.
- Our national retirement system is so unstable that, in the words of Federal Reserve chairman Alan Greenspan—not a guy who likes to scare people—it

could cause "fiscal catastrophe" in America in the next twenty years. Yet Washington is largely afraid to acknowledge the problem; rather it continues to look for quick fixes and settle for more long-term studies.

- The federal government has run up trillions of dollars of unfunded liabilities—payments the government owes or will owe but does not now have the money to pay. This includes most of Social Security, Medicare, and all future benefits now assessable. The Baby Boomers alone have been promised $14 trillion more than they have contributed in federal payroll taxes—and that's just what we can estimate today.

- Medicare, the primary health care entitlement for the retired, costs working Americans almost a quarter of a trillion dollars a year—an amount that will skyrocket as the number of beneficiaries doubles over the next thirty years. Even worse, the Medicare trust fund will be bankrupt by 2008 absent drastic reforms to the program. Despite this dire situation, last March a national bipartisan commission once again failed to reach agreement on how to repair it, leaving Medicare on a rapid road to insolvency.

- By 1996 a fifteen- to twenty-four-year-old was more than twice as likely to die by suicide or homicide than someone from that age group was in 1970. A black teenager today is three times more likely to die of gun violence than of natural causes. And a young black male in Harlem is less likely to live to forty than his counterpart in Bangladesh, one of the

poorest and most miserable places to live in the
world.

- In 1995, 32.2 percent of all African American men
were in jail or prison or on probation or parole—
and it's estimated that 28 percent of all black men
in America will be in state or federal prison at some
point in their lives.

- In 1980 minorities made up 33 percent of all federal
prisoners. By 1995 the number had nearly doubled,
to 64 percent of the total federal prison population.
Per capita incarceration rates for African Americans in 1993 were seven times as high as for whites.

- We spend over $20,000 a year on average for each
of our nation's 1.3 million prisoners and only
$6,500 a year per public school student. And that's
an average. Oregon spent over $77,000 per inmate
in 1997, and most states spend over five times more
per prison inmate than per student.

- During the 1990s, New York State increased spending for prison inmates by $761 million. During the
same time it cut higher education funding by $615
million. Today, the state spends more on prisons
than on public colleges and universities combined.

- Forty-two percent of all Americans under the age of
thirty-five are uninsured. And infant mortality in
the United States is higher than in all other of the
eighteen industrialized nations of the world.

- Since the mid-1970s, poverty among eighteen to
thirty-four-year-olds has gone up 50 percent while
the median income of young two-parent families
has fallen by 33 percent, an average of $10,000 per
family.

- In 1969 full-time employment at minimum wage was enough to support a family of three. In 1997 minimum wage left that same family almost 20 percent below the poverty line.
- Since 1972, the prison population in the U.S. has increased 600 percent.
- Between 1968 and 1994, voter participation in federal elections fell by almost 40 percent. Today, less than half of eligible Americans vote.
- Between 1979 and 1999, the per capita rate of violent crime among adults in their thirties and forties doubled, leading to an increase of more than half a million violent crimes a year.
- Every year 3,000 American kids die as a result of gun violence and another 2,000 from abuse and neglect.
- An estimated 5 to 9 million Americans were homeless at some point in the latter half of the 1980s.
- Washington, D.C., the nation's capital, has the second highest per-capita income in the nation. It also has the highest rate of poverty—almost 22 percent.
- Sixty-seven percent of New York City fourth-graders cannot read.
- America's toxic waste problem is so bad it would cost almost half of the entire annual U.S. budget just to clean up what has already been dumped.
- Compared with children in 25 other industrial countries, under 15 kids in the U.S. are 12 times more likely to die from gunfire, 16 times more likely to be murdered by a gun, and 11 times more likely to commit suicide with a gun.
- Nearly 50 percent of all adult Americans lack basic literacy skills, and cannot balance a checkbook or

read accurately from a map. The number of illiterate seventeen-year-olds has doubled in the last ten years, and today 7 million American high school students are functionally illiterate. In fact, America has the largest number of functional illiterates in the industrial world. Compared to our international competitors, the U.S. ranks second from last in percentage of national output invested in K–12 education.

- We live in the most advanced technological society in the world, yet in a 21-country study, U.S. students performed among the lowest in math, science, and physics, including general math and science knowledge considered necessary to function effectively in society as adults.

- Our national infrastructure is in such bad shape that it would cost almost $500 billion just to repair roads and bridges. Almost two-thirds of our roads need repair, and over 40 percent of our bridges have been deemed structurally unsound. New York State alone has an estimated need for $92 billion in infrastructure improvements over the next decade.

- One in five American kids lives in poverty. One in three will be poor at some point in childhood. One in three is a year or more behind in school. One in seven has no health insurance. And one in eight never graduates from high school.

Statistics never tell the whole story, but they almost always tell some of it. Since 1968 there has been a 250 percent increase in violent crime, a 300 percent increase in births to unwed mothers, a doubling in the rate of teenage suicides (tripling among five- to fourteen-year-olds), and an almost

80-point drop in Scholastic Achievement Test (SAT) scores. Poverty among under thirty households has doubled, while average weekly earnings have fallen almost 10 percent; the national debt has increased more than fifteenfold, median home prices (adjusted for inflation) increased over 100 percent, and the cost of attending a private four-year college has more than doubled. Between 1981 and 1989 alone homelessness tripled, leaving as many as 2 million people homeless at some point during the year. The number of children living in poverty has increased almost 30 percent. The number of guns in America has more than doubled, to over than 200 million, and annual deaths by firearms have increased tenfold. Arrests for juvenile violent crimes have doubled as have the number of kids in the United States who have trouble speaking English. And there has been a steady decline in real wages (except for a marginal increase in the last three years), even as the cost of living has steadily and dramatically increased.

It's not just in the numbers. Our cultural, moral, and ethical values have toppled as well. Everything has become relative. Everyone justifies his or her own self-interest. Sacrifice is seen as foolish. Trust and honesty as naive. No one wants to take responsibility for anything. Movies and TV programs are jam packed with violence, hatred, and gore—which we watch and pay for, all the while condemning those who feed on the message and mimic the behaviors. We have become no better than what we condemn. Remember the fans in Madison Square Garden when Mike Tyson took a bite out of Evander Hollyfield's ear in 1997? They were as disgusting as he was, turning the whole place into a shameless brawl. It's not as if we haven't made progress since the days of the Roman Gladiators and the Coliseum, but you'd think that by the year 2000 we would have come a little bit further.

Sure, we've become more prosperous, more technologically advanced, but if you think about it, are we really getting
any nicer? It seems the opposite is true, that we're more cut-
throat, more cruel, and more disconnected from one another
than ever before. I listen to yet another news radio report
about yet another mother who dumped her baby daughter on
the side of the road and I wonder: What's wrong with people?
What kind of society have we created that this kind of behavior is so widespread? Some days I look at the world and I just
don't know if I want to bring a child into it. I'm not proud of
that fear, but I also know I'm not alone. Am I crazy?

Why are we all so desperate? It seems we can't get
enough of anything anymore. Everyone wants more, better,
now. We can't change channels, fashions, and fads fast
enough. People line up outside department stores at 6:00 A.M.
the day after Thanksgiving to start shopping for Christmas.
Adults act like children to get their hands on the last new
gimmick toy to please their insatiable kids. Beanie Babies,
Giga Pets, and Teletubbies. Buy it today. Trash it tomorrow.
The stream of images that shapes, directs, and then redirects
our wants and desires is staggering. It's as if were on some
sick Roman orgy—stuffing our faces until we puke and then
going back for more. I've been at the trough. Haven't you?
I'm not talking about traditional values; right and wrong is a
relative thing. I'm talking about a degree of decadence and
insatiability that has permeated our society, leaving us temporarily full but ultimately hungry. This too is part of the
falling down of America.

There's another side to the last thirty years. Despite the
loss of ideals and direction, a lot of good has happened as
well. We saw unprecedented technological advances, including the possibility of universal, instantaneous communication. We landed a man on the Moon, a rover on Mars, and

sent a spacecraft around Jupiter. We created the Internet and digital TV and discovered the ability to map, manipulate, and re-create human genetics. We made enormous strides in medicine and nutrition. As a result, many people are healthier and living longer. We made huge strides in closing the gender gap and—thanks largely to the civil rights movement of the 1960s—in stomping out the most blatant racism in America. We watched the fall of communism and of the Berlin Wall and finally saw the Cold War come to an end—an event that, in turn, generated the biggest peacetime dividend in world history. And we have experienced the longest and highest rise in the stock market since it began and the most widespread distribution of its returns—ever.

It's not that we haven't made progress in the last 250 years, but we seem to be stagnating—sitting on our laurels, not pushing ourselves to become the best that human society can be. It's almost as if civilization itself has advanced but our civility, our decency, our humanity hasn't grown commensurately with it. Think how often you step around a homeless person on the street, or look right past the crazy person on the subway, or avoid the drug addict living on the other side of town in a rat-infested tenement. The problems aren't any one person's fault, but our willingness to look past them is certainly a collective sign of where we stand as a civil society.

The economic, scientific, and technological triumphs of the past thirty years raise a specter of promise and opportunity for the new millennium, but they also highlight a sad contradiction. For the first time in our national history, America at last has the financial, technological, and practical ability to take on, and possibly even put an end to, some of the most stubborn and insidious problems in the history of humankind: widespread and systemic poverty (especially among children); racial conflict and gender inequality; crime and the cycle of violence, broken families, and lack of education that breeds more crime; the destruction of the environment; cancer, AIDS, and genetic illnesses; and the lack of opportunity that exists for whole classes of people. We also have the chance to create the most inclusive and broad-based citizen democracy in history, giving every single American unprecedented choice, autonomy, and personal power, and for the first time in history to give everyone the opportunity to maximize wealth, leisure, and happiness.

Yet despite the awesome opportunity, in spite of unprecedented human and financial resources and the once-unimaginable technological tools for communication and problem-solving that now exist, we wait, somewhat indifferent to or even unaware of the almost limitless power of a real democracy like ours. Instead of facing the world's demons or realizing our greatest aspirations, we have retreated, hiding our ideals behind our daily concerns and clinging fast to the past, to old models, worn-out assumptions, and the failed policies and politics of previous generations.

A national retreat from our ideals. Apathy from coast to coast. The steady erosion of the American dream. Could a single, final devastating event have triggered all that? Had Bobby Kennedy lived, had he become president, the world would be a different place, sure. But Bobby Kennedy wouldn't have—simply couldn't have, no matter how extraordinary he was—solved all the problems America would face. No one person could. But as a nation, as a people, we could have—with or without Bobby. And for whatever reason, we chose not to.

Maybe Robert Kennedy's assassination was the knockout punch. Maybe it was one too many blows. Or maybe it was just an excuse to run from our ideals, a reason to take the easy way out. Whatever the reason, however we want to explain, justify, defend, or excuse it, that is what happened. During the last thirty years we have, for the most part, silenced our national ideals. We put them in a box, sealed it, and sent it away.

It started with the Baby Boomers. My generation just followed suit. Often I'm tempted to think it's all their fault, that we never had a chance—and to a certain extent that's true. Certainly more than any other generation, I think the Boomers carry the bulk of the responsibility for what has and hasn't happened in America during the last three decades. But we all share the blame.

My generation can try to spin ourselves as different. I know I have. But who are we trying to convince, them or us? We checked out early, and the Boomers checked out late. We all seem to have lost our faith, our willingness to try. I look at most of my friends, most of the younger people I meet in my daily life and the thousands I met as a twentysomething political activist, and they don't want to make the effort any more than the Baby Boomers. Like the rest of America, most people in my generation think it's a waste of time. Just like their parents, they're all too happy not to rock the boat. Things might not be perfect, but they could be worse. We're mostly just doing what everyone else is doing. No one wants to be the one to go out on a limb.

At Stanford Law School, for example, one of the top three law schools in America, the students should consider themselves the chosen people. The world is theirs to conquer. Five hundred of the smartest, most able people in America, earning a credential so powerful that collectively they could change the course of the nation. There isn't a door these bright young minds can't open, not a challenge they can't collectively help America conquer. In the 1960s, Stanford was one of the hotbeds of political activism. Today, sadly, it's mostly about jobs and money. On the whole (with a few wonderful exceptions), my classmates at law school were about as far from a group of idealists as you can get. Insecure and afraid, they competed with each other to be the first in line to a life of professional subjugation. They begged for the chance to be exploited—to give eighty hours a week and all their loyalty to whatever firm would take them. During interview week the desperation was palpable. These weren't the future leaders of America. They were the most influential group of lemmings I'd ever encountered.

Stanford is not unique. And the students there are no worse than or different from those anywhere else. They're simply a microcosm of the rest of America, a reflection of the prevailing attitudes that sweep across the nation. They're no different from people I know in Hollywood who get paid a fortune to make crap and hide their guilt by arguing that someone else would have done it anyway. They're no different from people I know in Washington who work for political leaders whom they don't respect because there aren't any whom they do respect and they want a job. They're no different from the millions of us who every day make up excuses for why what has gone wrong in America is not our problem or responsibility and who justify not having done more to try to fix our collective national problems. No one else is doing it. Why should I have to go first?

To knowingly allow the loss of an ideal as powerful and transformative as the American dream is treasonous. Yet that is exactly what we have all done. America's democracy offers each of us the opportunity to realize our true selves—to be everything we dream of—regardless of our race, birth, or economic status. The lack of a formal class system, a language that makes no gender distinctions, and the presence of equality under law all combine to create an opportunity that is spiritual as much as material. Free speech, broad protections against the government, and the right to your own beliefs are much more than constitutional concepts; they're a kind of equal opportunity employer that gives every person in this country the chance to succeed beyond his or her wildest dreams. But careless and self-serving political leadership and our national complacency and cynicism about political change have put all that in jeopardy.

Why would we let that happen? Is it because when we look too deeply, when we dig beneath the surface of America, we don't like what we see? Maybe it's just too painful to honestly acknowledge the mess we, or those before us, made, to acknowledge the depth of the inequities, to look our kids in the eyes and tell them the truth. Besides, to own the problem would require us also to acknowledge the causes and confront the solutions, however hard they might be to swallow. And that would mean challenging some deeply held beliefs about ourselves, about our nation, and, more important, about our democracy and its foundations.

Questioning deeply held political and cultural beliefs is the hardest thing any person can do. It requires being willing to abandon the security of what is familiar for the pursuit of what is right. It means risking short-term stability and comfort in order to get long-term growth and generational prosperity. It means challenging tradition in order to find truth, embracing moral authority over political authority, and no longer looking at what has been but rather at what could be. It means challenging our elders, our leaders, our friends, and our colleagues—even our own families—until we're sure the path we're on is right. Questioning one's deeply held beliefs is definitely the hardest thing that any person can be asked to do.

I know. I had to do it.

4.

Blind Faith

WHEN I WAS SEVEN YEARS old, I sat in the living room of my parents' house and watched my little brother die. Jimmy died of heart failure, caused by a high temperature brought on by scarlet fever. Not many kids in America died of scarlet fever in the second half of the twentieth century. But in Christian Science families, kids die of everything from untreated infections and broken bones to measles, malaria, and scarlet fever. I didn't visit a doctor, get inoculations, take any medications, or receive any kind of medical treatment until I was in my early twenties. In my childhood I had everything from the chicken pox to the flu, to near-death fevers, infections due to rusty nails, and that particular spring scarlet fever.

I remember waking up to the sound of my mother's frantic cries in the living room. Wandering downstairs I went from cloudy sleep to wide-awake terror as I saw my father cradling Jimmy in his arms, trying to revive him with mouth-to-mouth resuscitation. I watched in horror as he looked up from his youngest son with a face full of fear and helplessness that I have never forgotten. Then my mother's scream; then the sobbing and gasping, and then—and only then—the call for help. When the ambulance and the paramedics arrived, I sat at the top of the stairs watching my little brother, Jumbo Jim as I called him, disappear in a cluster of big hands and funny machines. But it was too late. He was already dead. I didn't understand why he had died, why my parents and their faith didn't save him. I never understood and no one ever explained. My brother was cremated, his ashes interred in a vault somewhere, and that was pretty much the last anyone said about it.

The topic was off-limits. The very mention caused my mother to burst into tears. Certainly my parents never intended this to happen, and years later, when I was a teenager, my mother told me she believed that there was nothing more that could have been done to save my brother—that he would have died anyway, even if he had been hospitalized. "Medicine doesn't always work," my parents would say. "Look at all the people who die in hospitals from all kinds of things: from medical malpractice, or misdiagnosis," our church leaders would remind me. It was a standard Christian Science line of reasoning. Look at the medical failures, not ours.

Don't get me wrong. None of this was malicious. It was simply misguided. My parents thought they were doing the right thing. Their religious faith told them it was the right thing. So they convinced themselves that the alternatives wouldn't have changed the outcome. And they believed, somehow, that there must be a moral justification, that a loving God must have some reason—either punishment for something they did or a vehicle to strengthen them for something yet to come—for taking their child away.

My parents meant well, and the suffering they experienced—especially my mother—for the rest of their lives was real and, in my view, incalculable. They got their punishment; they had to live with the loss and pay the constantly rising price of relentless denial. But all that still doesn't excuse what they did or didn't do, and it doesn't erase the fact that there was something they could have done, however hard, however much it would have forced them to challenge their preconceptions, question their faith, and risk the support of their friends and their community.

As much as I loved them, I could never completely forgive their stubborn adherence to blind faith, however well intentioned. Because maybe they could have saved Jimmy's life. They could have called an ambulance before it was too late. They could have gotten him simple medical attention sooner. They could have inoculated him. None of this may have made a difference. I'll never know. All I know is that one spring morning I watched my little brother die in their arms. I watched them pray and I watched him die. I've never looked at a doctrine, authority, or institution the same way since.

My parents weren't mean, thoughtless people. They were loving and caring people who believed with all their hearts that if they prayed hard enough, my brother would live. They weren't indifferent. They were indoctrinated, and they were not able to get beyond their own limited belief system about the world and to make the changes—very real and very hard changes—that would have allowed them to take a different course of action.

Their faith was premised on deeply held beliefs, passed down for over a century, reinforced by their church and by their religious community, and protected by a society that allowed them to make the choice they did. To my parents, these beliefs were absolute, inviolable, and self-evident—and it would have seemed heretical to counter them. They were unwilling, maybe even afraid, to challenge what they had been taught. Instead, they bought their religion's party line about faith healing hook, line, and sinker—and my baby brother died as a result.

What my parents did was extreme and, in this instance, tragic, but looked at from a broader perspective, it was not unique. All of us to greater and lesser degrees cling to our beliefs—to the things we grew up with; to the ideas and values that our parents, church leaders, and teachers taught us; to the norms that our communities, friends, lovers, and families share, whether they're about deeply rooted concepts such as race, gender, sexuality, religion, or politics; about parenting, dress, body art, or pornography; or about crime and punishment, rights and responsibilities, the cause of social ills such as poverty, crime or homelessness; or expectations about what is necessary, possible, acceptable, or unacceptable in civil society.

Although my brother's death may seem an odd way to set up a discussion about making change in America, there's an unmistakable similarity to what is happening today with our country. As a little boy, I watched what happened when good and well-meaning people cling to a set of dogmatic beliefs. And I'm watching it today, as an adult in America, as we cling in that same way to a limited way of thinking about our democracy, about our rights and responsibilities, about the social and political problems we face as a nation, and about our system of government and how it should operate.

We have our own national dogmas, from the belief that you have an inalienable right to own a weapon, to the belief that all government is inherently bad; that the free market is always right; that poor people are poor only because they don't pull themselves up by their bootstraps; that more money won't solve our social problems; that divided government is the best government; that voting is a right, not a responsibility; that state interests should always trump federal ones; that privacy is not a fundamental right; and perhaps most frightening of all, that whatever the founding fathers wrote, said, or did must be right.

It's as if we have a national religion, and our bible is the Constitution. Just as with the doctrine of Christian Science that I was raised to believe, our national religion has a series of premises and tenets that the faithful consider unalterable and beyond examination. A number of these tenets make sense and have proven themselves over time. Others are irrelevant, outmoded, or just no longer beneficial to our society and the times we live in. Some are even fatally flawed. But none of these premises, doctrines, or tenets, no matter how sacred, should be beyond examination—now or ever.

The consequences of clinging blindly to false beliefs, whether in a parochial religion like Christian Science or in a secular religion like democracy, is too often destructive. Lives are wasted, dreams are squandered, and opportunities for real and transformative growth are passed by. These consequences, although almost never intended, are too often predictable. The failure to address them in advance, to avoid them if at all possible, and to take whatever steps necessary to minimize their damage is irresponsible, costly, and in some cases immoral. At a minimum, this willing ignorance amounts to a kind of national political negligence. And while it is easily rationalized and explained away today, through

the lens of history and hindsight, it will not be easily forgiven
. . . or forgotten.

We are condemning an entire generation—and perhaps
those that follow—to an uphill battle of epic proportions: to
struggle for decades to pay down trillions in squandered national debt at the expense of needed current investments; to
deal with a level of poverty and violence unheard of in the
rest of the industrialized world; to confront an irreversible
global environmental crisis; and to work with a political system so badly broken that most of us have written it off as
irrelevant. All this, and on top of it, a level of apathy and
indifference that offers no hope for, no reason to, and no
benefit from caring.

This is what my generation and those that follow will get,
unless we all act differently today. It really isn't too late, but
it's later than most of us realize. And continuing to hide behind the superficial gloss of good times is nothing more than
rearranging the deck chairs on the *Titanic*. It's a recipe for
national suicide, even if the worst of it doesn't happen until
after you're dead and buried. There's no such thing as an
unsinkable ship, and, if we ignore the underlying deficiencies
long enough, even the most powerful empire will fall.

I've already made the case for a national housecleaning,
starting with Congress and the president. I really believe that
if we set our minds to it, we could see something close to 525
new members of Congress in January 2001, and a president
who is beholden to neither the Democratic nor the Republican party. But that is only a first step.

The ultimate goal is to create a sustainable America for
future generations. To do that we have to look at our government's operating system and modify it accordingly. That

means asking some hard questions about our government, our leaders, and our rights and responsibilities as citizens in a democracy, and then doing something about the answers we come up with.

Solution #2

- Within a year of taking office, the new American Congress should convene a national convention to rewrite the holy book of American democracy— our national political bible—the U.S. Constitution.

The U.S. Constitution has been considered almost a sacred text. What it does or does not say has been used to justify everything from slavery, to allowing the internment of millions of innocent Japanese during World War II; from justifying various invasions of privacy and censorship of speech, to creating a criminal legal system that is backlogged, inefficient, and almost completely devoid of justice; from allowing people to own AK 47's to denying public funding for kids in religious schools. It's also done a lot of good and helped American democracy survive for over 200 years. But that doesn't mean that it can't be improved. Clinging blindly to a certain set of principles makes sense only if those principles support and reinforce the values, needs, and considerations of our current situation. Besides, the only reason we have the Constitution to begin with is because the Founding Fathers were willing to be radical in their own day. For the times they lived in, some of the stuff they stood for was revolutionary. Are we willing to act with the same courage and integrity today? And if not, why?

Amending the Constitution will be the hardest single thing America as a nation has done or will do since the Civil War. It will force us to question who we are and what we stand for as a nation. But it also will give us the chance to ensure the survival of American democracy for generations to come. It will require more thought, effort, and care than almost any other action taken in the history of our nation. It will challenge us, it will threaten us, and it will transform us. It will be, quite possibly, the most meaningful, beneficial, and revolutionary event since the founding of the country.

We put the whole kit and caboodle on the table, and then it's up to us to make it better. What are we afraid of, making it worse? Who are we kidding? It's not as if the country is running smoothly. Constitutional jurisprudence is convoluted, inconsistent, and illogical, not to mention impractical and basically incomprehensible to the average American.

Here are just a few core examples:

- We can't pass a federal law banning guns within a certain distance of any school in America, because the Supreme Court has held that the Commerce Clause (it's the clause in Article I of the Constitution that says Congress has the power to "regulate commerce among the several states") doesn't apply in this instance. The Court's legalistic reasoning is that guns in public schools don't have a "substantial effect" on interstate commerce, a necessary condition according to the Constitution, so Congress can't regulate them in that environment. What's more, the Second Amendment clearly allows gun ownership. So that right trumps. Forget about the kids. Forget about what makes sense.

- XXX movies are in your local video store and on TV in five-star hotels. Porno stars are going mainstream, you can buy pornographic magazines at 7-Eleven, adult content dominates the Internet, and

Playboy has giant billboards promoting its on-line site announcing that "the revolution has just begun." But, believe it or not, these things are not necessarily protected forms of speech. Although the First Amendment is supposed to protect the right of *free* speech, the Supreme Court has held that the Constitution does not protect obscenity—and pornography is very often, at least according to the Court, obscene, regardless of how many of us watch it. So today you have a right to own obscene material—as long as it's not child pornography—but do not have a right to sell it. Now, that's a double standard if I ever heard it. Besides, what exactly is *obscene*, and according to whom?

- You have an explicit constitutional right, written in the Fourth Amendment, against having your home, papers, person, and effects searched without a warrant, but warrantless searches in homes, cars, electronic documents, and even body cavities have been allowed because of the vagueness of how this constitutional right is worded.

- The Constitution prevents discrimination against one state by another. So according to the Supreme Court, this means that a state cannot require that all trash or hazardous waste dumped within its state borders must meet certain environmental standards—because that would discriminate against states that don't meet those standards. Is that just about the dumbest thing you've ever heard? Yet it is not discrimination for one state to refuse to honor a homosexual marriage made legal in another state because the Court does not interpret the Constitution to recognize the validity of gay marriages, only straight ones. Nor does the Court think the Constitution requires equal protection to gays and their lifestyle choices, although they do think it does if the discrimination involves race—say a law treating a black person differently from a white person. The reason for this dichotomy is that race and national origin are the only classifications that the Supreme Court has decided get the highest level of constitutional equal rights protection. Everything else, from gender to wealth, to age to sexual orientation or mental condition, gets a lower level of protection. Why? Because the Supreme Court says so. They say that's what the Constitution says and what it intends, although, in fact, the Constitution doesn't say anything at all about it directly.

You see, although many of the core principles of the Constitution are still valid, its outdated language and lack of specificity about many modern issues has made it ripe for all kinds of interpretational abuse. That's hardly shocking. Just look at the environment in which it was written. When the all white and educated men who started the country wrote the Constitution, black people were slaves—therefore considered three-quarters of a person; women couldn't vote; there was no mass communication; people lived in small communities and defended themselves with local militias (thus the need for guns); there were only thirteen states, all in the East; California hadn't been discovered, at least by us; there were no cars, trains, planes, or freeways; a jury of your peers was not only possible but probable; there was no such thing as birth control; genetics wasn't even a word; and New Jersey was an oasis. Need I say more?

The times have changed, but the document hasn't—not at least in the ways it needs to. The changes in the Constitution that have been made over the last couple hundred years are kind of haphazard; it's almost like we gerry-rigged the thing to work. That's why, for example, the fourteenth Amendment—which was passed primarily to force all states to comply with the end of slavery—has been used to apply all kinds of laws having nothing at all to do with race relations to the states. I'm not saying a lot of these other changes weren't for the better, but an equal number make no sense at all. And the bottom line is that there is no intellectual or moral integrity in applying the Bill of Rights to the states by fiat.

If we want the Constitution in all respects to apply to the states—which I firmly believe it should—then let's pass an amendment that says just that: "Everything in the Constitution applies to the states." Otherwise, let's stop using the fourteenth Amendment, the purpose of which was clearly specific to one issue—racial equality—to try to achieve broad application of the entire Constitution to the fifty states. The truth is that the Founding Fathers probably didn't want the Constitution to apply broadly to the states. But maybe that is what we want now. It's what I want, and many other Americans do too. But if that is, in fact, what we want, then let's do it honestly and thoroughly rather than with the kind of haphazard whatever–the–current–Supreme Court–wants approach that we use now. The ends don't always justify the means, and living that way just sets us up for bigger problems down the road.

We need some accountability in this country, and the Constitution is a great place to start. Look, I'm not a constitutional law scholar, but I had the benefit of studying with some of the biggest names in the field at Stanford. I took a full year of constitutional law and read hundreds of cases and thousands of pages of analysis. I've met several Supreme Court justices and have known a number of Supreme Court law clerks. I can tell you this: It's a carefully preserved fallacy that the Constitution is airtight, that the Supreme Court is impartial and unpolitical, and that the justices make logical and consistent decisions based only on the law and the Constitution, not on their own personal and political ideologies.

Neither the Constitution nor the long and complex series of Supreme Court decisions that have been handed down over the last two centuries is consistent or based solely on the law. In its own way the Court is as political as Congress. The justices rule as much from ideology as from law. And the Constitution is so full of holes when applied to twenty-first-century America that it looks like Swiss cheese.

What's more, our current hands-off approach keeps constitutional jurisprudence above the intellectual reach or comprehension of the average person, and therefore out of the control of the populace. It keeps the Constitution in the hands of a limited number of people, mostly lawyers, all who have a vested interest in keeping it the way it is. That is not an interest the rest of us share.

So there are several powerful reasons to have a national Constitutional Convention.

1. *Force us to accountability*. It's time to stop pretending. Let's say what we mean and do what we say. It's that simple. No more smoke and mirrors. We need a Constitution we can live and abide by.
2. *Provide simplicity and clarity*. Only when we all can understand exactly what rights we have and what

rights we don't have, when we have all agreed on the rules, will we be able to start acting accordingly both as individuals and as a society.

3. *Make our Constitution fit our times.* A Constitutional Convention will provide a means to make the necessary adjustments so that the Constitution is better suited for the society we actually live in— a vast, technologically sophisticated, multicultural, gender-neutral, economically, racially, and educationally diverse modern society, not the one that our Founding Fathers lived in 1776 or the one they might have imagined for our future.

The end goal of a updated Constitution will be a better, more useful national operating manual, and the best way to get there is to make the whole affair an inclusive national process. To bring people into the process and up to speed we hold a series of town meetings across the country—all televised—and hosted by everyone from Ted Koppel, Larry King and Peter Jennings, to Matt Lauer, Oprah, Maury, Rosie O'Donnell, and even Jerry Springer. Get the people who talk to America teach America.

Next, we make easily understood materials available everywhere, not just post offices. We put them on-line, at Kmart, McDonald's, Starbucks, and the Hard Rock Café. We run two-minute trailers at the beginning of big movies with movie stars talking about getting involved in the process. We market the process, and the need to participate, just as we market anything else. We use celebrities, and humor, and sex. And in the end, over the course of a year, we all learn about the Constitution.

We learn about the issues. We talk about the issues. We

fight about the issues. And then we do it: We update the Constitution, making necessary changes to the current amendments and, where needed, adding new amendments. We'll
end up with either a cleaned-up version of the current Constitution or possibly a completely rewritten document that
incorporates the core premises of the old one that we want to
keep and simply adds and subtracts to that. What I'm talking
about is not a revolution, just a modernization—a critical
difference. The former would send the country into a tail-
spin; the latter is ultimately the best way to keep us out of
one in the long term. Most likely we'll emerge with some kind
of a compromise—an improved version of what we have now
but still keeping to the basics of the big document that have
served us well.

The last step is getting the changes made. Article V of the
Constitution sets out the rules for amending the Constitution. A majority vote of two thirds of the state legislatures
would first have to vote to convene a convention. Then, any
actual proposed amendments would require the support of a
majority of the members of three fourths of the 50 state legislatures.

In a nutshell, that's the basic process. People will still say
that it's too risky, that revisiting any of the Constitution will
open a can of worms, that the majority of us will not pay
attention and a minority will have their way with America.
Well, on that last point, they already do. But overall, I think
the opposite is true. I believe a Constitutional Convention
would energize us, bring people out of the woodwork, create
a situation in which a majority of Americans paid attention
to something other than a tragic accident, a horrific crime, a
scandal, or a national sports championship. You're talking
about changing some pretty sacred and fundamental things.

Americans are smart. We know when something's important. This would be. We'd all know it. And we would show up for the party.

We can also amend the Constitution without a convention. And if we're too scared to hold one, we should still consider making some long-overdue changes, even one amendment at a time. In the amendment-by-amendment approach, proposed amendments first would be introduced in Congress, where they would have to pass muster with two thirds of both the Senate and the House of Representatives— something an all-new Congress would make a lot easier. After that, the changes would need to be ratified by a majority of the members of three fourths of the 50 state legislatures. But again, a constitutional convention is the better route, since it would involve more of us in the process, ensure a more citizen-controlled outcome, and allow us to do a more comprehensive and honest job of bringing the Constitution up-to-date.

That said, here are the most important things I think we should do. Rob's constitutional reforms in a nutshell. Just remember, these are *my* ideas, nothing more. Some of them may work; some may not. Some people will agree with all of them. Some people with agree with none of them. I hope you will agree with some and disagree with others. Because that is exactly where we need to be—in a dialogue, at the beginning of the journey, not at the end result.

I've broken my proposed reforms into two categories: the *Necessary Changes* and the *New Amendments*. I've taken a minimalist approach—sometimes less is more—and focused on the areas that I think are essential to moving America into the next century.

THE NECESSARY CHANGES

The Second Amendment

First off, I say let's just get rid of the Second Amendment altogether. It's not serving the purpose it was designed for— to allow citizens to form militias to protect against foreign invasion. Not even close. So we need to either change it to reflect a modern and useful purpose or eliminate it altogether. If what we really want is for people to be able to have guns to shoot their spouses, kids, and neighbors, or to protect against crime (which technically is what the police are supposed to do), or to just have in the event of a violent emergency, then let's make the Second Amendment say that and be done with it.

I'm not kidding. Guns do kill, despite the fact that the National Rifle Association (NRA) says only people do (but with guns in their hands, so go figure). But that doesn't mean we aren't OK, with that. There may be a time and a place to have and to use a gun. And the cost of allowing for that may be that accidents happen—lots of them. From the massacre at Columbine High School in Colorado to abusive husbands and jealous wives who in a fit of rage shoot their spouses, or kids who find a gun under the bed and accidentally shoot their siblings, friends, or themselves. But maybe we're willing to pay that price for the freedom to pack a weapon. Maybe it's worth it to us for the emotional safety factor, to be sure that the only people who have guns are not the police and criminals. Then let's just say so and be done with it. Cut the crap; you want a gun, here's the deal. A clean amendment, not subject to lots of interpretation and not weighted down by any historical bullshit. It should say this:

You have the right to own a gun, subject to reasonable and limited restrictions on type, place, and registration requirements, which shall be decided on a state-by-state basis.

Otherwise, let's just delete the whole amendment. All the current amendment is doing is fucking things up. If the mayor and city council in New York City or Miami want to ban guns, why shouldn't they be able to? The streets in most American big cities are tense and dangerous enough without armed citizens. Who are we kidding when we pretend that the Constitution intended to protect the right of an urban motorist to carry a gun to shoot at another citizen in a road rage explosion? The America of the Founding Fathers *needed* an armed and prepared citizenry. The last thing we *need* in America today is armed citizens, especially in urban America.

On the other hand, why shouldn't you be able to have a gun in Kentucky or Wyoming or West Virginia if that's what a majority of those citizens want, whether for hunting or for safety or just because it runs in their blood, and that's how they define liberty? Besides, having spent my teenage years in rural Wisconsin, I can understand someone not wanting to wait a half hour for the police to arrive.

The bottom line is this: Gun laws ought to be a state-by-state choice, not a constitutional issue. Every state should be able to decide, based on what a majority of its residents desire, the appropriate level—if any—of gun control. From total bans, to allowing concealed weapons. The problem now is that because of this 200-year-old dinosaur of an amendment, every time anyone tries to put any kind of a limitation on gun ownership, however reasonable, and however much the people of a given community want it, the restriction runs into this big constitutional hurdle—because the Constitution states that you and every other citizen have the right to own a gun. And the NRA and other gun advocates use this argument every time, effectively prohibiting the federal government from acting in a way that ensures a minimum level of gun control and regulation at a national level, and distorting the real issue—which is what the people of a given state want—when it involves a state gun control law.

Eliminating the Second Amendment will also clear up a sticky constitutional question of whether the amendment actually applies to the 50 states and the laws they pass or only to federal government and any laws or actions it takes. The issue remains hotly debated by legal scholars, and is clouded by less than clear language in the two major cases that first addressed the question over a hundred years ago. (For those who want to know, the cases are U.S. v. Cruikshank and Presser v. State of Illinois.) Either way, there's enough ambiguity surrounding the decisions, that because of the Second Amendment, no state could get away with a total ban on gun ownership—even if every one of its citizens wanted it—and even the most minimal gun regulation by the federal government is made unnecessarily difficult.

It's ridiculous. The Second Amendment was written to provide national security for America and Americans in a very different time and against a very different kind of threat. The decision today whether to allow citizens to be armed or not armed should not come down to a 200-year-old national security issue. By that reasoning, if the Second Amendment had been written today, it would preserve your right to own tactical nuclear weapons in the event the government is overthrown by terrorists and we need to organize citizen militias to fight back.

Today the right to own a gun, if there is one, has nothing

to do with well-being of our nation or our need to protect ourselves from our own government. In its modern context, it's really more about balancing the freedom to live free of state interference and the social mandate to minimize the opportunities for random and unnecessary violence, of which handguns are a main cause in America. That's the real debate, and the one we all should be having. Clinging to the old constitutional framework creates a political barrier that the Founding Fathers probably would have thought was preposterous. So let's do their memory and our world a favor— let's do what they did in 1776 and would have done today: Make an amendment that fits the needs of the people of America and the realities of the times we live in. Nothing more and nothing less.

The First Amendment

We need to bolster the First Amendment. It's probably the only amendment most of us know off the top of our heads—or at least the free speech part: "Congress shall make no law . . . abridging the freedom of speech, or of the press . . ." But despite what a lot of us think, speech is less protected today than ever before, especially if you consider the degree to which speech has expanded—both the range and volume of outputs, and the diversity of types of speech and media for expression.

Today all kinds of speech, from hate speech and obscenities to commercial speech (advertising) and artistic expression, can be restricted and even banned. Only so-called political speech is fully protected—ironic, since it's the least practiced and probably least meaningful type of speech in America today. Among other things, that means that you can't put a limit on what someone can spend to run for office (since trying to get yourself elected is considered a form political expression), although you can limit what a person spends on someone else. (According to the Supreme Court, that's not the same kind of political expression.) You can't censor what a racist like David Duke says at a political rally, but you can keep an artist from expressing herself, or keep a company from advertising, or kick Howard Stern off the air for swearing—although not for talking about how horny he's getting looking at a topless woman with big tits. None of it makes much common sense.

The reality is that the terms, definitions, and standards set by the Supreme Court are confusing, inconsistent, socially and culturally outdated, and naive. Take the pornography example I gave earlier. The Supreme Court has created a three-part test that includes as the first prong whether "an average person, applying contemporary community standards" would find that "the work taken as a whole, appeals to the prurient interest." OK, who decides who is an "average person," what "contemporary community standards" are, and whether something is "prurient"? One justice in a famous line said he couldn't define it in words, but he'd know it when he saw it. First off, they probably won't see it; and second, I really doubt that the nine justices of the Supreme Court have a standard of what is pornographic or obscene that would align with mine, with that of most people I know, or maybe even with yours.

Besides, I don't want nine bookworms who live in constitutional law texts to decide what I can or can't look at and what is or isn't illegal knowledge for me and my friends. Do you? A couple years ago I met Justice Breyer. A friend of mine who is an actress was visiting me and went with me to a cocktail party. In conversation, she told the justice she was shooting a sitcom pilot that was a little like a modern-day *Dick Van Dyke Show*. He looked at her with that blank look of incomprehension and said, "I don't watch a lot of TV." I'm not kidding. He didn't know who Dick Van Dyke was. I don't know about you, but I don't want that person deciding what I can and can't look at.

There is an easy solution. We need to prescribe broad protection for all types of literature, language, pictures, information, and speech—including pornography and obscenity and all on-line and electronic communications, regardless of content or medium. It should not be subject to a wacky subjective reasonable-person type test but provide explicit and comprehensive expression protection. The amendment could read something like this:

> Congress shall make no law restricting the right of free expression in all communication media now developed or to be developed. This protection shall apply to all types of language, literature, pictures, information, and speech, including pornography and obscenity and all on-line and electronic communications. The only exceptions shall be to protect the physical security of a person or a community or the national security of the nation.

The Fourth Amendment

The Fourth Amendment is in some ways the most fundamental right against government intrusion into your life. It's the search-and-seizure amendment, the one that states: "The Right of the people to be secure in their persons, houses, papers, and effects, against unreasonable searches and seizures, shall not be violated . . ."

In the real world of late twentieth-century America, that protection simply no longer exists. The fact is that the Supreme Court has whittled the Fourth Amendment down to where the police can search and seize almost anything they want. The standard the Court has developed is a reasonable expectation of privacy—in other words, whatever a reasonable person would expect to be considered private. If you or I or some other "reasonable" person wouldn't have a reasonable expectation of privacy, then the police can come on in and look—without a warrant and without your permission.

The problem, other than that no two people have the same expectation of privacy, is that the Court's concept of what is reasonable is anything but. The Court held that a man who built a ten-foot wall around his property to shield it didn't have a reasonable expectation of privacy on the grounds that it was in plain sight of a plane flying overhead. The Court considers it unreasonable to expect privacy on anything that is in plain view. The problem is that the Court considers something in plain view even if the police are flying over your property, using flashlights, binoculars, aerial surveillance with a $22,000 camera that can identify an object one-half-inch in diameter, or have attached a beeper to your car in order to follow the radio signals. The Court also holds that you have no legitimate expectation of privacy as to the numbers you call from your home phone; or to a package that the government opens so long as someone else—say, the Federal Express people—already have opened it, even if that was without your consent; or to your trash once it's in the garbage, even if the garbage can is on your property.

The Court has held that a person doesn't have a reasonable expectation of privacy on his or her private property unless it is within what justices call the "curtilage" of your property, an area that is defined as immediately around your actual house. Next to your barn if you live on a farm wouldn't count, only the farmhouse. So that means even if you've walled off your property and put NO TRESPASSING signs every ten feet around the perimeter, if the area in question is more than 100 feet from your house, it's not reasonable to consider it private, at least to the government. You could have me arrested for trespassing, but it's not off limits to the police if they want to search it. Sorry, pal—it's not in the curtilage.

In what is possibly the most bizarre example of "reasonableness" reasoning, the Supreme Court has held that you have almost no expectation of privacy in your car. The Court in its infinite wisdom has decided that a car, unlike a house, is not a place most Americans consider private. I don't know about you, but I consider my car a very private place. I wonder how the justices would feel if after leaving their ivory-towered courthouse they saw strangers sitting in or on their cars. I think they'd be really upset. I know I would. I know some guys who treat their cars better than their girlfriends—which is not to say that makes them great people, but it certainly does suggest they consider their cars to be private places. And I see people do things in cars that I know they wouldn't do in a completely public space—put on makeup, talk on the phone, pick their nose, and have sex.

The car is a home away from home for many people, the most expensive piece of property a lot of us own, and a highly personal space that usually reflects the owner's personality, income level, and taste. So how can the Supreme Court say that you have almost no reasonable expectation of privacy in your car? *Because the justices don't want it to be private.* That's why. It's not that they really think a car isn't private. They're not that out of touch, although the Dick Van Dyke comment might make you wonder. It's that the car, precisely because it is so private, has become a place people can hide things from the watchful eye of the government. And since the Fourth Amendment doesn't say anything literally about cars, and how could it since they didn't have cars (it specifically protects houses, papers, persons, and effects), the Court conveniently has made cars accessible to the police. In other words, they've done an end run around the Fourth Amendment, which is not a good thing to allow if we value our privacy in other areas.

Then there's the Warrant Clause. Sometimes, before the police can perform a search, they are supposed to obtain a warrant from a judge, describing the place and specific property to be seized. The ostensible reason for the Warrant Clause is that when practical and reasonable to obtain, the police should get judicial approval for searches and seizures of private property. The text of the Constitution says: ". . . and no Warrants shall issue, but upon probable cause, supported by Oath or affirmation, and particularly describing the place to be searched and the persons or things to be seized." Warrants, however, slow the police down, and despite a long jurisprudence upholding the basic notion that searches without warrants should be the exception, not the rule, the Supreme Court has come up with so many exceptions to the Warrant Clause that it takes up a whole chapter of criminal procedure.

For starters, there's the obvious—that you consent to the search. That one makes the most sense. After all, if you say yes, it's your problem—although sometimes the police make it impossible to say no. Beyond consent, it's all downhill. The rest of the exceptions are for most part built on constitutional sand. There's the *plain view* exception, which, as I described earlier, includes things that could be viewed by high-altitude surveillance cameras in an airplane; *the search incident to an arrest* exception, meaning after a supposedly legal arrest the police can search you; the *exigent circumstances* exception, which arises when the police confront what they consider extraordinary conditions, such as when they are in hot pursuit of you for something they *think* you did, when they *think* you have a weapon, or when they *think* you might destroy evidence that they *think* you have. Of course, they don't have to be right, they just have to *think* it. Then there are exceptions for almost any type of *automobile searches*. In fact, even if you're handcuffed in a nearby squad car, the police can search your car without a warrant on the grounds that you might be able to escape from the police car and get to a hidden weapon say under the backseat of your car. I'm not kidding, the Court said with a straight face that Houdini-like acts are possible, and this exception was necessary to protect against that. Finally, there are a wide variety of *regulatory searches* allowed without a warrant, including health inspections, border inspections for illegal aliens, and police sobriety checkpoints. All, of course, in the name of public order, and all violations of our fundamental right to privacy from government intrusion into our lives.

The same is true with regard to your house. Despite a remarkably clear constitutional prohibition against letting the government into the private homes of American citizens without a warrant, today in America the police can in most cases find a way into your house and, once inside, find a way to search for just about anything. Technically, the Court has limited a warrantless search of your home to the area in your immediate control, and this exception is justified only as a safety precaution for the police to make sure you are not within reach of a deadly weapon. Fair enough, but to me, this would seem to be a very small area—say within ten feet of where you are standing. The Court, however, has defined this area to possibly include rooms other than the one you are in, faraway hard-to-reach spaces, and closed places— even perhaps a cabinet in the kitchen or the bathroom where the police suspect something very unlike a gun is resting. That I'm handcuffed to the floor facedown with three armed police officers standing over me doesn't make the need to search for those "weapons" any less valid in the eyes of the Court.

I'm making light of it because the Court's reasoning is so ridiculous and absurd and deeply offensive to the sensibilities of any thinking person. The police aren't trying to get to weapons. They're not trying to protect themselves. More often than not, they're trying to get evidence, generally drugs, and they don't want to have to get a warrant to do it. So determined is our government to win the war on drugs (which nonetheless it is losing) that the Supreme Court even has allowed the police to break into private property without a warrant, find incriminating evidence (again, it's almost always drugs), and then come back and say after the fact that they would have been able to get a warrant based on what they found inside.

Do you trust the police that much? I don't. What if they planted the evidence? Even if they didn't, it's a dangerous precedent to allow, because at some point they will. Only by then it might not be drugs they are finding but something different that they, the government, has decided is impermissible—which is exactly why the Fourth Amendment was written in the first place: to keep the state at arm's length, to keep a wall between the authorities and us, and to ensure against abuse of our civil liberties.

We should make a choice. No should mean no. And yes should mean yes. If we want so badly to stop crime and illegal drug use that we are willing to let the government get in our pants, then let's stop pretending that they aren't allowed to. Let's stop making half-ass excuses, which only end up creating an unbelievable amount of litigation, wasting precious time and money, and generally resulting in arbitrary outcomes.

If we want to say yes to the government searching our private property, if that's a right we are willing to do away with to a substantial degree (and remember, we already have in practice), then we should rewrite the Fourth Amendment to say clearly that the police have the right to search your private property if they suspect you have committed a crime. Forget about reasonable expectations of privacy. Forget about warrants and probable cause. If they think you did it, they can check. If you did, too bad for you. If you didn't, then the government should have to pay some kind of a penalty, either financial or retributive. Maybe the cop who makes the mistake should have to go to jail. Or he or she should have to pay you out of his or her salary as compensation for the intrusion.

Otherwise we should make the Fourth Amendment an airtight safety latch against government intrusion into our private lives. Plain and simple. Just like in the good old days. No more complicated exceptions that take years to work through the courts. No more twisted and tangled interpretations of common sense. A clear, bright-line standard. No intrusion into the private space, broadly defined, of an individual, without a warrant. No exceptions. Ever.

What we are doing now is the worst of all. We have a right that is inherent and inalienable, and we are letting the government trample all over it. In the former Soviet Union, people could vote for the Communist Party candidate or for no one. What kind of a vote is that? It's a mockery of an election. And our Fourth Amendment jurisprudence has become just that, a mockery of a constitutional right.

We can amend the current Fourth Amendment to make clearer the line between the state and the individual. That may not be enough, however. Our modern notion of privacy is now much broader than the "search and seizure" of personal property that Founding Fathers contemplated. The best solution to fixing the Fourth Amendment is probably to abolish it altogether and establish a whole new right—a fundamental right to privacy. That's the first of my four proposed new amendments.

NEW AMENDMENTS

Establish a Fundamental Privacy Right

We need to write the word "privacy" into the Constitution. Right now the Court goes back and forth on what privacy is and what it isn't. For example, you have a right to get married—that is, if you're straight—procreate or use contraception, and raise a family—including keeping your kids from receiving medical attention—all with minimal or no state interference. Why? Because the Supreme Court says that these things are privacy rights alluded to but not expressly outlined in the Constitution.

The Court in a series of decisions beginning in 1965 said the right derives from the Fifth Amendment's reference to no loss of liberty without due process, from the Fourteenth Amendment's application of the due process clause of the Fifth Amendment to the fifty states, and from what the Supreme Court called the "penumbra" (OK, with a word like that, need I say anything more about the need for some clarity?) of the other first ten amendments. Penumbra, for those who don't have a Ph.D. in language, is kind of like saying it comes from the gestalt of the Bill of Rights—you know, the general, unspecified feeling the Supreme Court thought or wanted to think the drafters of the Constitution had at the time they wrote it.

On the other hand, you do not have a right to have sex if you are gay. You do not have an unqualified right to have an abortion and, as I pointed out, you do not have a right to privacy in your car. The reason? The Supreme Court says these are not among the things that the Constitution, in its "penumbra," includes as privacy rights. Sounds completely inconsistent and insupportable to a lot of people, and—with all due respect to the fact that the justices were trying hard to work with something that wasn't there—it is.

The truth is, the Constitution is silent on the whole matter. It doesn't say squat about privacy in literal language, either for it or against it. The word isn't written in the text of the Bill of Rights. And in the one place that the Bill of Rights does provide guidance and explicit protection against government intrusion into our private lives—the Fourth Amendment ban on unreasonable government searches and seizures of people and their private property—the Constitution is so vague and the language so outdated that the Court has been able to water down the protection to where, in reality, you have almost no protection.

For example, the Court has upheld a warrantless search without probable cause of a woman's alimentary canal. In 1985 Elaina Hernandez was held for twenty-seven hours at Los Angeles Airport without a warrant, strip-searched, and ultimately subjected to a rectal examination. Don't ask how, but the Supreme Court actually held that being detained for twenty-seven hours in an airport without a warrant did not constitute more than a brief and "noncustodial" (read informal) stop, and that—OK, this is the really harsh part—an anal cavity search was not an unreasonable intrusion into a person's privacy that would necessitate a warrant or even an arrest based on probable cause.

All I can say is bend over folks, because what we have right now is a Supreme Court and a judiciary that is willing to let the police look up your butt at an airport without probable cause, without a warrant, and without arresting you— all in the name of law enforcement. Which makes me think that the justices on the Court are either so out of touch with their own anatomy that they actually think they're being reasonable—in which case they may need an anal cavity check so they can understand—or they're such elitist theoreticians that they have no concept of the practical realities that inform the rest of our lives—in which case they need to be reined in.

Either way the point is the same: Absent a clear and unerasable line in the sand that says that we have a fundamental right to privacy, a line that defines that right and one that forbids the government without due process of law from taking that right away, the Supreme Court is likely to keep eroding what little privacy rights it now acknowledges, whittling away what little protection the justices have artificially read into the Constitution over the last half century and allowing the state to reach deeper and deeper into our personal lives, our private spaces, and our biological, intellectual, and physical sacred realms until the person standing accused, naked and spread-eagled in front of a bunch of guys with guns, is you, in your home, as they download your computer, check what you've read, bought, and thought, examine and evaluate your sexual habits for social and political correctness, and take a couple of DNA strands for a national data bank. All with the backing of the U.S. Supreme Court, under the authority of the U.S. Constitution, and unwittingly authorized by us, the American people—the only ones with the power and authority who could make sure such a terrible outcome doesn't occur.

It hasn't happened yet. But we're already way too close, and the wall that can prevent it from happening doesn't exist. So it's time we put one in place. It's a simple task. Let's write a privacy amendment into the Constitution.

The text might read something like this:

All persons shall have a fundamental right of privacy in their homes, vehicles, and dwellings; in, on, and with respect to their personal property; with regard to their bodily integrity; in their medical and repro-ductive choices; and in all their personal communica-tions, in whatever medium now in existence or to be developed in the future.

"No person shall be denied this right without due process of law. This fundamental right of privacy shall apply to the states as well as the federal govern-ment."

Now, for those of you who worry that criminals will run ram-pant, don't. Because they won't. This right won't create a blanket prevention against any and all government involve-ment or intrusion in our lives. It's merely a check. There are some things we want the government to keep a watchful eye on—say monitoring against child abuse, or pursuing crimi-nal activity, protecting consumers from fraud, or making sure restaurants are clean and buildings won't collapse. And with adequate procedural process—that's what due process of law is—the government still will be able to come into your house, search your car, and even get your files off the com-puter. But right now the wall is too low, the safeguards too inadequate, the terms of privacy too undefined, and the potential for and reality of abuse too great.

A privacy amendment will lift the bar, setting a much higher standard before the government can intrude. It will demand that the police use procedural precautions before violating your privacy, and it will enable courts, legislators, law enforcement, and citizens to operate on the same page, with the same clarity about what is and isn't private, and with the assurance that there's a minimum expectation of privacy that no one can undercut.

It will make a difference, and it will work. Believe it or not, just as the Court worked with the framework of what it had before, it will do so again over the coming decades, massaging the new privacy amendment to adjust to the realities created as new challenges, issues, and complexities arise. In this way, a privacy amendment will do more than create a necessary shield for our current lives; it also will pave the way for a new constitutional jurisprudence in the area of privacy law and allow the Supreme Court and the American people to deal with privacy issues in a framework more appropriate to the era in which we live.

Place Term Limits on the Supreme Court, Congress, and the President

The Founding Fathers wanted to create a balance of power in the federal government. In theory, they did—making a powerful legislature, a much weaker chief executive, and a judiciary to oversee, but not overpower, the both of them. But in practice, and over time, things have changed. Today Congress is probably the weakest of the three branches. The president has enormous power by virtue of the office, the prestige, and the visibility, although this power is somewhat limited in practice and governed by some strict constitutionally mandated guidelines. But the judiciary—in the form of the Supreme Court—has become a juggernaut, something of a council of kings. The justices get appointed for life, and then they just sit there for decades wreaking havoc on the whole country with no recourse.

OK, don't let anyone try to fool you otherwise. The Founding Fathers never intended the Supreme Court to be so powerful. In fact, a lot of the Court's power was self-created back in 1803 in a famous case called *Marbury v. Madison*. John Marshall, the famous first Chief Justice of the Supreme Court, basically told outgoing president James Madison to screw himself by refusing to uphold political appointments Madison had made after losing the election but before leaving office. The immediate effect of the decision was a big political welcome gift to incoming President Thomas Jefferson, with whom Marshall was politically aligned. Jefferson, who had just defeated Madison, could now fill the spots with his own friends. But the long-term effect was to claim for the Supreme Court far more power than the other two branches of government. That might be OK in theory, but not in practice when these guys can sit in power for fifty years.

So I have an idea. There's no need to weaken the Court's power directly. Instead, we just put a limit on how long these guys can stay there. Right now they're appointed for life, as if they are priests or something. But with the Supreme Court you don't have a choice about whether to go to church and worship—it's mandatory adherence. So to fix that, let's pass a constitutional amendment that creates a single ten-year term for each justice.

Term limits on the Supreme Court would keep the Court from ruling our lives arbitrarily, put a check on the unlimited political power the nine justices now have, and keep the Court politically balanced and in touch with the times. Justices of the Supreme Court should, at least to some degree, reflect the values of the American people at any given time and the times in which those people live. And the only way to ensure some healthy relationship between the America we live in and the laws that govern us is to require change and turnover on all levels—even the high Court.

While we're at it, why don't we establish constitutionally mandated term limits for all nationally elected offices? Even if Congress passes statutory term limits (meaning it makes a law saying there are term limits), the Supreme Court could—and probably will—say they are unconstitutional. That, or future Congresses could try to repeal them. A constitutional amendment is the only way to make the term limits permanent (at least until the next Constitutional Convention).

Constitutionally mandated term limits also would give us the opportunity to fix once and for all our messed-up national election cycle. Right now we have four-year terms for the president, two-year terms for members of Congress (or the House of Representatives), and six-year terms for U.S. Senators. This is crazy. It means every four years we have a big election and every two a small one. Every two some senators are up for election and some are not—who can keep track?—and basically no one has any time to focus on being in office because their all too busy worrying about the election cycle.

So let's unify the whole thing, with a comprehensive Term Limit Amendment to the Constitution that creates one ten-year term for Justices of the Supreme Court and two four-year terms for every elected national office—senators, congresspersons, and the president. They all get two terms maximum—that's eight years total. Fair and square. Easy to remember. The incumbents' lock on the system will be broken. Special interests lose. The public wins. Our government runs better, and we think about elections only half as often and, I hope, twice as hard.

Make Equality a constitutional fact

We should pass an Equality Amendment, guaranteeing, at least in formal terms, equality under law for all people, regardless of race, gender, sexual orientation, or religion. Its wording could be simple and straightforward:

> It shall be illegal for any state, state agency, or representative of the state to deny any person any job, promotion, service, or benefit—or to discriminate in any other way against a person—based on gender, race, national origin, religion, or sexuality.

An Equality Amendment essentially would bring to an end the long legal battle over fairness. It would implicitly forbid quotas and affirmative action—which, however well meaning, were seriously flawed attempts to force equality that ultimately created a double standard and held minorities down and only exacerbated racial tensions. At the same time, an Equality Amendment would make unconstitutional legislative actions like the Defense of Marriage Act and other religiously or conservatively motivated restrictions against gays and other minorities.

Deal with the Death Penalty

Opponents of the death penalty often argue that the Eighth Amendment's ban against cruel and unusual punishment makes the death penalty unconstitutional. In practice, however, because of the more conservative makeup of the Court today, the cruel and unusual punishment argument doesn't work anymore, and capital defense attorneys focus instead on alleged procedural and substantive rights violations of the defendant while in the criminal justice system. The defense attorneys go through every piece of paper in the file and in the court records and try to find a Fourth, Fifth, or Sixth Amendment right that was violated. The whole thing takes up a lot of time and energy Sixth and still keeps very few people out of the chair.

Even if a future Court swings back to include more traditionally liberal justices, the eighth Amendment argument is weak. Like the NRA with the Second Amendment, it's longstretch reasoning. The Founding Fathers didn't think death was cruel or unusual. They passed laws allowing people to kill their slaves. They had duels in the streets. They had public hangings. We, however, may feel as a society that death is an inappropriate punishment for the state to mandate on a citizen, no matter what the crime. After all, it's not a very civilized response.

On the other hand, justice is sweet and there are some people who just seem to have forfeited their right to life by the horrific nature of their criminal acts. Then again, maybe the bigger issue that we as a society need to confront is whether we want the state to have the power to take life, under any circumstance, regardless of the nature of the crime or character of the criminal.

Either way, just as with gun ownership, let's face the issue head on and stop beating around the bush and taking up all kinds of time and energy—legal, emotional, and intellectual—because we can't as a society make a clear choice about a vital social issue. Let's just step up to the plate and either allow the death penalty or disallow it.

Choice A:

No state shall be allowed to execute a citizen, regardless of the crime. However, life imprisonment can be made mandatory for any crime that results in the death of another person or that involves a substantial level of violence.

Choice B:

The death penalty shall be allowed, for certain statutorily defined crimes (however, only for those that involve intentional taking of life), and shall be decided on a state-by-state basis. The method of death shall be up to the convicted defendant, and shall be limited to death by lethal injection or the taking of a poison pill with the last meal.

That's my list of proposed constitutional changes. It isn't comprehensive, but I think it's a good start. We don't have to change what's working, but we need to decide as a nation what we think works and what doesn't. As I said before, everyone is going to have his or her own idea, and we'll just have to battle it all out in the court of public opinion.

There's no doubt that a Constitutional Convention will be a big deal. It will be hard. It may be divisive. There's no guarantee that we will make the Constitution better—although it's hard to imagine we wouldn't. At the end of the day and if we want to enough, I think we can find agreement on what we want to do and the means to do it. Without a doubt, the outcome will be infused with all the intelligence, imagination, and spirit that our nation possesses.

A major overhaul of the Constitution can be done, and it should be done. The elitists will cry wolf, worried that the American people aren't up to the task and that, even if the current system is broken, trying to fix what's wrong will only make things worse. I believe that we are more than able. Even Thomas Jefferson, who helped write the first one, said he thought we should convene a Constitutional Convention every twenty years "for periodical repairs" so that each new generation could have "the right to choose for itself the form of government it believes most promotive of its own person." We've stalled for long enough. Let's give ourselves a millennium present. Let's put in place a constitutional framework that fits the world we live in. We deserve it. We will benefit from it. And besides, we can't continue to prosper much longer without it.

5.

Nightmare on Main Street

IN APRIL 1997 BERT KAY got an offer he couldn't refuse. NASA offered him a great job in a small, affluent community in northern California, with some of America's best
public schools, one of the nation's great private universities,
and streets you could let your kids play on at night. It didn't
take long for Bert and his wife to decide to take their three-
year-old twin daughters from the urban chaos of New York
City to the serene Palo Alto.

Palo Alto is about as white bread a community as you can
find. Its tidy streets are populated by executives at top technology companies, Nobel Prize winners, and Olympic athletes. It has one of the highest per capita incomes of any city
in America. The houses are big, the lawns luscious, and the
streets shared evenly among cars, bicycles, and pedestrians.

At around 10 P.M. on June 12, Bert picked up his keys and went for his nightly "thinking" walk. He left his wallet at home and set out to enjoy some private time. Half an hour later he ran into six teenagers on the grassy promenade in front of city hall. Bert never came home. The next morning police found his battered body behind a park bench, a block away from the police department. The victim of a random gang assault, Bert had been kicked and stomped to death by members of the True Blue Crips, a Pacific Islander gang from East Palo Alto—which, in direct contrast to its affluent next-door neighbor, has one of the lowest per capita incomes in the country, less than one-third Palo Alto's.

Maybe the Crips killed Bert because he didn't have any money. More likely, it was part of a gang initiation—Bert dies and a new kid makes the cut for the gang. Either way, Bert was dead, leaving his wife without a husband and his twin little girls without a father—and the six assailants had just closed the book on the rest of their lives. Proud of their act, they left a blue bandanna on his body to identify their gang as the culprits. The police arrested all six of them within a week.

On Tuesday October 13, 1998, a German tourist Horst Fietze, his wife, and a friend were taking a walk along the wind-swept boardwalk of Santa Monica, a beach town twenty-five miles west of Los Angeles. As they walked directly across the street from the swank four-star hotels that line the beach-front, a stranger shouted at Horst. He turned, apparently misunderstood their demand for money, and seconds later lay dead in the street from gunshot wounds.

A mile away and two hours earlier, in an unrelated event, Omar Sevilla walked along a boulevard returning from his twenty-second birthday party. A car drove by filled with people he'd never met, and never would. They fired five shots at Omar, killing him on the spot.

Less than a week before the shootings in Santa Monica, Matthew Shepard, a gay twenty-two-year-old college student at the University of Wyoming in Laramie, was picked up at a bar where he hung out, taken to a remote area, robbed of his wallet and shoes, beaten, burned, and then lashed like a scarecrow to a wooden fence, his skull smashed in with a .357 Magnum. His crime: coming on to one of his assailants in the bar earlier that night.

On Monday morning, April 20, 1999, two high school seniors in Littleton, Colorado, walked into their school carrying guns, pipe bombs, and a plan to blow the school and everyone in it to ashes. Two hours later fifteen people were dead, twenty-five were wounded, and the country was left staring in disbelief at the worst school shooting in American history.

Littleton, Colorado, is a comfortable, middle-class suburban community. The kids live in big houses with two-car garages, have computers in their classes, and have been given every economic, social, and educational advantage there is.

Palo Alto has one of the highest per capita incomes in the country, and one of the lowest crime rates.

In 1997 Santa Monica had one homicide all year. In October 1998 it had two in one day. By November 3, election day, the homicide count for 1998 had climbed to six, and Santa Monica was on the verge of a gang war.

The Laramie, Wyoming, police commander said that in

his twenty-five years on the force, there had been a few hate crimes but "nothing anywhere near this."

According to the United State Bureau of Justice Statistics, crime in America is decreasing. According to the aggregate statistics, the rate of violent crimes decreased almost 20 percent from 1993 to 1997. Similarly, rape, robbery, and assault rates all declined. So did burglary, theft, and auto theft. Homicide rates declined as well. Tell that to the friends and families of Bert and Horst and Omar and Matthew. Tell that to the families and friends of the dozen dead and two dozen wounded kids from Columbine High—to the members of an entire city that will never be normal again.

Statistically, crime rates may be falling, but in the larger sense, crime in America is anything but on the decline. Horrendous, violent crimes of the type most of us could hardly have imagined twenty years ago are commonplace. Littleton, Colorado, was the worst—so far—but not the first. It happened eight times in 1998 alone: students in junior high and high school opening fire on their teachers and classmates, making postal worker rampages seem like petty theft. Preteens have been charged with violent sexual homicides. Today the median age of sexual assault offenders (not victims) is thirteen. Teenagers are now the leading perpetrators of homicides and the leading victims. Between 1985 and 1994 juvenile arrests for murder increased 150 percent and arrests for aggravated assault and weapons charges doubled. It's not just kids, however. Thirty-four-year-old George Pierre Hennard took a Glock 17 pistol and a Ruger P-89, got into his Ford Ranger, and drove right into Luby's Cafeteria in Killeen TX in October 1991 and shot fifty-five people—twenty-three of them dead.

Random acts of violence unheard of thirty years ago in America are more and more common. Two years ago Timothy McVeigh blew up the Oklahoma City federal building, killing over 100 people and starting a new trend in U.S. terrorism. Someone, probably fugitive and suspect at large Eric Rudolph, bombed the Atlanta Olympics. Bombings at abortion clinics are common, as are hate crimes, drive-by shootings, murderous acts of road rage, gang rapes, child kidnappings, wildings, and, possibly the most brutal and shocking, the gang initiation similar to what probably happened to Bert Kay, where the initiate must kill an unsuspecting and random victim to become a member of the gang.

Gangs, once the exclusive province of big cities, have flourished and spread to the small towns of the Midwest and the open plains of Montana. And gang violence has reached epidemic proportions in both degree and frequency. Remember *West Side Story?* Show that family picture to an urban fifteen-year-old today and they'll laugh. Honestly, Charles Manson and the Tate murders seem almost tame compared with the nature of many crimes that happen, and happen often, today. The truth is that even the most shocking crimes no longer surprise us. They make the news for a week and then they're history, replaced by the next sensational event. Can you remember the major crime stories of a year ago? Was there a shooting rampage, a gang rape, or a horrific abduction and murder in the last month? Would you really remember if there were? And more important, would you really care?

It seems that, for the most part, we've become immune to the violence, almost unaware of any incident that doesn't affect us in some way personally, unless of course it becomes a national news story. Even then it's like watching a wreck on the freeway—we watch because we can't look away, not because we really care. And once it's over, just like a football game, we change channels and move on to the next newsbreaking event for amusement. Other than a morbid fascination with crime and taking enormous precautions to protect ourselves, we've kind of checked out, turned off the TVs in our heads, and simply decided to accept the horror as a part of modern American life. After all, what else are we supposed to do?

But are we really indifferent—or are we just really scared?

Despite the quiet calm on the surface, just a few feet below, the waters are troubled. Jaws is out there waiting, and we all know it-even if Roy Scheider hasn't closed the beach yet. Increasingly, no place in America is really safe. At least, not safe by the standards of the society my parents grew up in. Not safe enough to let your children play outside unsupervised, much less talk to a stranger; not safe enough to let a female friend walk to her car alone; not safe enough to make the mistake of cutting off a stranger in traffic; or accidentally to walk down the wrong street or drive through the wrong part of town. America is not getting safer, violence is just getting more common and seems less shocking when we hear about it. In fact, in 1982 a Gallup poll found that 3 percent of the country thought crime was the most important problem facing America. In 1998 the number had gone up to 20 percent.

Even the superficial statistical decline in crime rates is somewhat of an illusion. The current drop is from the record highs of the 1980s and early 1990s, not over the longer term. Compared to the 1960s and 1970s, or to any other period in American history for that matter, the rate of crime in the United States is astronomical. Since 1968 the incidence of violent crimes nearly tripled, with the number of aggravated assaults going from 300,000 to over a million in 1996, forcible rapes increasing from 32,600 to almost 100,000, and murders rising from just under 14,000 to nearly 20,000.

Crime has increased throughout the world in the last thirty years, but nothing like in the United States. The dramatic increase is not happening everywhere else—or *anywhere* else. When you look at the United States compared to any other industrialized country today, our crime rates are staggering. In 1990 there were 23,440 homicides in this country. Germany had 3,000; Canada had 1,561, and England only 669. Israel, a country most Americans think of as racked with violence, had only 118. There were 102,560 rapes in the United States in 1990. In Germany that same year, there were 5,112, one-twentieth as many; 3,391 in England; and just 687 in Italy. Even in China, with almost 2 billion people, the number of rapes was only 50,000—half of what it was in the United States.

Crime isn't going away. What's happening is that we're basically just putting a lot more people in prison and avoiding the real underlying issues. The number of prison inmates per 100,000 U.S. residents almost doubled between 1990 and 1997. In the one-year block between mid-1996 and mid-1997 alone (a period when crime rates were supposedly falling) the number of people in prison increased almost 5 percent, to over 1.7 million people.

By the beginning of 1999 the number of people behind bars had increased to almost 1.9 million. In addition, 3.9 million adults were on probation or parole at the end of 1997, an increase of over 100,000 during that year alone. That means that there are almost 6 million U.S. residents currently under some form of state or federal correctional control, and the number is increasing daily.

The United States has the highest recorded rate of incarceration of any nation in the world—passing both South Africa and Russia, countries that used to hold that dubious distinction. We incarcerate six to ten times as many people, per 100,000 population, as most of the other industrialized nations of the world. Between 1985 and 1998 the U.S. rate of incarceration increased 113 percent. In New York State alone, the prison population went from 12,000 in 1973 to over 70,000 today. It's stunning and frightening, and it leaves us with a twofold problem.

First, we don't have enough prisons for all the prisoners. At the end of 1997, state prisons were operating at between 15 to 27 percent above capacity and federal prisons at 19 percent above capacity. And that's after a ten-year building spree. Between 1990 and 1995 America built 213 new jails or prisons—that's nearly one new prison a year per state, with the trend continuing in the last five years. In the last 15 years, California alone has built 21 new prisons—compared to only 1 new university campus.

We're spending a fortune on punishment. State government prison expenditures increased more than 450 percent between 1982 and 1993, from $4.2 billion to over $19 billion, and the amount of direct government expenditures, local, state, and federal combined, for corrections activities in the United States increased since 1982, from 35.8 billion to over $100 billion annually. At a cost of between $20,000 and $30,000 per inmate per year, that means that we are spending upward of $35 billion a year to lock people up-roughly double the national budget for welfare. Talk about throwing good money after bad.

Second, we're dealing with the symptom not the problem. Our solution—locking more and more people up—is a Band-Aid that eventually won't be able to hide the ugly growth that festers beneath it. There's a big difference between a genuinely lower rate of crime and simply rapidly upping our prison population. When most of these people come out, and eventually they will, I promise you they are not going to be better than when they went in. They are not going to have the social, educational, and psychological skills to compete in the workplace, to have satisfying relationships, to raise families, and to contribute to the greater good. They are not going to be good role models, great parents, or employees of the week. They are going to be poorly adjusted, unproductive, and angry. They will be the products of a system devoted punishment instead of rehabilitation. Given our current prison model, almost without exception they are going to be worse when they come out than when they went in, and that is really not a good thing.

When you take your basic inmate, we're not talking about a well-educated investment banker who fudged the numbers one too many times and got caught. In 1996, 48 percent of jailed women had been physically or sexually abused before incarceration. Twenty-seven percent had been raped. One-third had some form of mental or physical disability. In 1997, a majority were unemployed and 90 percent made less than the national average. Thirty percent were between the ages of thirty-five and forty-four. 82 percent were high school dropouts. When it comes to the majority of the prison population, we're talking for the most part about people who start out behind the curve. Absent a miracle, under the current system of incarceration they will come out even farther behind.

Not surprisingly, recidivism rates are sky high. A study of prisoners from eleven states, representing over half of all prisoners in U.S. prisons, found that 63 percent of those released were rearrested for a felony or a serious misdemeanor within three years of their release—23 percent for a violent offense—and that 42 percent were returned to jail. Recidivism rates were highest among men, blacks and Hispanics, and persons who had not completed high school. The older the prisoner, the lower the rate of recidivism. Is anybody surprised? You can't cage a person like an animal, do nothing to help him change, and hope he's different when he gets out. It just doesn't work that way.

So here's the fuller picture. Crime rates are dropping. True—but that's relative to the recent past. The rate of crime in the United States is higher today, and the nature and magnitude of crime is far worse than when compared to thirty, twenty, or even ten years ago. (Forget about comparisons to other countries.) And while it's true that we're locking more people up, eventually they're going to come out again. Almost all of them. And when you combine what happens in prison with the makeup of most of America's inmates before they go in, it's just a matter of time till we have a new generation to incarcerate, because we're not really fixing the problem. In fact, we're only making it worse. **The third of my common sense proposals—three radical reforms to our current approach to crime & punishment—would change that**.

According to a 1996 Gallup poll, 49 percent of us thought the most important goal of prison should be rehabilitation. Another 33 percent thought it should be crime prevention and deterrence. Only 14.6 percent thought it should be punishment. Yet that is exactly what prison in America does today—punishes people. Which is kind of like cutting off our nose to spite our face. Because as I've mentioned, most of these people, when they have served their time, will come out, no better off and most likely much worse than when they went in. And we will have paid for it. Every single dollar.

Why not give them a chance to come out better than they went in—to go straight and to begin a new life after they have served their time? I'm not saying let's make a nice home for people who rob yours. I'm saying let's make incarceration productive. Let's provide essential job training; basic literacy and educational skills; help people learn self-respect and social skills, rage control, discipline, self-respect. We can make them learn, work, and improve themselves. We can give them an incentive, give them role models, give them mentors. And we can give them a chance to start again, with decent odds, after they pay their dues.

True, some people are beyond any and all help—but that's a minority, and one that probably should be treated differently. If you commit a crime for which you receive a life sentence without the possibility of parole—meaning a crime that is so violent, offensive, and shocking that we never want to let you out on the street again—then we can keep you like a caged animal. Maybe then you have lost your right to a second chance. Maybe then you have lost your right to any help. Maybe then we want you to suffer so badly and our need to punish you is so great that we really should just lock you up and throw away the key. But that's not most people in prison today.

For the rest, for the vast majority of people living in the state and federal prison system, people who are not beyond help, people who do deserve a second chance, being caged like a wild animal serves no purpose and has no utility, for them or for us. It doesn't cost us less, in either the short or the long term. It has no rehabilitative value—which makes it a pointless and self-defeating response to crime because, even if some criminals can't be rehabilitated, many could be. And it doesn't deter crime. At least not in the long term, and that's what really counts.

So, the first step in reforming our crime and punishment system should be basic but systemic. Let's reserve the current (put-'em-in-a-cage-like-an-animal) incarceration structure for the most violent offenders. For all the rest, for the vast majority of the million and a quarter people in prison, why don't we try a more constructive, socially productive, and civilized approach—one that highlights our humanity, not our vindictiveness?

Here's what I propose:

- **The federal government should replace its current incarceration system with a military model for all federal prisons and provide corresponding federal incentives for any states that adopt a similar model.**

Let's convert our prisons into military like bases—fenced and surrounded with towers and armed guards—and put prisoners who commit violent crimes into them for a minimum three-year stay, complete with boot camp, basic and hard physical training, prison police (who act like MPs), curfews, no leaves, martial law once you're inside, serious penalties—including physical punishment—for violating rules, and deadly consequences for trying to escape. Once inside, there would be little free time. Instead, inmates would be subject to a highly regimented schedule morning to night—exercise, work, study—all of it designed to teach them self-respect; respect for law and order; discipline; and social, workplace, and academic skills,-and to give them a fighting chance at starting over once they get out.

Only the worst offenders, those who are never going to leave and those who consistently fail to comply with the rules of the base, would end up caged, alone and held like an animal in a cell. The rest would live in barracks, have drill instructors, address superiors in formal military titles—

captain, sergeant, general—wear military-style uniforms, be placed in platoons, receive summary punishment, have a "brig" for solitary confinement, and be given a public graduation ceremony when they leave. They would be given demanding physical labor, drug and alcohol counseling, mandatory therapy, academic education, vocational training, and ongoing rigorous drills. Just like the military, the camps would be an experience of total immersion, including summary and severe discipline, hard work, physical and mental training, and unquestioning obedience to authority.

A military model for prison makes sense and can be done. A number of states have experimented with boot camps for prisoners since 1983, with the first one in Georgia. However, none of the seventy-five boot camps in the United States today is intensive enough, keeps prisoners long enough, and makes the stay hard enough. The average stay in a boot camp is 180 days; that's not enough time to do what the military does. They don't have martial law inside the camps, and typically they provide only low-level, parole-type supervision once the prisoners get out, rather than the intensive aftercare that would be necessary to make the changes stick. A successful program needs to be comprehensive and widespread—basically a replacement model for prisons, not an alternative for a small and limited number of prisoners.

Rehabilitating those whom we will eventually let out and caging those we won't also might help us solve the dilemma around the death penalty. Perhaps we'd feel better about eliminating it (which is really the more civilized thing to do, no matter how much we want certain people to suffer and die) if we reserved the most inhumane treatment exclusively for people whose crimes now allow for a death sentence.

Right now we treat everyone pretty much the same once they're locked up. If you're in prison for fraud or possession of cocaine with the intent to distribute, you're right there beside the guy who cut someone's liver out and ate it. Equal treatment for unequal acts doesn't seem fair to either them or us. So we naturally want to up the ante and do something worse to the worst offenders; thus the death penalty. But how much more sensible and socially productive instead to create a helpful and hopeful framework for those who can be helped, and isolate and metaphorically banish only those who are beyond redemption, at least in this lifetime.

A military model for prisons also is a good business and social investment—putting our justice system resources toward a future gain rather than just pouring more good money after bad. Based on the first ten years of model boot camps, the cost per offender was about the same as that of a prison inmate. That alone makes it worth doing. But there's another reason, equally important. It would be good for us as a society. The great Russian writer Dostoyevsky said that a society should be judged not by how it treats its upstanding citizens but by how it treats its criminals. Based on that standard, America wouldn't get very high marks.

What we're doing now is really a kind of learned helplessness. We're so overwhelmed by the crime problem, and so familiar with the historical way of treating it, that it's hard to believe in a fundamentally new approach or to know how to begin pursuing it. So instead we just lock more people up, and then, at least for a little while, we feel better. But for how long, and to what end? How much safety do we really get? How lasting is the satisfaction? Does it solve the problem?

Put him away—that'll teach him. But will it? At the end of the day, does retribution for crime leave any of us feeling like winners? The victims are not restored to where they were before the crime, and the offenders are not less likely to do it again. We're no better off, nor are they. How much more satisfying would it be to feel like we actually won some-thing, made something better, different? How much more satisfying would it be and how much more would we get from the act of forgiveness that is required to give someone another chance?

We've proven we can terminate. We've shown how un-forgiving, how tough, how lacking in compassion we can be. We've shown how much we can punish people. That was the easy part. The real question we need to ask, the real chal-lenge for America in the twenty-first century, is whether we can learn to do less and, in doing less, do more. Do we have the courage to admit that the current approach is failing and to try a new one?

Adopting a military model for all prisons would be the most significant change in the American criminal justice sys-tem since the founding of the country. It would be progres-sive and enlightened and would do more to solve the crime crisis in America than all the combined so-called reforms of the last decade. If this was all we did to improve the current criminal justice system, we could pat ourselves on the back and move on to other social problems. We would have done a socially redeeming thing for our country. We would posi-tively affect the lives of millions of people now incarcerated, while at the same time saving millions of us from becoming the victims of crimes not yet committed. We would change our destiny. As remarkable as that would be, it is still only a first step in dealing with the crime and punishment dilemma facing America. There is another level we could go to if we were willing, a second step that would actually allow us to start moving the crime clock backward rather than just put-ting it on hold.

If you're a tough-on-crime, zero-tolerance kind of person,

you probably won't like what I am about to propose, because it changes the paradigm that we have all become used to when dealing with crime and punishment. Crime is a somewhat relative concept. In other words, at least to some extent it is our judgments and attitudes about what is criminal and what is not that condition the actual behavior of those who commit crimes. The more we criminalize behavior, the more criminals we have. The less we make criminal, the fewer criminals we have.

At the same time, the worse we punish someone for an act we collectively define as "criminal"—even if it's an act that the perpetrator thinks is justified from his or her vantage point—the more likely that person is to do it again, and maybe even do something worse. We're all social beings, and our behavior is a product of not just our circumstances but also of how others look at us and our behavior. It's just a sad truth of human nature: Someone beaten as a kid tends to beat his or her kids. You raise a person to think that he is an elephant and he probably will grow up acting like one. You tell someone he's a criminal enough times and he thinks of himself that way. It's just the way we are.

Even if we think there's a code of behavior that defines right and wrong, it's not absolute. It's always changing, with the times. Jesus told the disciples that they had a right to steal corn from the fields—even though the fields were the private property of the Pharisees—because he said God put the seed there for them as much as for the people that owned the land. Yet one of the Ten Commandments is Thou shalt not steal. Who was right, Moses or Jesus? At the end of the day, maybe it just depends on which side of the fence you're on, whether you're a landowner or a peasant. Regardless of what you think about the disciples illegally pocketing corn, the bottom line is the same: Crime is not absolute. It's relative to the times and to the situation and to the circumstances in which the act happens.

Punishment should be relative as well. We already look at many acts, while bad or dubious in nature, as noncriminal. That's why we have a civil justice system. If I destroy your floor while repairing your plumbing you can sue me, but you can't put me in jail. Yet if I steal a painting from your home while repairing your plumbing, you can put me in jail. Why the difference in punishment?

In addition to putting in place a more humane, productive, and rehabilitative system of incarceration, we also can find more humane, productive, and rehabilitative ways to punish people than simply incarcerating them. In fact, it's kind of barbaric that we haven't already. As we enter a new millennium, it's time we took a more enlightened view of criminal behavior and of the best way to punish people for acts that do not involve violence.

- **The federal government should statutorily eliminate prison terms for all nonviolent offenses, or at least for all nonviolent property and drug related offenses, replacing a stay in prison with a system of enforced restitution, work, and community service. It then should establish incentives for state governments to do the same.**

In 1996 less than half of all inmates incarcerated in state prisons were there for committing a violent crime. Twenty-three percent were in for property offenses, 23 percent for drug offenses, and 7 percent for public order offenses. Among federal inmates, only 12 percent were in for violent crimes. Eight percent were in for property crimes, 19 percent for public order violations, and 60 percent for drug offenses. Sixty percent—that's 56,000 people put in federal prison for drugs in 1998 alone. That's compared to only 16 percent—or 3,400 people—who were locked up for drug offenses in 1970. Almost 130,000 Americans are currently behind bars for the simple possession of narcotics.

It's barbaric and kind of absurd. We're throwing people in jail for years because they do drugs. Or worse, for living in a dirty house. I'm not kidding. In November 1998, the Santa Monica district attorney sought a prison sentence for a woman who was charged with violating heath department regulations in her home by living in unsanitary conditions.

Is that really the best solution we can come up with for a slob? It's the beginning of the twenty-first century and we are still imprisoning people for crimes that don't involve violence: tax fraud, embezzlement, drug use, and unarmed property theft. In 1996, of the 13.5 million offenses known to the police, 11.8 million—87 percent—were *nonviolent* property crimes.

In a civilized society, no one should go to prison for a nonviolent property crime or for crimes that involve harming only yourself (literally), such as drug use, suicide or illegal possession of pornography. I'm not saying these acts are good or bad, just that they aren't acts that should put you in prison. I am no more upset if someone robs my house while I am at work than if the plumber carelessly fucks up and destroys the same property while I am at work. Either way I want my property back, repaired, or replaced. Either way I want an apology and some assurance that the person won't do it again and that he or she has paid a fair price for the actions. But why lock that person up? I don't need to see him go to jail. I don't need to see her life wrecked. How about just making the person pay for it; come over and apologize; lose

some privileges—like a curfew or home arrest; and be publicly shamed? Why destroy lives and rob people of all their
freedoms for a property crime? Seriously, it's primitive.

It sounds radical at first, but if you let it soak in for a
while it starts to make sense. Think about it. Treating radically different kinds of "criminal" offenses differently would
do more than create "fairness" in the justice system. It also
would create a real incentive for potential offenders to find
nonviolent ways to commit crimes. It might seem crazy to
want to incentivize criminals, but let's face it: The economic
and social realities of our world ensure that, for the foresee-
able future, people will continue to break laws in both violent
and nonviolent ways. So why not encourage them to do so in
the least destructive way possible?

Just because you break a law does not mean you are
necessarily a "criminal." People make mistakes. People get
desperate and do things they shouldn't. People get impulsive
and act without thinking. As long as the crime isn't violent,
why don't we give people another way out—a better way to
make it up, a more humane and productive form of punishment?

Again, the key is nonviolent, so if violence can be proven,
then you could go to prison. What this means is that if you
got drunk and drove over someone you could go to prison. If
you got caught standing on the street corner smoking a joint
you couldn't. Nor could you go to jail for stealing a car—
unless you did it when occupied, thereby requiring coercive
use of force. You wouldn't go to jail for burglary, unless you
were carrying a weapon, in which case you could and you
should.

I remember reading in high school about how in the old
days they used to throw people in prison for owing money—
debtor's prison. It seemed so backward. It's like, lock me up

for not being able to pay my credit card. If we did that today, think of all the people we'd have to put in prison: students who bail out on their loans; farmers who can't pay the mortgage; businesspeople who go Chapter 13; all the people in Debtors Anonymous. But we don't.

We've progressed. Crime is relative. It's what we, at any given time in society, think is criminal. It's still not OK to walk away from your debt, but we don't lock you up for it. So why do we lock someone up if he steals a car? Or robs a store? Or possesses illegal drugs? I'm not saying these things are good—but just because they're wrong doesn't mean we should necessarily imprison someone for doing them. There are other ways to punish people.

We all break the law at one time or another—and most of us more often than we realize. Speeding; failing to get a new license when you move; cheating on taxes (and that includes underreporting income); bumping someone's car in a parking lot and driving off; driving while drunk; having oral and anal sex in states where they are illegal; trespassing; lying to the insurance company; smoking a joint; throwing out jury duty notices; expensing things that aren't really expenses; taking towels from the hotel—and so on.

If there's anyone out there who is so sure they're perfect, that they never, ever break the law, step forward and take a bow, because you are some kind of freak. But for the rest of us, why are we so sure the way we do it is right? Why is stealing a radio from a car, nonviolently, worse than, say, going 90 miles an hour on the freeway when you're late for a meeting or driving home after a couple too many drinks? The worst that can happen from the stereo theft is that the victim has the hassle of replacing it and walks around for a couple days with that awful feeling of being invaded—a feeling I'm not minimizing. But at 90 MPH, or when you've had just a little too much to drink, you could maim or kill someone. It happens all the time. When you look at it that way, it seems that maybe our priorities are a little messed up.

Or how about this: If you rent a videocassette player at Blockbuster, you have to put down a deposit. If you fail to return the player, after a certain number of days, the store keeps the deposit. End of story. Blockbuster isn't happy about it, but it has its money. But if you walk into that same store and pick up that same VCP unit and walk out, the store will call the police, have you arrested, charged with theft, and put in jail. Why? What's the difference between the two acts? Nothing. Same VCP. Same value. The truth is that it's all about how we define crime and what we have gotten used to thinking about as criminal. We think there's a difference between the two because we have gotten used to seeing it that way. But what if tried seeing it a different way?

Restitution wouldn't let "criminals" off. It would simply shift how we make them pay their debt to society from a model of incarceration to one of forcing them to apologize and repair the damage. It would allow for creative sentencing-punishments that fit the offense, the offender, and the victim-and ensure that the victim gets compensated by the offender, who is forced to pay a price for committing a crime.

The restitution or forced work framework could work something like this. For enforcement, offenders would be given bracelets to monitor their whereabouts and even put under electronic surveillance, including telephone and Internet monitoring to ensure that they perform their work or community service and don't violate the terms of the sentence. They would be put under curfews, and even home arrest, with the penalty for violating any of the conditions of the sentence being imprisonment. There also could be required employment and education, intensive probation, and mental and physical treatment for substance abuse and emotional problems as well as community-based residential confinement. In addition, the offender would be forced to pay back financially, either in a means-based approach or through straight-up restitution.

The traditional punishment model we use now does nothing to restore the victim and never makes the offender truly accountable. In fact, the first thing a good defense attorney does for his client is plead not guilty since because our current approach focuses on legal and technical definitions of guilt. Restitution is a restorative justice concept; it seeks to make the victim whole, or more whole, and make the offender account for the criminal act and make amends as well as pay an additional price, both emotional and physical.

How nice would it be if someone took your wallet to have him apologize, make it up to you, pay you more than you lost, and learn why not to do it again—versus see him in court, watch him deny it, get convicted, and go to jail—or worse, be acquitted because of a technicality. Wouldn't an approach that focused on healing the wrong and making the victim more whole, rather than incarcerating the wrongdoer, make more sense? Wouldn't it make you feel better? Again, I'm only talking about nonviolent offenses. In 1996, of the 15 million arrests in the United States, only 730,000 were for a violent crime. That's less than 5 percent. The other 14,300,000 didn't involve violence.

The same logic is true for nonviolent crimes involving drug use. Why lock up someone whose only crime is using illegal drugs? Arizona—the one and only state that has decided not to lock up nonviolent drug offenders but instead require a mandatory treatment program—saved more than $2.5 million in its first year and found that 77.5 percent of the probationers subsequently tested free of drugs—a much higher rate than for offenders on probation in other states. Arizona found that it cost only $16 a day for the probation with mandatory treatment compared to $50 a day for housing an inmate in prison.

So why not? The current approach is not working. Does anybody really think it is? Why not try something different? There must be a state out there—one that is progressive, a little antigovernment, maybe a little bit socialist leaning, one with a progressive tradition—that would want to try not incarcerating all these people. Maybe Vermont? Minnesota? Wisconsin?

Which brings me to the core of the crime and punishment issue. What we consider criminal is subjective. It is the state in all its power that statutorily defines crime and then subsequently prosecutes and punishes those people who commit the statutorily prohibited acts. If it isn't on the books, you can't go to jail. In many states, watching a person commit a crime is not a crime. Nor is doing nothing about it, even if you could have stopped it. That's why David Cash, a seventeen-year-old who watched his best friend rape and strangle a seven-year-old black girl in a Nevada casino in 1998, couldn't be charged with a crime. But smoking pot in that same rest room would have been a crime. So would stealing the toilet seat. You could go to jail for taking that seat but not for watching someone drag a screaming kid into the bathroom stall and strangle her on it.

That's how the law works—it's criminal only if the state says it is and not otherwise. That's an enormous amount of state power, and we ought to be careful with how easily we relinquish it. After all, it's really up to us, the people—not the state, not law enforcement, not judges or legislators—to decide what we want the standard to be, what we want to be legal or illegal, and how we want to punish people who break the law. That's why we live in a democracy. Just because something is defined by the state as illegal doesn't mean it should be—and vice versa. It's really up to us. Certainly, for the good of basic law and order, we need some basic laws, and we need to have them on the books. But we've gotten to the point where we are criminalizing just about everything. In one city in California, it's a crime to let your kid walk across the street alone. Granted, no jail time, just a $250 fine, but it's the trend that's scary.

You want to eliminate all criminal behavior? We could. Enforce a 10:00 P.M. curfew in every major city, require visible tattoos on everyone for identification, install hidden cameras in all public places, surgically implant chips that record where people go, monitor all private transactions through a smart card. Let's just change the name of the FBI to the Federal Bureau of Information and then authorize it to know anything and everything about any of us at any time, and I promise you we will stomp out all criminal activity. Every single bit of it. We're a ways off, but that's the trend we're on and it seems to me like a very dangerous route because at some point the snowball turns into an avalanche that will bury us all. Do you really want to live in a society that has criminalized most behaviors, or all the acts that the majority in power at the time think of as antisocial? Do you really want a government to have the power to monitor and enforce those prohibitions? I don't.

Well, that's what we're heading toward. Kind of blindly and haphazardly, but nonetheless in that basic fascistlike direction. Let someone else tell us all what to do, it's so much easier. It seems like most of us have just stopped paying attention. We've abdicated responsibility, shifted into autopilot, and no one is really watching where the plane is heading.

It doesn't seem like the direction we're going is one that benefits most people, even those who consider themselves (in the traditional sense) lawful.

As we statutorily forbid more and more acts, as we regulate, prohibit, and criminalize more and more types or behavior, we are giving the state more and more power, more and more control over our lives, and ever narrowing the scope of freedom and liberty that we allow ourselves. We rationalize the suffocation of choice as necessary for law and order, morality, or the public good, but it's a slippery slope, easier slid down than climbed back up. Soon the definition of what is moral, necessary, or in the public interest isn't the same as yours or mine, and one day you are going to wake up and something is going to be illegal that you don't want to be illegal, something is going to be criminal that you never thought could be criminal—like the kind of places you can go to; or the kind of pictures you can look at; or what websites you can visit; or whether you can have a baby, or shave your head, or have a visible tattoo, or have sex on Sundays—and it's going to be too late to say no because you and I and all of us will have given all our power away. Because we were afraid to keep it for ourselves. Because we were unwilling to take the risks, pay the costs, and deal with the consequences of allowing ourselves more rather than less freedom.

Which leads me to the third major reform—one of the single most morally challenging and socially positive changes we could make in America today. It would change the face of crime and punishment, radically reduce violence, and give a second chance to millions of younger Americans.

- **Starting with the federal government, we should enact a limited legalization of drugs. We should create a federal government agency to regulate all**

addictive and dangerous substances, including alcohol and cigarettes, and we should require and provide drug treatment for addicts, with stiff penalties for refusal.

It's something that's been talked about over and over again— and we never do anything about. We're afraid to take the necessary steps toward dealing with it. Few mainstream politicians want to come out in support of legalization—and those who do are usually from drug ravaged cities like Baltimore, Miami, and New York. Yet what we are currently doing, however well intentioned, is not working. In fact, it's a total disaster. In 1993 the senior judge of the Eastern District of New York announced that he would no longer handle drug cases. In a personal and passionate explanation he wrote: "I need a rest from the oppressive sense of futility that these drug cases leave. . . . I simply cannot sentence another impoverished person whose destruction has no discernible effect on the drug trade." Locking people up for drug use isn't slowing down the drug trade, just raising the cost of policing it, costing us billions in prison costs, and creating a whole new class of ex-convicts—people whose crime was using or supplying a drug.

I know all the arguments against legalization: Illegal drugs are dangerous, addictive, immoral. So is alcohol. It's just legal. Although it's hard to believe it ever wasn't legal, there was a time. And Prohibition proved to be one of the greatest social failures in American history. It's one of the few things in America that had two constitutional amendments to deal with it. One to ban it, the other to make it legal again. Not only didn't Prohibition stop drinking (as if anything could), but it succeeded in launching a cottage crime industry—bootlegging—which created a massive underground economy, earned some people over $30 million a year during the depression, and triggered a violent crime wave unseen before. That is, until recently, when the birth of the modern illegal narcotics industry created the most profitable crime industry and the most violent society in world history. Prohibition also led to blatant hypocrisy as top business, social, and political leaders, including the president, went to speakeasies and had private booze parties, all the while publicly condemning the use of alcohol. Sound familiar?

The comparison between Prohibition in the 1920s and the use and sale of illegal drugs today is so obvious that it seems pathological that so many of us still don't get it. You can't make something go away by prohibiting it—you only push it underground and make it more desirable. Look at what's happening with teenage smoking. The harder the government and the antismoking crusade work to discourage, prohibit, and punish teen smoking, the more teens smoke. Teenagers are the only category of people showing an increase in smoking in the last five years—up to over half of kids between the ages of thirteen and eighteen. Just say no most often leads to yes and to please sir, may I have some more?

It's not just true with drugs, it seems to be kind of a basic thing about human nature: We want what we can't have. Take nudity, for example. In Europe, upper-body frontal nudity is no big deal—magazines show it, ads show it, and while men may get a little titillated, boobs aren't the obsession they are here. Go to a topless beach, which most in Europe are, and nobody looks twice. Here, where you have to be an adult and go to the X-rated section of the newsstand to get a peek, we have made nudity shocking, forbidden, and somewhat inaccessible—and so we want it more and lust after it harder.

Put most American men on a beach in Europe and they can't stop turning their heads. But breasts aren't addictive (at least for most people), and drugs are. You have a real problem when you take a highly addictive substance, ban it, and then create stiff criminal penalties for both use and distribution. First the demand goes up, and the supply goes underground. Then the price goes up in order to compensate for the limited supply and the high costs, risks, and difficulties of providing the illegal substances. Finally, the enormous profit potential, the complete lack of regulation, and the severe consequences of getting caught take the whole enterprise to a new level, making violence both necessary and somewhat inevitable.

The entire process is counterintuitive if the goal is to reduce drug use. Instead of decreasing demand and controlling supply, criminalization most often leads to a widespread, financially lucrative, and wholly unregulated underground industry, where there are a few big winners and an enormous number of losers. Add in the human and financial costs of law enforcement to try to cut off the supply and stamp out the demand and we're looking at the biggest waste of money and lives since Vietnam. Now, not only are we losing the addicts and the dealers and the random victims of drug violence and abuse, also all the money and people in trying to stop a monster that just keeps getting larger, growing stronger, and burying itself deeper and deeper underground.

We are spending over $17 billion a year in drug control at the federal level alone—a sixfold increase since 1986—and around another $10 to $15 billion at the state level. We are incurring an incalculable cost in lost and wasted lives, shattered dreams, and unrelenting social discord. Think what we could do with that money, with all those lives, and with all the time, energy, and thought we now put into keeping drugs illegal. And the stupid, obvious, and painful irony of the whole thing is that if we legalized drugs, the entire process would change.

So why do we continue to make drugs illegal and to punish offenders by putting them in prison? If it's about morality, we've not only failed, but we're walking on thin ice. Letting the government act as a moral arbiter never leads to good results in a free society. If it's to promote social order, we've failed yet again. Only an idiot could think that the current approach has created confidence in either the police or the government or left any of us believing that the problem is under control. It can't be for financial or economic reasons, because there's no economic benefit in what's being done now. And it's certainly not out of humanitarian concerns, because there is nothing remotely humanitarian or compassionate in the way we as a society now treat drugs, drug users, addicts, or dealers.

Which leaves us with the last and probably the true reason we refuse to legalize drugs: It's politically and socially safer not to. The bad we know is better than the good we don't—a cultural mind-set that the state, law enforcement, and politicians promote. Keeping a major social enemy out there helps the government keep us in control. The war on drugs keeps us from thinking we are too safe, from wanting too much freedom, too much liberty, too much control. It makes the power of the state seem more necessary. Look at how dangerous it is out there without the state to protect you.

I'm not kidding. And I'm not a wacko. It's not a conspiracy, but the state and its desire for power isn't an abstraction either. Institutional government, law enforcement, the political establishment all are entities. They may be nonsentient, but they're nonetheless organic and self-protective. They cannot allow themselves to be minimized any more than you or I can. It's the insidious way that institutional power continues to legitimize and empower itself. By scaring us and keeping us in the dark. There's danger beyond the gates of the city—so you need us and, in exchange, you will not disobey or replace us.

There's also a financial incentive. The modern prison industry creates tens of thousands of jobs, generates billions in revenues, and creates deep political and corporate ties and a revolving door between the public and private sectors of the so-called corrections community. There are prison industry trade shows, conventions, and mail-order catalogs. There's even a Corrections Yellow Pages that lists more than 1,000 prison service vendors.

I'm not saying that "illegal" drugs aren't dangerous or that there's no danger of misuse. I'm just saying that narcotics use is an inevitable and not necessarily bad part of human society. Recreational drug use has been around for thousands of years. The Native Americans who hosted our sorry asses before we took over the whole place smoked the peace pipe with us. Today we'd have to lock up the whole bunch, Pilgrims and generals and all. Cocaine was actually an ingredient in Coca-Cola until 1905. Heroin used to be a cough suppressant. Sherlock Holmes was written from Arthur Conan Doyle's opium high. President Kennedy's doctor gave him daily doses of an illegal painkiller, and, according to his wife, the late Sonny Bono—a Moral Majority conservative—was a prescription drug addict.

In 1997 nearly 30 million Americans used *illegal* drugs. That's a big chunk of the population breaking the law. But the truth is that almost all Americans are drug users of one kind or another. There are more than 50 million smokers and 10 million people with serious drinking problems. Let's not even talk about caffeine. If we want to be consistent, why not make alcohol and caffeine illegal as well? I mean, it's really hard to see how alcohol is better than marijuana, which, last time I checked, was not responsible for untold billions of dollars lost and lives wasted due to liver disease, domestic violence, addiction, and car fatalities.

Besides, there's absolutely no evidence that legalizing drugs will lead to more users, more addicts, or more social damage than we have with the current illegal racket. In fact, if we spent half of what we do now for enforcement on regulation, treatment, and upfront investments to give people more hope and prosperity so that they didn't need to turn to drugs in the first place, we'd be twice as far ahead socially—and still have half the money left to spend on other investments. In addition, our prison population would decline dramatically, our courts would become unclogged, our inner cities would become less violent—and our children would grow up in a saner and safer world.

Reform the prison system, eliminate prison sentences for property crimes, legalize drugs: These are three vital reforms we could and should make to the current criminal justice system. But in the bigger picture of American society, they too become only the beginning. When it comes to crime and punishment in America, it's less about what we can do and more about what we want to do. It's all about choice.

We have the choice about the kind of society we want to live in. We can build all the prisons in the world, we can lock up everyone who breaks the law, no matter what their reasons or how sympathetic their stories, and we can try to look the other way, closing our eyes to our own complicity in whatever social structure we have allowed to develop. But at the end of the day, we are all in some measure responsible for the state of our society—for its successes and its failures, for its heroes and its criminals.

We can judge those who slip, even dramatically, thinking of them as different from and somehow inferior to the rest of us, branding them as outcasts, and then banishing them from our community. Or we can take a harder look at ourselves—at our role in creating or our complicity in tolerating the problems that have led to such failures and at our responsibility for not doing more, for not doing whatever is within our power to right these social wrongs and to avoid their inevitable outcomes.

Take Hollywood, for example. Every year it punches out a string of new movies showing more and more horrific crimes, usually committed by someone we all recognize, a movie star, a role model, a hero. Kids watch them. Then they repeat them, and we're always shocked. Why are we shocked? You blast provocative, violent images and ideas into the minds of a bunch of emotionally immature, testosterone-high teenagers and offer almost no antidote; what do we expect? Yet each time it happens, hypocritical Hollywood reacts with surprise and concern. We've all heard the soundbite of some celebrity or studio executive saying how upset and bewildered they all are that anyone wouldn't know the difference between a movie and real life.

Gimme a break. Show what you want, but own the consequences. Sure, the studios warn the public that no one should repeat these crimes. What's that all about? It's all talk. I don't see those same studios doing anything about the problem. I don't see them turning around and pouring millions into helping clean up inner cities, improve the quality of education, or teach kids the real difference between right and wrong. No, they're making money hand over foot—and then reacting in shock at the horror that their products help create.

I'm not saying that Hollywood alone is at fault for the extraordinary level of violence, but Hollywood is in some measure responsible if not for helping create the problem then for not doing more to combat it. And we are all responsible in some measure for the outcome since we go to see those movies and make it profitable for the industry to make them. And all the actors who get paid fortunes to make all those movies, they too are responsible—and so on. I'm not saying we shouldn't go to see them, or that the actors shouldn't be in them, or that they shouldn't make them. Maybe they shouldn't and we shouldn't, but that's a separate issue. All I'm saying is that we should own the choices we make, stop denying the effects those choices may have on the bigger picture, and take collective responsibility for the resulting problems that our choices, however indirectly and unintentionally, help perpetuate. The sooner we accept that maybe there is more we could do and better ways to do what we're doing now, the sooner we really will get a handle on crime—not by putting out the fires after they start but by changing the environment that causes them in the first place.

What if all the A list actors in Hollywood said they would make really violent movies only if 10 percent of the movies profits went to educational and quality-of-life improvement programs aimed at the kids who go see the movies? What if we demanded the same in exchange for going to those movies? What if we just owned up to the fact that in accepting the status quo, we're each in our own way making these images more prevalent and doing nothing to help stop the violence they encourage?

I'm not casting blame, just refusing to erase responsibility. No matter how much we dislike the thought, we are all in some way responsible. And in taking more responsibility, even if we do nothing about it, we still move the ball forward. We might find that crime is not as black and white as we think, that justice is not as simple as we would like, and that our own denial might be a much bigger part of the problem than we ever realized. I learned this the hard way, from a kid in the ghettos of Washington, D.C. His name was Norman Hawkins.

Norman Hawkins was born on March 6. He was the sixth child in the sixth generation of African Americans born in the United States since the Civil War. He was born at Children's Memorial Hospital in Washington, D.C., discharged into a low-income housing project, and a childhood of physical and spiritual neglect, emotional abuse, and all-around hardship. Norman's mom defined the term "welfare queen." Seven kids, from several different fathers, no husband, no steady job, a permanent public housing tenant, on welfare for nearly thirty years—and still refusing to take responsibility for her life, her choices, or her reproductive capacity.

By the time Norman was thirteen, when I first met him, his environment already had begun to take an irreversible toll. He was a smart kid, with a winning smile and a keen intuition about people. But years of malnutrition, abominable living conditions, and no stable role models left Norman unable to concentrate for more than a few minutes, barely able to read or do basic addition and subtraction, and leery of school, studying, and people.

I met Norman through a volunteer tutorial program

called Project Northstar. He refused to talk to me for the first hour. When he did, it was merely to inform me that he hated white people. Norman stared at me from under the hood of his jacket. Never had I seen such fear and hatred. At first, all I could do was stare back. I wanted to look away, I wanted to get up and leave but I knew I couldn't back down. So I began to talk.

I told Norman everything I could about my life, my childhood, my parents. I told him why I thought that he and I needed each other. Looking back, it kind of surprises me, but right then and there, I made a commitment to be part of Norman's life—and I let him know it. After about an hour Norman looked up and smiled shyly. "I don't hate *all* white people," he said.

We started with reading and math, and moved on to dealing with people, time management, social skills, spirituality, and even rock climbing. I got him a job, helped him navigate through his first sexual experience and his first gun. For two years, I was Norman's tutor, big brother, surrogate father, role model, and guiding light. Then I left.

But not before I watched him grow into a six-foot one-inch-tall young man with a love of people—black and white—a passion for knowledge, and a deep desire to do right. And not before I had a chance to see the violence of his world. In 1993, while walking to the subway to meet me, Norman was knifed through the chest. The reason—$1.00. He ran a mile and a half with a punctured lung to his housing project, where an ambulance rushed him to Children's Hospital—the same one he was born in. There a team of surgeons sewed him back together. They closed the knife wound but not the fear it caused. A year later Norman was an accomplice to an aborted car theft. Rather than send him to jail, the state agreed to let Norman move into the foster care of an aunt living in Alaska. Norman got on a plane, and I got on with my life.

I kept in touch for a while, but I felt my commitment had been fulfilled. I had other things to deal with. I was beginning law school and had a whole host of problems of my own to confront—from moving, to studying, to stressing about the massive debt I was accumulating. I justified that it was for the better—he needed to take responsibility for his own life. I rationalized that he was too far away for me to be much help anyway. And I convinced myself that it was meant to be. Besides, Norman was happy in Alaska. It seemed to calm and center him. He told me how amazed he was that he didn't have to lock the door at night and that he could see mountains and fields from his window. Two years later Norman graduated from high school. After going home to visit his mother in Washington for the summer, he planned to return to Alaska, work for a while, and then attend a community college.

But Norman was barely back in D.C. before he got into trouble again. This time it meant jail. Three months for attempted car theft. Always one to look on the bright side, Norman did his time, setting his sights on the future—and planned his return to Alaska right after Thanksgiving, less than a month after his release. Norman knew D.C. was bad for him. But somewhere deep inside, he believed that with a little luck and a little more time he could get his life back on track. He never got a little of either.

Norman died much as he had lived—suddenly, tragically, and probably without understanding fully what was happening or why. The night of his release, he was the unlucky passenger in a car wreck; the young driver was drunk and ran from the scene of the accident, unharmed and unwilling to take responsibility for his actions. It was the last in a series of bad choices Norman would make in his short life. But Norman's life wasn't much of a choice to start with. A wreck from day one—it was one big accident waiting to happen.

There are millions of Normans in America. Kids living in urban and rural poverty facing daily degradation and suffering. Many of these kids are black and Hispanic, but the fastest-growing percentage is white. Whatever their color or ethnicity, they share one thing in common. They are children—children who lack adequate health care, live in unsafe and unsanitary environments, drink polluted water, suffer daily physical and mental abuse—and all of it with probably even less hope and less help than Norman had.

Yet most of us continue to avoid the issue—and those kids—refusing to accept any responsibility for the problem, denying our ability individually or collectively to alter the situation, and finding all kinds of reasons for why we shouldn't have to. "It's not my problem, it's not my fault, and there's nothing I can do anyway. I didn't raise them. I didn't even know them." I've heard it so often it makes me sick. I've heard it from my friends, family, business leaders, social activists, and even the clergy. I've even heard it from myself. And nothing, nothing at all, could be further from the truth.

Maybe that's why the problem seems so intractable and why it's getting worse instead of better. Maybe that's why there is still a nightmare on Main Street. We don't think Norman is our charge. We don't think we have the time, energy, or responsibility for people like Norman. And we don't think our action or inaction will have any impact on our lives or on the lives of the people we love. It's a dangerous and shortsighted misperception. Our indifference will have practical costs: in lost lives, theirs and ours; in billions of dollars wasted on prisons, rehab programs, remedial education, and repairing the aftermath of vandalism, drug abuse, and neglect; and in an incalculable cost in lost human potential. But there's a deeper consequence.

What's at stake is more than the plight of millions of Americans, many of them children; more than the wasting of billions of dollars, most of them from the pockets of taxpayers; more than economic well-being of you and your kids. What's at stake is the very essence of America: its ideals, its values, its honor. What's at stake is our humanity. This is the moral cost of our denial: a national consciousness weighted down by the burden of widespread human wreckage and suffering, a toll that regardless of whether each of us directly added to it, we all could have done something, however little, to ameliorate.

Years after my brother's sudden death I used to have a recurring dream. I watch my brother lay dying on an island, within sight but out of reach. Beside him is my father, helpless and afraid. I can save my brother, if only I can get to the island. I have a surfboard with a motor, but I can't start it. And for some reason, I think it will take too long to swim. After what seems even in dreamtime like an eternity, I start the engine. Racing to the island, I run to my father with a wide smile on my face. "I'm here, Dad, I'm here," I say. "I can save Jimmy." My father, motionless, looks back at me, silently shaking his head. "No, Robert, you can't," he says. "It's too late. He's already dead."

There was nothing I could have done to save my brother Jimmy's life. I was an eight-year-old kid, sick myself with scarlet fever, indoctrinated by a dogmatic faith that didn't believe in medical treatment, and scared beyond belief.

There was a lot I could have done to save Norman's life. I was there in the beginning, but then, as events in my own life took over, and as I became more consumed with my own problems, Norman's life seemed less and less relevant, and his future something I thought I couldn't or shouldn't be responsible for.

What difference would I make in the long run anyway? Norman was who he was and was what life had made him. What's more, the problem was bigger than one kid. It was bigger than Norman, bigger than me, and beyond my ability to affect meaningfully. Besides, I'd already done more than most people; what was I supposed to do? I wasn't my life, he wasn't my child, and I had other obligations—other priorities. When I ran out of excuses I lied to myself, promising to do more later, when I had more time, when I could be more effective.

Later never came. And as I stood in front of Norman's public housing project watching his teary-eyed mother drag on a cigarette in the shivering cold of a rainy fall day, listening to her talk about what it was like to lose three kids to the grave, I realized how wrong I was.

If we are going to bring the crisis in our cities to an end—if we are going to restore moral and civil order, clean up the streets, wipe out the crime, put an end to the depravity, violence, and moral disorder that wracks urban America—it will require a national commitment based on personal commitment, at least at a moral and intellectual level, of each American to take responsibility for finding and supporting a solution. It is not the task of any of us to solve the problem single-handed, nor should any of us be expected to sacrifice our own lives for the cause—although some of us will. But we have to lend our support to those who will lead. We have to create the moral authority for action. And we have to be willing to acknowledge the problem, the urgent need for a solution, and the hard truth that failure to find a solution is a failure not just of our leaders but also of our nation, of our ideals, and of ourselves.

6.

Saving Norman

I WAS SITTING IN THE heart of Montana Terrace, a ghetto in northeast Washington, D.C. A twelve-year-old kid sat on my jet-black Yamaha Maxim 650 motorcycle, pretending to ride it. Next to him, two kids fought over my helmet, declaring they were going to kill each other if they didn't get to wear it. It seemed so nice, so normal. Kids playing, wanting to be adults. They were black. I was white, but at their age, it didn't really matter. I came and went to their neighborhood. The younger kids liked me. I had a motorcycle. I wore jeans and a T-shirt. I had been on TV. The older kids in the ghetto just ignored me. Norman told me they thought I was an undercover cop. He thought that was funny.

As I pulled the twelve-year-old off my bike, I asked him what he wanted to be when he grew up. He smiled and said a fireman. I turned to his friend. What do you want to be, little man? I asked him. He looked at me, warm sweet eyes smiling out of his dark-brown face. He frowned. "I just want to grow up," he said. Two days before another teenager had fucked up and gotten killed. It was on all of their minds. But it wasn't just that. Norman had already lost one brother to a shooting. Most of the kids knew someone who had died a violent death—before eighteen. They all knew it was a fate that might claim any of them, and there was nothing they could do, except hope for the best. Looking around Montana Terrace that day, it struck me how much of a long shot growing up was.

Over 30 percent of African American males in their twenties are in prison, on parole, or on probation, and 35 percent are expected to end up there before the age of twenty-five. A black teenager is three times more likely to die of gun violence than of natural causes. If you're black and live in Harlem (which is no longer even close to the worst place in America to live), you have less of a chance of living to forty than your counterpart in Bangladesh, one of the poorest and most desperate nations in the world. Black infants in Chicago, Detroit, and Philadelphia have a greater chance of dying in their first year than do infants born in Bulgaria or Cuba. Now that's depressing.

I'd been to Norman's house. I knew his family, friends, and community, and I could see why his life prospects were so bleak. He lived in a dump. Ratty and stained furniture sat atop aged yellow shag carpeting. The windows were broken. Roaches crawled across the junk on dirty floors. Norman had a two-year-old nephew, the son of his seventeen-year-old sister, a beautiful young woman who was doing her best to be a mother before she should have been. Sad, but not as sad as the fact that Norman's youngest brother, the eighth child of his welfare-dependent mother, was a year younger than her daughter's baby was. Both babies probably were subject to unhealthy levels of lead—which causes brain damage, learning disabilities, and emotional disorders. Norman needed to do his homework, but there wasn't a pencil or pen in the house. Even if there had been, concentration would have been nearly impossible. In the living room the TV was on so loud I couldn't hear myself think. The older kids were screaming, the babies were crying. Norman's mother was sitting in the kitchen overwhelmed.

Norman had a father, but he rarely showed up. Neither did his older brother, except to cause trouble. One day Norman's mother told me she didn't have enough money to buy formula for the babies and milk for the other kids. I came back the next day with two bags of groceries. Two days later Norman told me the food was gone. How could it be gone? I asked. His older brother, a sometime resident, had come home with friends and eaten it all. His mother had pleaded that it was for the kids. They told her to shut up and finished their dinner. Great male role models for Norman.

When you talk about crime and violence, you can't help but come back to the causes—the roots of the crisis, the heart of the problem. An entire generation of young people is growing up in poverty-stricken communities; in broken and trash-infested homes, surrounded by violence; without solid male role models; attending schools that lack adequate resources; undernourished, sleep deprived, and psychologically damaged. They watch their friends and siblings go to jail or die in the street. They see their mothers become drug addicts or prostitutes. Half the time they don't ever see their fathers. They close their eyes to the realities of their daily lives, try to hang on to their childhoods, but they can't. They live in a nightmare they can't wake up from, trapped in environments that do not nurture children but destroy them. Eventually, and all too soon, these kids have to grow up. Which they do: dysfunctional, angry, poorly educated, and dangerous.

Of all age groups, children have the fastest-growing rate of poverty in America. Twenty percent of all kids in America live in poverty—that's over 14 million—and kids make up 40 percent of all Americans living in poverty today. At some point in their lives, one in three American kids will experience poverty, in the richest nation on earth. Over a million kids are homeless in America. Eleven million are uninsured, the highest number ever reported by the Census Bureau, and the number grows by 3,000 a day. In the last decade, 4 million kids dropped out of high school, and the number of illiterate seventeen-year-olds doubled. Seven million high school students are functionally illiterate. One in eight will never graduate from high school, and half will never complete a single year of college. And poverty is to blame for most of this.

Poverty sucks. And if you're a child, it can ruin your life. A baby born into poverty is less likely to make it to his first birthday than a baby born to a mother who smoked during pregnancy, and poverty puts kids at greater risk of falling behind in school than being born to a single parent or to teenage parents. Poverty increases the likelihood of dying in childhood, of stunted growth, anemia, having emotional and learning disorders, physical and mental disabilities, being blind or deaf and dying by an accidental injury. It makes someone less likely to go to college, more likely to end up on welfare as an adult, and, of course, more likely to end up in jail, prison, or on the wrong side of the law.

Whatever we do or don't do to people after the fact, after they cross the line and end up "in the system" is ultimately only a Band-Aid because we're still only treating the symptom and not curing the cause. If we really want to solve the crime problem in America, we are going to have to look at what happens before someone ends up in jail—at the broken infrastructure, rotting public education system, drug crisis, and especially at the poverty that is crippling a generation of kids. Then we are going to have to focus on early intervention aimed at getting to those kids before it's too late.

At a minimum, we need to make urban schools a full day, twelve months of the year, and restructure them on a community model, complete with day care, sports programs, mentoring, and tutoring. We need to pump more money into programs like Head Start—which provides critical education, healthcare, and nutrition for kids—and drug treatment programs, which save per dollar spent about twelve times what we will otherwise pay in future social costs.

We should increase the minimum wage; pump up education and training programs for workers—especially those leaving the welfare system; make sure child care is affordable—full-day child care today ranges from $4,000 to $10,000, but the average poor family with children made only $8,600 in 1996, and although there are assistance programs, only one in ten eligible children now gets the help needed; and we should increase funding for youth development and job training programs at both the federal and state level.

Money won't solve all our problems, but it will help with this one. We're spending over $20,000 a prisoner and $6,000 per public school student. That's smart. The per family average monthly AFDC (Aid for Families with Dependent Children) payment—the primary social welfare program that the federal government used, until recently, to help lift children out of poverty—declined 10 percent between 1970 and 1993 despite steadily rising living costs. That decline is nothing, however, compared to what is happening now.

AFDC was eliminated with President Clinton's "historic" welfare reform, as were most of the programs designed to deal with poor children or poor people of any age. Ending welfare as we know it may have been the single most cynical act of politics by a president and a Congress in the last twenty-five years, and it certainly was the ultimate sign of the level to which our compassion has declined and our ideals bottomed out. A nation solidly in the grip of its most prosperous era ever, with a Democrat from a poor family who got aid and scholarships his whole life in the White House, in a single, benevolent stroke cut the floor right out from under the poor in America. We took them off the welfare rolls, and we told them to get a job. But we didn't provide them any of the necessary supports to ensure that they made it—such as healthcare, child care, job training, or the assurance of a living wage. We did this with a straight face, pretending it was somehow justifiable, even long overdue. Political leaders from both parties claimed it was the right thing, the best thing, and the most generous thing to do. A historic victory for America. Sure, as long as you weren't one of the poor.

It's easy to criticize poor people as lazy, happy not to work, or just plain undeserving of something that they didn't earn, and to feel good about denying them financial assistance, no matter what their hardships or backgrounds. Yet it is a fact that we give far more financial assistance to rich people in the form of tax breaks, which are just another form of taxpayer-supported subsidy, than we do to the poor in direct aid. It's easy to say "Get off your butt and get a job." However, will you be the first one to give them a job? It's easy to ignore problems such as the cost of child care, the lack of adequate training, the numerous financial disincentives for poor people to work, and the long-seated effects—psychological, physical, and mental—that poverty has on people.

But forget the logic, forget the economics, forget that fact that there but for the grace of God goes any one of us. Think about the kids. Welfare *reform* and our stubborn refusal to deal honestly and humanely with the poverty crisis in America have pushed millions of kids to the edge—kids whose only mistake was to be born to the wrong parents, to parents who were less intelligent, less successful, less well off than the rest of us who were blessed to be born out of poverty. And this selfish and shortsighted action has put them—and us—in real trouble down the road.

We may have started to lower the welfare rolls with welfare reform—although the consequence is that millions of former welfare recipients are now jobless and unaccounted for—but we haven't dealt with the undeniable and inexcusable fact that whatever we think of their parents' fate, millions of American kids are currently living in, and will continue to live in, poverty. And no matter how much we want to wish the problem away, no matter how much we blame the parents, no matter how much we justify denying these kids the resources necessary to succeed, they aren't going to make it unless we make it possible. At a minimum, that is going to cost money. Lots of it, and so what?

If we can give multimillionaire retirees Social Security payments (and don't tell me it's their money because they're all getting back a lot more than they every paid in), then we can give poor kids in America the money to eat well, live safely, and get a basic run-of-the-mill public education. If we are going to make a choice, and I'm not saying should, the winner is clear cut in my eyes. Hands down I say pull the cash from the rich old geezer and give it to the hungry child.

But it doesn't have to be a choice. We spend less than $500 million annually on welfare for kids in America, less than one-twentieth of 1 percent of the total budget. God, are we that cheap? Are we that selfish that we can't, as a nation—the richest, most powerful nation in the world—afford the extra several hundred million dollars a year it would take to ensure that all our kids, regardless of where they live and who their pathetic parents are, are cared for?

Money is the first, and probably most critical, aspect of ending child poverty and giving these kids a fighting chance in the future, and the sooner we stop being so cheap about alleviating the suffering of the youngest and weakest in America, the better off we will all be. Beyond money, however, we need to start providing more choice and expanded opportunities for the parents of poor kids, and create a primary school system that ensures all kids in America a real education.

SOLUTION #4

- **To give all kids in America a fighting chance, we should move toward complete privatization of the nation's public school systems, giving all parents education vouchers to put toward the school of their choice, and we should establish a uniform National High School Exit Test, which every high school senior has to take to graduate.**

A single, standard, uniform, this-is-the-basics-you-have-to-know-to-pass-go, get-out-of-school, and join-the-real-world test. You don't pass it, you don't graduate. It's that simple. No exceptions. No excuses. No whining about how we can't make a test that tests black kids the same as white kids. Or Latinos who grow up in Spanish-speaking homes the same as kids who grow up with English-speaking parents. In this day and age we certainly can test whether a kid has the basic building blocks to function and survive socially and financially in the world we live in. We have to if we want to give everyone an equal chance at making it. A uniform test is the best way to make sure that all schools in America teach what kids need to learn and then make sure they learn it. It's fair to the kids and forces the schools to make sure kids know what they have to know before they push them out into the streets.

As for privatization, it's just time. Most public school suck. I went to two of them for twelve years, one a big city and the other in a rural community. Neither was worth the time I spent. I didn't get close to the education my friends who went to private secondary schools got. They learned more, from better teachers, with more resources. They came out better prepared and with more opportunities. They also worked harder and were rewarded more. My high school guidance counselor basically told me I didn't need to go to college—you know, the it's-not-for-everyone thing. I just graduated Stanford Law School. Go figure. That's the public school system at work.

I remember President Clinton making a big deal out of his opposition to vouchers for public school kids and then sending Chelsea to the best private school in Washington, D.C. It seems like it's always the people who can afford to keep their kids out of the system who are the biggest fans of keeping everyone else in it. If I had it to do over, I'd beg my parents to find a way to send me to a private school, secular or parochial. Just keep me off that asphalt jungle of a grade school and that first-grade teacher who kept hitting my left wrist with a ruler because she insisted I was writing with the wrong hand.

Seriously, privatizing the public school system will be the

best thing we do for our kids. Some people say that it's the states' responsibility, that education shouldn't be a profit-making business, that our kids' learning will become hostage to the fiscal realities of running a business. The state is doing a terrible job, and kids' learning is now hostage to the fiscal and political demands of the teachers union. As for profits, if it would make schools work, who cares if it makes someone else money?

The American Association of School Administrators has declared one in eight secondary schools substandard places for learning. In most public schools there's no incentive for teachers to teach or students to learn. Worse, we have a two-tiered education system—public and private schools, divided largely on race and class lines with a few really good public schools that stand out from the rest. The incentives of the market place are the surest way to make sure that the schools work; you're no good and no one will send you their kids. Besides, what are the kids getting now? Crap. And anyone who tells you otherwise is either deluded or has a vested interest in the current system.

To be fair, I know there are people out there with big hearts and good minds who want what's best for the kids and who oppose privatizing public schools. I think it's a scary thing to take something that has been for so long a public commodity and shift it into the private realm. We are afraid of making a mistake. But how long are we going to let our fears stand in the way of what's best for the children of this country? The current public school system is by and large a national disaster. Privatization is its best and maybe its only shot for salvation. Privatization removes the high overhead and bureaucratic costs of the public system, allows for economies of scale in resources and facilities, creates an environment that demands better teachers and will pay more for those teachers, and allows for the best approaches to win out.

Most states already have made limited moves toward school privatization, from charter schools (where the schools remain public, but control is in a private entity that gets funding depending on how successful it is), to tuition vouchers and scholarships—like the Milwaukee Parental Choice Program—that allocate a certain amount of money to parents to use at the school of their choice, to education tax credits and tax exemptions. Thirty-three states and the District of Columbia have charter school laws, and there are more than 1,000 charter schools in operation across America. Twenty-nine states have some from of public school choice, and three states have tax credits. But these efforts are only a beginning and stop short of the necessary big step.

I'm talking all-out privatization. Let's gradually start eliminating the public school systems in every school district across America and replace them with privately held entities to run all schools and educate all our children. Every school district would have one or more private entities that manage and run the school system. All the money now used for public schooling would go into vouchers, ensuring that every kid had the ability to get into at least one privatized school, and the schools would operate off the tuition payments, with additional assistance as each state and district found necessary. Obviously, this has to happen state by state, since the federal government can't go telling the states how to run their schools, but we're already heading that way, so why not speed up the process? In addition, the federal government could tie allocation of federal money to the states for education to having a privatized system in place. Who knows, maybe we could even abolish the federal department of education, or at least reduce its size and focus it on a singular mission of helping privatize the public schools.

There will be problems, and the transition will not be without mistakes. But it can't be worse than what most kids in public school have today. Everything won't be even. Some schools and systems will be better than others, and the rich will still be able to get the best for their kids, as they always have and always will. But so what? They do already. With privatization, less advantaged kids will be able get a better education than they do now, all families would have greater choice in the schools they send their kids to, and we would do away with the inefficient, broken and disheartening system we have now.

We can be afraid, but the evidence doesn't support our fear. In every single area that we have privatized, it has worked. Basically, America is a privately owned society. That's how we do things, with few exceptions. And those exceptions, our public goods, are generally not very effective. Even national defense, probably the best example of a public commodity, is essentially a shared public/private operation if you think about it. We're just holding on to the current model of education because we're used to it. And again, most of us who cling most tightly to the current model, who defend it the hardest, are those who either have something to lose if it changes or who can afford to make the choice to avoid it. But what about for all those who can't?

Think about your own choices. You discover a tumor and have to go for a biopsy. If you have a choice, which do you choose: a private hospital or a public one? You have to send something that absolutely must get there the next day at 11 A.M. without fail. The U.S. Postal Service or FedEx? You break the law and you need a lawyer. The public defender or a private attorney? You're after-dinner coffee works too fast. A public rest room or a private one? Still not convinced? The Los Angeles public prosecutor against the Dream Team? I'll take the Dream Team every time. Honestly, if you had the choice—if money wasn't an issue—would you really send your kids to a public school?

There are a million facts, statistics, stories that could defend the status quo, and I could come up with a carload of my own data to support privatization, but at the end of the day, the argument that sways me is that privatizing the public school system simply makes sense. It just does. Intuitively. Logically. Fiscally. In hindsight, it will be as obvious as McDonald's or FedEx, because it will work.

All it would take is enough of us to give our communities the permission to try. The thinkers and entrepreneurs to create the structure would emerge. The money would be raised. The parents would start sending their children. And we'd start paying down the education deficit in America. Why do we settle for the bad we have instead of the good that could be? Why do we stick to a badly broken and seriously flawed public education system when there are better alternatives? Because that's how it's always been. That's how it was when we were kids, and when our parents were kids, and their parents, and so on. So it's hard to imagine doing education in a way that's radically different from the way it's always been done. But that's a copout, and we all know it.

It's the same copout we use when it comes to all aspects of saving Norman and the millions of kids like him.

I was the only white person at Norman's funeral—crammed into the back of a packed inner city funeral home with gangbangers, young mothers, crying babies, and teary-eyed gray-haired seniors. It was a community gathered, not a people divided. My computer sat in a nice shoulder bag outside with kids on the stoop. No one took it. No one dared. I stood pressed against a young gang member. I got no attitude and gave none. Death does that. It unifies us. Humanizes us. The minister eulogized the loss of "yet another one of our children" and asked the gathered congregation to help put a stop to the senseless violence and social decay that was robbing the black community of its young.

Afterward, the minister came up to me in the street. "I noticed you in there," he said. "I guess I sort of stood out," I replied, smiling at how odd it must have looked to see a white guy at this black kid's funeral. "Why did you come?" he asked. I explained but admitted that I almost hadn't. I said I felt I didn't belong, like this was no longer my business. "I'm not really part of the community," I said, looking around me. He nodded.

"Norman was a good kid," he said. "Yeah," I answered. "He had a big heart. A really big heart." I turned to walk away. The minister reached out and took my hand. We were in the middle of the street, traffic stopping to get around us. On the sidewalk people from the funeral watched. The minister leaned in close, his big hand on my shoulder. "Norman needed you, whatever your color," he said. "We can't win this war alone. It will take all of us, or we will all lose."

The next American war should be the war to save the next generation. If we let yet another generation of kids go down the drain, socially, economically, educationally, we will watch them sprout back up as criminals, addicts, and social outcasts. And the farther away we push the problem, the deeper underground it goes. The more we disassociate ourselves from the solution, the worse it will get, because the real enemy is within us, not out there on the streets. We are the most powerful nation in the world. We have tapped human potential in ways that people would not have even believed possible thirty years ago. We have landed a spacecraft on Mars, cloned life from itself, split subatomic particles, begun to create artificial intelligence. We've cured polio, wiped out the plague, and found a way to combat AIDS and cancer—and someday we will cure these as well.

But despite our phenomenal social, medical, and scientific accomplishments, we haven't figured out how to eliminate poverty. We still have ghettos in the richest nation on the planet. We still have the highest infant mortality rate in the industrialized world. We still have millions of children who are hungry, cold, and unsafe. It's staggering. It's shocking. It's pathetic. Worst of all, we consider poverty a normal and acceptable part of life in America. No one likes it. No one thinks it's good. But we all accept it. We tolerate it. We allow it. We justify it. We even think it's inevitable.

Well, it isn't.

We haven't solved the poverty problem in America for one reason and one reason alone: because we haven't chosen to. There is nothing this country can't do if we set our individual and collective consciousness to it. If we take the time, spend the money, make the effort, and want it badly enough, we can do it.

Poverty is a disease, a sickness, that wastes lives, destroys communities, and kills people, especially kids. Just like any other sickness, we end it when we find a cure, and not before. Like finding a cure for anything else, it will take time, money, and commitment, but it can be done. And sooner or later we are going to have to do it, because poverty has infected our society, spread through our nation. And whether you yourself have it or someone else does, eventually, in both tangible and intangible ways, it affects us all. We are only as strong as the weakest among us. And if a million or 2 million or 10 million or 20 million are poor' than we are, to that degree, all poor.

Poverty infects our economy, slowing growth, reducing productivity, and costing billions in remedial and dependency costs. The Children's Defense Fund estimates that childhood poverty alone will cost America at least $130 billion in lost future productive capacity, and that's not counting additional costs like remedial education; medical, insurance, and social services for the poor; and the cost from increased crime.

It's more than just about money, however. Poverty affects our social structure, creating a massive and permanent underclass, lowering the aggregate quality of life for all Americans and acting like a noose around the neck of our nation. In allowing this needless suffering, in refusing to take responsibility for eliminating it, in making excuses for why we can't do it or why it can't be done, we soil the garment of our national identity, make a mockery out of our national ideals, and suffocate the soul in ourselves and in our country.

SOLUTION #5

- **We should launch a Twenty-first–Century War on Poverty—a no-excuses national campaign to cut poverty by 50 percent in the next ten years and to ensure that all Americans, regardless of income, have food, shelter, and basic medical care.**

The poor will not always be with us. They will be with us only for as long as we allow them to be. We have the money. We have the knowledge. We have the power to wipe poverty from the face of our nation. Once we commit, the rest will happen. I have no doubt that the cynics and critics, the scholars and experts will say that I'm naive, that it's just not that simple. But they're wrong. Commitment alone won't solve the problem, but it's the first and most essential step, and until we take it and make it, nothing else matters. There are hundreds of possible approaches, countless strategies, unlimited potential, and none of it means squat if we haven't first made an unequivocal, unilateral, nonnegotiable commitment to the end result: Cut poverty in half in ten years. No matter what it takes.

I'm not trying to oversimplify a complex problem. But we've made progress so complicated that we're frozen in place, unable to move forward. Pledging to tackle poverty would at a minimum break the logjam and trigger a national debate on how to do it—a debate we could all participate in and that would inform us, motivate us, and guide our decisions. A national commitment also would enable us to cut through the forest of misconceptions, find and channel the necessary resources, and generate the needed public support to empower political and community leaders to take action. And it would give us something unbelievably positive to be about, a national goal worthy of the greatest of nations.

I know the arguments against it. Poverty is inevitable, systemic, and even necessary to keep an economy functioning. It's part of the human experience. Yeah, as long as it's not *your* experience. How can we say that? How can we excuse or justify poverty in twenty-first-century America? "Well, after all, it's their own fault. Those people are lazy. They don't want to take responsibility. They want a handout." I don't buy it. I don't buy any of it. Nobody wants to be poor. And a handout may be easier than working, but at the end of the day no one likes the way it feels to have to beg, entitlement or not.

Most poor people don't know how to be poor. It's learned behavior that has to be unlearned. But regardless of whose at fault, poverty in America—especially among children—is an inexcusable and intolerable situation. We've had an eight-year-plus bull market. Unemployment is lower than it's been in decades. The engine of American capitalism is running at full tilt. Isn't this the time to make it right for those who can't or haven't been able to for themselves? Isn't this the time to be generous with our national prosperity, not selfish?

Besides, when you think about it, what exactly have we got to lose in trying? The closest we've come to tackling poverty on a national scale was a brief attempt in the 1960s, one that was quickly overshadowed by Vietnam. If that was a war effort, it's no wonder we lost it. Lyndon Johnson's "war on poverty" was essentially a government-funded initiative that had limited private sector participation and minimal public support. It was overshadowed by a nasty and divisive war in Vietnam, and headed by a president who was losing the confidence of the American people. That's not a war. That's Kosovo. When we fought World War II, the entire nation united around a common objective—beating Nazi Germany and the fascist states of Italy and Japan, and ensuring democracy for generations to come. We all joined together, public and private sectors, and made the necessary sacrifices to beat the enemy. Neither effort was easy—unifying the nation or winning the war. But we did both. The rest is history.

The same thing is necessary today. The enemy is poverty and our apathy and indifference toward beating it. If poverty wins, the price we will pay will be the loss of yet another generation, and then another, and another, until the social, economic, and human costs will be too heavy to sustain, the immorality of our indifference too hard to ignore, and the wound inflicted on the growing and entrenched class of poor in America too deep to heal. At that point, we will lose our nation. There is only one way to solve the crime problem permanently in America, one way to heal the racial divide, one way to stomp out the violence, drugs, and ignorance that has permeated our landscape and flooded our shores—that is to break the cycle of poverty before it's too late. Either we break the cycle of poverty or it will break us.

There's no half-baked way to do this. It has to involve all of us. It has to be a unified national commitment. It won't happen any other way. The actual plan of action is secondary. We'll figure that out as we go along. Like any social problem, the solution isn't static. It's an organic process. The course we take will depend greatly on what happens after we begin the journey. We will need to find innovative new approaches, combine new federal programs with joint public–private sector initiatives, and create massive incentives to bring in private capital and to ensure broad participation.

There will be radical steps and conservative ones. Rights lost and responsibilities added. In exchange for people getting assured food, shelter, and healthcare, they may have to take jobs they do not want, even limit the size of their families. If the parents of poor kids refuse to act responsibly, even after adequate resources are available, then they shouldn't continue to be parents. That said, we have to give people every tool necessary to make it. We need to tear down the ghettos, rebuilding them with decent housing, good schools, and adequate incentives to attract real business development. We need to create effective, ongoing, and universally available job-training programs, provide child care for parents, and ensure that there is a job—with a living wage—for everyone who will work. This is the minimum we should do for the significant number of Americans who are missing out on the prosperity and the opportunity the rest of us enjoy.

Not everyone will be happy; in fact, some people will be downright mad. Breaking the cycle of poverty in America will cost money—lots of it—and require all of us to take a leap of faith. It will not be easy, and it will not be quick. But if we did it, if we tried, the effect on all of us would be dramatic. Making a national commitment to cut poverty in half in the next decade would transform the social and economic landscape of America, create hope for millions, and trigger a spirit of nation renewal that we have not seen in a century. It could possibly be the most defining moment in American history.

There are enormous economic and social gains to be made from winning a war on poverty. But there's a moral mandate as well. Poverty is not just a social stigma, not just a necessary evil in a good society, not just someone else's misfortune. One day we will realize that it is a moral disgrace, intolerable and unacceptable in a compassionate, civilized society. We call ourselves a Christian nation. America was built on a Judeo-Christian ethic. Well, there is nothing even remotely Christian in poverty. Or remotely humanitarian. Whatever our respective and diverse religions and spiritual beliefs, whatever our politics, personal ideologies, and values, to accept poverty, to turn away from it, to allow it, tolerate it, excuse it can be nothing less than a national sin, a collective national blasphemy. A stain on the moral fabric of our nation.

If we want to save the Normans of the world, if we want

to put an end to crime, drug addiction, and generation upon generation of inherited and learned bad behavior, if we want to save America from a terrible race and class conflict in this new century, we have to make one essential commitment—to stamp out poverty in America.

7.

The Great American Rip-off

SHE SAT IN THE CIRCLE, holding hands with the man and the woman on either side of her. A man with tears in his eyes was telling of the day he finally realized he had gone too far and needed help. It was all he could do to get through the day without doing it again, he told the group. At first he rationalized the problem away, but finally he had to admit it, he had to own his disease. He was out of control. He needed help. And he knew it.

This was not an AA meeting. It was not a Narcotics Anonymous meeting, a meeting for sex addicts or people who were habitual liars, hypochondriacs, or shoplifters. It was a meeting for people who couldn't control what they spend, who live always beyond their means, who shop like there's no tomorrow. It was a meeting for Debtors Anonymous.

My friend was there because she had recognized her problem and was ready to seek help. She was done pretending. She was ready to heal. She said the Serenity Prayer, learned the twelve steps and starting taking it day by day. The meeting should have been attended by every representative of the government of the United States, because in the last thirty years Washington has run up a national debt tab so large it makes my friend and every other member of Debtors Anonymous look like pennypinchers. Seriously, the U.S. government is addicted to debt.

In 1960 the cumulative national debt of the United States was $290 billion. Today it's almost $6 trillion dollars. That's less than $300 billion in 184 years, and $5.7 trillion in 40 years, or $1 billion a year for almost two centuries and then over $100 billion a year average during my lifetime. It's true, as a lot of economists point out, that not all debt is bad. But $6 trillion of debt is outrageous, I don't care economist John Maynard Keynes and his protégés might say.

Gross interest payments alone on that much debt total over $300 billion a year—50 percent of all personal income taxes-nonrefundable, and due annually for as long as the debt is outstanding. Three hundred billion dollars a year in interest payments? What, are we crazy? That's almost 20 percent of the entire U.S. budget being spent on finance charges. Not a dime of it toward principal. That's my future getting spent to pay for the past, and it really pisses me off. If someone told me he was living, relatively speaking, as far over the edge as the United States is, I'd be sending him to the Debtors Anonymous meeting with my friend. If you live that way you are going to destroy your life, and if you have kids and loved ones you are going to destroy their lives. Which is exactly what we are doing in America.

What about the budget surpluses you hear so much

about? In 1998 that surplus was $70 billion. Wow. What are we going to do with all that money? Go out and buy ourselves a new freeway? What's wrong with us? We're patting ourselves on the back for a $70 billion surplus in this year's annual budget when we're still $6 *trillion* in debt from the last thirty years.

Think about it. How can we really have a surplus when we are nearly $6 trillion in debt? It's like saying you are in the black because you finally can pay your monthly minimum payment on a credit card even though you still have a balance of $50,000. That's $50,000 on which you are accruing monthly interest; all of it is money you can no longer use, and all of it is a debt that continues to grow one that ultimately will come due one day.

A balanced budget is the least we should do, not the most. As long as this country is so deeply in debt, we are not in surplus just because this year or the next we actually take in more than we spend. Our annual surplus is just a slow-down in the overall growth of our debt, which actually continues to grow even with surpluses $113 billion in 1998 alone because it is already so large that it accrues more through interest than the so-called surpluses offset. But all that's academic in a way. If you do the numbers without all the fancy fiscal footwork our political leaders use to make things look better, we don't even have the surpluses they say we do. The truth is, in real terms we're still running up a deficit (the amount we spend over what we take in) every year and thus actually making the cumulative national debt even larger. Washington is just making it look like we're not on paper.

That's the ugly truth. The so-called budget surpluses of 1998 and 1999 are nothing but fiscal fantasies, the result of some egregious number shuffling. The federal budget is in the black only if the $90 billion Social Security Trust Fund surplus is included, and that's money that the government doesn't have a right to use to offset current spending, since it's already been promised to future retirees. Without stealing from the retirement fund to push up the numbers, in 1999 we actually would still have a deficit of over $20 billion. But $70 billion up or $20 billion down, either way, it's still only a superficial response because at core nothing has changed. We have not made a dent in our nearly $6 trillion debt. We have not as a nation dealt with the underlying problem that led to our massive debt buildup in the first place—our insatiable desire to consume, even at the expense of tomorrow. Our politicians have not chosen to be more accountable, either to us or to future generations, nor have we demanded it from them. And probably most disturbing, we have not confronted the massive entitlement crisis that looms in the first part of the next century.

Instead, we have chosen collectively to cover up the real problem in the American economy: that we are now and have been for several decades living dangerously beyond our means. We have spent what we do not have, mostly on things we did not need, too often on things that were politically expedient expenditures for the moment rather than on more valuable but less politically beneficial long-term investments in the future. We poured trillions of dollars down the drain. Sooner or later we will have to face the consequences—and the later it is, the harder it will be and the more damage we will have done to those who come after us.

We are stalling, because for right now we can. Just as with so many of the major challenges facing our country, we have chosen to look the other way, to settle for the status quo, to believe the shallow lies from those in power, and to remain, individually and collectively, dangerously and irresponsibly in denial. But deep down we know the truth; I know we do.

Maybe we avoid the truth because we don't want to deal with the mess, because it would mean giving up some of what we now have, which is something most of us don't want to do and something our leaders are afraid to ask us to do. So they tell us it's fine. They assure us that the situation is under control. They point to the market indicators and show us the charts that say surplus, and then they smile, look straight at the camera, and promise that prosperity is permanent. If we just reelect them. Ever watch those lemmings in the *National Geographic* special?

We can close our eyes. We can ignore the underlying tell-tale signs. We can point to the stock market and the low unemployment numbers and the calming words of Alan Greenspan. But at that end of the day, we can't hide from the truth. America is deeply in debt. We can look the other way, or we can stop lying to ourselves and do something about it. We can stop talking about the annual budget surplus' of 1998 & 1999 and start to deal with the debt.

That means no more creative accounting Washington style.

Right now there's a couple of number games Washington uses to make it look like we're doing better than we are. For instance, Congress takes things that cost us money today and puts the cost off to the future; this concept is called fiscal outlays. In other words, if something will cost $1 billion over ten years, Congress says that it will only cost $50 million this year and for each of the next five ($250 million total); it puts off the other $750 million until the last five years. Sounds good, except it's not really accurate. In the long run it just means we are going to have budget deficits again, because in reality we are going to have to pay what it costs, and more often than not the costs are being incurred now, even if they're being put on paper as future expenditures. Congress and the president also frequently ignore or underrepresent the cost of future programs, such as the inevitable and dramatic growth in entitlement spending—primarily Social Security and Medicare—for the rapidly expanding class of senior citizens, or the rising costs of repairing our deteriorating infrastructure or cleaning up our environment, or the price tag for housing the expanding population of prisoners. Rather than face the fiscal realities, they raise growth assumptions and lower cost estimates. Rather than pick up the check for certain expensive social problems, they put off for tomorrow what should be done today.

Finally, and this is the whopper, when calculating the budget—and the deficit or surplus—the budget makers completely exclude the costs of Social Security—even though it consumes up an estimated 23 percent of total federal expenditures. This last act of fiscal sleight-of-hand—taking Social Security "off budget"—is the most deceptive and, given the size and projected growth of Social Security, the most dangerous of all.

The government rationalizes keeping Social Security off budget by arguing that it is a fully funded and self-supporting program, financed by the payroll tax. It's supposed to work like this: You put the money in and you get it out later, with interest, when you retire. Except you won't. There is not now and there never was a big bank account for Social Security, where your money is being saved for the day you retire.

Social Security is a pay-as-you-go system. Fully 93 percent of what you pay in each month in payroll taxes (that's the FICA part of your paycheck) goes right back out to current recipients rather than being safely invested for the day you, the payee, need to start collecting on your investment. So much for that wet dream. As a result, the Social Security system is not "fully funded" (meaning able to pay what it expects to owe) as the retirement lobbies such as the AARP like to misrepresent. The fund is actually *underfunded* by at least $6 trillion. That's the projected amount by which Social Security is going to fall short when the Baby Boomers collect what they've been promised. If you add in Medicare and all other federal retirement benefits, there's a total unfunded liability of $14 trillion. Guess who gets to make up the shortfall?

Social Security is absolutely not separate from the rest of the budget, no matter what Washington and the AARP tries to tell you. There's one and only one budget pie. We pay our taxes to the government, and even though the government considers Social Security or the FICA tax separately from income taxes in how it collects and accounts for it, at the end of the day all the money goes to the same place—the government. The government collects that cash out of your paycheck and spends it however it, in its infinite wisdom, sees fit. The dollars you pay as FICA tax might go to pay for a new federal prison or a road repair, or for a $1 million outhouse in a national park (yes, that much was spent on one), or to foreign creditors who hold a chunk of our national debt and therefore are entitled to annual interest payments just like a bank.

That the government accounts for this money on paper separately from income taxes doesn't mean squat. It just makes the government a liar. Ask your accountant. If you or I got as creative with our money as the feds do with Social Security, we'd be in jail for tax fraud. In fact, if it is separate, why does the government use the trust fund surplus to offset the budget deficit? We can't have it both ways. Social Security can't be separate when we look at what it costs and then not when we want to make it look like revenues are higher.

But the bigger problem is with Social Security itself. It's in surplus at the moment—by about $90 billion as of the end of 1999. But that's a technicality in the biggest sense because the government already owes this money to future retirees-it just doesn't have to pay it out yet. The retirement boom hasn't hit. But it will hit, and then, just as with the national debt, the bill for Social Security will come due, and we—including our current crop of politicians—are going to be in real trouble.

Unfortunately both for *them* and for us—mostly us, because a lot of the *them* will be dead or in serious retirement by the time the problem erupts—we'd be a whole lot better of if they would just come out and acknowledge that the Social Security Trust Fund is not $90 billion in surplus but underfunded by at least $6 trillion and by as much as $14 trillion if you count Medicare. Talk about living in denial. All of which makes the much-heralded budget surpluses—which, again, don't really exist—seem like peanuts even if they were for real. Seventy billion? Pocket change. Money for the tip jar, baby, because when you add the projected shortfall in Social Security and Medicare to our nearly $6 trillion current national debt, we're looking at the possibility of a $20 trillion national debt load in the first half of the next century. All of it coming at you with interest, no payment plan, and extraordinarily bad fiscal consequences.

So here's the deal. Not only does Washington ignore that Social Security isn't really in surplus—because every dollar of that "surplus" is already promised to a retiree in the future, and the fund is still going to fall $6 trillion short—but in addition, the government uses this temporary and somewhat imaginary surplus in Social Security and considers it as revenues against the current budget so that they can, on paper, show a surplus in the overall federal budget. If, instead, the government was honest and didn't do that, we actually would have a $20 billion deficit in the federal budget instead of the $70 billion surplus we supposedly now have. So much for the era of budget surpluses.

If the Social Security Trust Fund is a trust, then the government should start treating it like one. Right now it doesn't even come close to meeting the traditional fiduciary standards of a private trust, in which the trustee (in this case the federal government) owes a duty both of loyalty and care to the beneficiary (us). Loyalty means that the trustee must not put its own interests above the beneficiary, and care means that the trustee will make prudent investment decisions on behalf of the beneficiary. Private trusts are governed by something called the prudent man rule, which means that they are supposed to behave the way a prudent man (or woman) would in regard to the choice of investments made on behalf of the beneficiaries. With regard to Social Security, the government is egregiously failing at both.

It's hard to believe that our national government could be so irresponsible as to knowingly misrepresent this issue to the American people. But it does. The lie is nothing new. In fact, Washington has been lying about Social Security for over sixty years, since FDR first proposed the program and called it a social insurance program for the elderly. Insurance is something you pay and collect on only if you have an accident—thus the name insurance. It's kind of advance payment in the event you are unlucky or suffer a big loss. If insurance was financed any other way it wouldn't work, because if the insurance companies gave everyone back the full amount they paid in, plus accumulated interest, the whole thing would go belly up—and there would be nothing left for those who needed more because of an emergency. That, or we would all have to pay so much that we couldn't afford the insurance in the first place.

Which is exactly why Social Security is not in fact insurance and why it is in so much trouble. Given the current structure, Social Security is either going to go belly up, or the government is going to have to charge us so much money (through increased FICA taxes) to support it that we will not be able to afford it. And when that day comes, no amount of shapeshifting is going to hide the fact that the debt will be exploding, our annual deficits skyrocketing, and our economy and the economic well-being of future generations hitting a massive fiscal brick wall. At that point, the shit will hit the fan.

January 1, 2011, is D-day, the day the retirement bomb drops. Beginning in that year the massive generation of Baby Boomers (everyone born between 1946 and 1960) will start turning sixty-five and retiring. Over 50 million of them, growing older, grayer, and greedier. Every single one of them will have been paying into Social Security their entire working lives—and they will want to get back what they paid in. They have a right to it; they were promised it. The problem is that "it" won't be there. Because beginning in 2011, there won't be enough reserve in the Social Security Trust Fund to pay for the Boomers' long and expensive retirement.

That's the unfunded liability—the $14 trillion in Social Security and Medicare that, beginning in 2011, the federal government is going to owe and not be able to pay. Medicare will actually go bankrupt earlier, by 2008, a fact that still didn't prevent a national bipartisan commission last March from failing to come up with a plan to salvage it. This unfunded liability is the potential source of what would be the worst generational conflict in American history. Senior citi-

zens, relying on the government's public and repeated assur-
ances, will expect to receive their full benefits from the
depleted Social Security Trust Fund for the duration of their
lives. They will be pitted against younger working Americans
who are already paying steep income and payroll taxes and
are unwilling to finance the liability created by generations
before them. At this point, the federal government will face a
politically divisive and economically costly choice: boost
taxes on my generation and the generation behind me to as
much as 50 percent for payroll taxes alone, or dramatically
cut back the benefits to retirees—people who have paid into
Social Security for their whole working lives and who right-
fully consider Social Security a sacred trust on the part of the
U.S. government—jeopardizing their financial security and
upsetting decades of careful planning and preparation for
retirement.

Either choice puts at risk the economic stability of millions of Americans, is likely to generate massive social and
political unrest, and ultimately would create a national fiscal
catastrophe that would make the Great Depression look
comfy.

It's a simple matter of arithmetic. The Boomers will generate the largest retirement wave in American history. In
1945 about a million people were receiving benefits. By 1965
it was up to 20 million people. In 1999 the number of beneficiaries was close to 45 million. By 2020 it will be nearly 70
million. Because of new technology and better health, tomorrow's elderly will live longer than the generations before
them, needing more and more expensive medical care and
facing increasingly higher costs of living. But at the same
time that the population of retirees and the costs of caring
for them are rising, the relative size of the workforce is
shrinking—fast. In 1950 workers outnumbered retirees by a

margin of 16 to 1. Today it's 3 to 1. By 2030 it will be only 2 to 1. That's two workers for every one retiree. That means every two of us still working will pay for one of those already retired. Is that a burden you want to put on your kids?

There's an age boom in America. In 1950 elderly Americans made up only 8 percent of the total population. Today they are almost 13 percent. By 2030 they will be 20 percent of the population and rising. If you look at the window between now and 2030, the number of elderly people in America is expected to double from 35 million to 70 million. That compares to a projected workforce increase of only 15 percent between now and 2025.

Making the whole thing worse, the growth rate of productivity is undergoing a long-term decline. Between 1946 and 1966 nonfarm productivity growth in the United States was on average, about 3 percent a year. But since 1973 it's averaged only about 1.1 percent a year, and from 1990 through 1996, only 1 percent. A similar pattern is true when you look at what is called multifactor productivity growth, a broader measure that includes capital investment as well as labor inputs.

True, there's been a spurt in productivity growth rates during the last two years, due at least in part to the Internet, but that's an aberration that might not be sustained. On average, over the last thirty years we haven't been growing as fast as we did in the thirty years before. That's bad, because the rate of growth of productivity determines the rate of growth of real incomes. As productivity growth rates fall, so will real wage growth, which in turn will lower tax receipts and savings and investment—which in turn will negatively affect productivity growth. All of which will mean less money to pay the ever-increasing and more costly population of retired persons.

So there you have it, the problem in a proverbial nut-shell. There will be too many retirees costing too much money and not enough of us workers working in an environment that is growing just a little too slowly. No matter how much we want to, no matter how much we care, we won't be able to make enough to pay for all of it and all of them. On top of everything else my generation will have to take care of, we will be facing our own higher living costs, trying to raise our own families, and worrying about putting away enough to cover our own retirements, since we can forget about getting back even a dollar of what we pay into Social Security.

Not in this lifetime. Let's face it, if you're under forty, you can say good-bye to a federally funded retirement program. It's ancient history. We'll spend our whole lives trying to pay for those who retire ahead of us, and even then, it won't be enough. Because just like a giant national Ponzi scheme, eventually the whole thing will come crashing down on the heads of those at the bottom of the pyramid.

You don't have to believe me. Go look it up for yourself. Nothing I'm saying is secret. The numbers are there in the public record—they've just been well hidden and widely denied by politicians and senior citizen lobbyists who are too afraid of the truth, too ignorant to know the truth, or just too dishonest and shortsighted to tell you. Lots of experts have warned about it, from former Commerce Secretary Pete Peterson to Federal Reserve Board Chairman Alan Greenspan, who finally admitted that Social Security could cause a fiscal catastrophe if it was not repaired soon. Judgment Day on this one is inevitable. Eventually no amount of creative accounting will hide the fact that there are too many retirees, living too long, needing too much money, with nowhere to get it from—except from an undersized and overtaxed workforce that will not and cannot dig America out of this mess.

That day is coming . . . sooner that you think. And although there's lots of talk these days about ensuring the long-term solvency of Social Security, for the most part that's all it is, talk. Despite the obvious fiscal imbalance, the Social Security trustees, the senior citizen lobbies, the president, and most of Congress have, with a few recent exceptions, insisted that Social Security just needs a little tinkering, such as adjusting downward the cost-of-living increase formula, marginally raising the retirement age, or increasing the payroll tax by several percentage points. And the people in power will continue to seek stop gap measures until we demand they do more.

These band-aids might cover up the problem, but they won't fix it. We can raise taxes, but for how long and to what end? Already the Social Security tax is six times higher and 100 times the financial burden for the maximum payers than it was sixty years ago when Social Security began. In 1937 it was 2 percent of the maximum taxable income of $3,000, or $60. If only. Even adjusted for inflation, the maximum Social Security tax increased almost 900 percent from 1951 to the present, compared to a rise in benefits of only 188 percent during the same period.

Even if we did agree to a massive tax increase, it's not clear we could survive the consequences economically. Using the Social Security Administration's own projections, former U.S. Secretary of Commerce and multimillionaire investment banker Pete Peterson has estimated that the payroll tax would have to nearly double from today's 12.4 percent to 22 percent—and that's not including the Medicare portion. With that added in, we're talking 35 to 55 percent of every worker's paycheck—*before income taxes*. Who can afford that and still pay the rent?

Raising the retirement age is a joke. When Social Security began, the average life expectancy of an American male was sixty-one and the age of eligibility was sixty-five. The average person wasn't going to be alive to collect. Today life expectancy for American men is seventy-three; for women it's seventy-nine. Age experts predict that with advances in medical diagnosis, microsurgery, bionics, organ transplants, pharmaceuticals, and even nutrition and lifestyle management, life expectancies could go into the eighties in the first quarter of the next century. Yet the age of eligibility is slated to increase only to sixty-seven, and even then slowly. But what are we going to do, make the new age of eligibility for Social Security eighty-five or ninety?

Nor is slowing down the annual cost-of-living increase adjustments a solution. The problem isn't inflation, it's age. You can't avoid a tidal wave by moving the beach back. Besides, exactly how are people on a fixed income supposed to pay for rising food and clothing costs, higher rents, and the constantly increasing cost of medical care if you don't adjust their allowance?

Continuing to raise taxes is unfair and dishonest, and raising the retirement age and slowing cost-of-living increases for retirees are mean-spirited and regressive. First we make you wait a little longer until we give you your money, and then we give you a little less of an increase each year, even though your costs of living are still increasing. The truth is that none of these three stopgap measures have any long-term or generational appeal. They only stall the inevitable. The problem with Social Security is that it is a fundamentally fiscally unsound program, built on false foundations and doomed to collapse. Until we face that fact, we're just blowing smoke up our own asses.

There's a way to make Social Security secure for the long haul and still ensure that the current recipients get what they need and deserve. It's all American, honors the ethic of the free market, rewards those more who work harder, and still provides a minimum level of protection for those who slip through the floorboards. And while we're at it, we can start today to tackle our debt problem in a way that goes beyond just hoping for annual budget surpluses from now on.

SOLUTION #6

- **Beginning immediately, we should privatize Social Security, establishing mandatory retirement accounts for all new and existing workers and a gradual phase-out from the current federal program for every working American under the age of fifty-five. For retired persons or those nearing retirement age, we should establish a post-retirement means test, which evaluates need and benefits based on one net worth after retirement.**

SOLUTION #7

- **Second, as a gift to future generations, we should establish a national lottery to gradually pay off the $6 trillion national debt.**

It's a one-two punch. By the time the Social Security crisis is expected to hit—around 2011—we will have put in place a comprehensive national retirement system that creates solvency and security for all Americans. Our national debt, while probably not gone, will be dropping daily as a result of the millions in revenues generated by the lottery and, thanks to the reform of Social Security, will be spared a $14 trillion blow-up. And we won't have to rely on annual budget surpluses real or fiscally fudged ones, to pay off the debt or to keep Social Security from collapse. Then, if the economic growth of the last eight years continues, we can put the increased tax revenues towards future goals rather than gambling on these uncertain gains to pay off an old debt.

President Clinton proposed a partial privatization plan in his 1999 State of the Union address. It was more smoke and mirrors. To begin with, Clinton opposed reform for as long as he could, arguing publicly for the first term and a half he was in office that the system wasn't even in fiscal imbalance. Now that he can't say that with a straight face, he's proposing a "partial" privatization. But he still wants to have his cake and eat it too, hoping to remedy Social Security without a complete overhaul. It's all politics.

Democrats used to oppose any changes to Social Security. Now they're starting to jump on the bandwagon for a half-baked reform, hoping to win votes—especially of the Baby Boomers—without really making the tough choices that would fix Social Security. Meanwhile, Republicans, some of whom were open to reforms before when they were unlikely, are now taking the place of the Democrats, arguing that Democrats want to destroy Social Security. Again, a cheap ploy for more votes from scared senior citizens.

The bottom line is this: There can be no partial remedies. Partial privatization will not solve the problem, it just will give us a false sense of security. Sooner or later we have to bite the bullet, admit the Social Security system is fundamentally and structurally unsound—not just fiscally and temporarily out of balance—and completely restructure it. No partial remedies. No keeping what we have for the most part but adding in a little variation. We can shift to a fully privatized system gradually and with sufficient regulatory controls to guard against disaster, but we have to make the shift—completely and to full privatization. And we have to begin immediately.

Starting as soon as possible, some portion of the current 12.4 percent payroll tax we all now pay (let's say 40 percent of the total FICA tax burden) should get shifted into mandatory personal retirement accounts for each working American, increasing to 100 percent within ten years. In this way each person would have a privately managed interest-bearing account, like an IRA or a 401K plan but subject to strict federal regulatory controls to ensure the safety of the investments. Then to protect those at the lowest end of the income spectrum, we should set a floor benefit that the government would pay to all workers in the event they didn't generate anything in their personal account.

With the core of the system changed, we also could do some smaller changes to buy a little cushion. We could increase the Social Security payroll tax a percentage point or two, raise the retirement age marginally to something like sixty-eight, and establish limited means testing so that high-income retirees get a reduced portion of their benefits, regardless of how much they paid in.

That approach would be more generationally equitable than the current system, because right now you get a check no matter what. You can be a billionaire and you still get your Social Security, even if someone in much greater need isn't getting enough to get by. That's just stupid. I don't care how much you paid in. If you're Bill Gates or Ross Perot, you will never need Social Security. Yes, both men paid in. Tough luck. Their grandkids' futures should come first.

Finally, we should invest some portion of the current Social Security Trust Fund in the stock market instead of in treasury bills where it's now invested and of course prohibit the government from using the "current surplus" to offset other federal spending as it does now. That way, whatever there is in holding will start generating a better return and will be protected from the government's strategy of robbing Peter to pay Paul.

It's true that the private equity market has risks that treasury bills don't, but when the government actually needs to collect the cash on those T bills, beginning in 2011, its credit isn't going to look so good either. Remember, the government already borrowed against those surpluses to pay off other liabilities and lower the deficit; eventually they will have to get that cash back by borrowing more, by raising taxes, or by defaulting on retirement payments to the Baby Boomers—something we all know isn't going to happen. So at the end of the day, what have we got to lose?

Honestly, I'll take my chances on the stock market over the federal government any day, even if it's going to have some slow-growth years. So would most people I know. Even if it wasn't essential because the whole system is going to collapse, it would still make more fiscal sense. Think of it this way: A twenty-two-year-old worker who enters the workforce today at a starting salary of $22,500, works to sixty-five, and dies at eighty would get a cumulative Social Security benefit under the current system of $12,500. How mediocre is that. Yet if that same person invested her wages (at the current 12.4 percent tax) in an annuity, she would have an $800,000 nest egg at retirement that would pay her $60,000 a year. What's to think about? Even if the return was 3 percent in the private market, most workers would come out ahead.

Privatization is not without risk, but nothing valuable in life ever is. There is no guarantee it will work. The current approach is going to fail, however. That is guaranteed. And privatization, whether the exact plan I describe or some variation, has a hell of a good chance of saving Social Security from collapse and thus sparing America a fiscal catastrophe and helping us avoid a massive generational conflict.

Unlike the current federal scheme, a privatized retirement system would be a progressive approach to retirement. The current Social Security system is supposed to be progressive. In reality, it's regressive, costing the wealthy less and paying them more. It's regressive on the payment side, capping taxable income at $72,600, so that the less you make, the larger a portion of your income that you pay in.

For example, if you made $40,000 a year, you would pay 12.4 percent of that entire amount, or $4,960 a year. Someone making $400,000, ten times as much, would pay only $9,000, just 2 percent of his or her total income. That's one-tenth as much of a percentage tax burden for someone making ten times as much income.

After retirement, the same regressive scheme holds true. Social Security pays more to those who have more money to start with. Although the elderly poor tend to get more than they paid into Social Security, they still get less than the rich, who, because they often have other retirement funds, don't even need Social Security. A person in the highest income-earning bracket will get more than twice as much each month as a person in the lowest income bracket gets—even though the lower-income person needs it more, and the system is strained and underfunded. It's just plain stupid.

In generational terms, Social Security is even more inequitable and regressive, paying more today to those in the older generations than it ever will pay to those who are younger. And the younger you are, the worse it is, regardless of how much more the younger among us pay into the system. An average one-earner couple today will get back almost $125,000 more than they—and the employer—put in during the worker's lifetime.

In fact, according to a former chief actuary of the Social Security Administration, 96 percent of retirement benefits payable over the next seventy-five years will go to people who are already alive today. That's very bad news for those not yet born and not very good news for anyone under forty. Even with a significant FICA tax rate increase, beginning in 2025 the average rate of return for a worker born five years from now will be just 1.7 percent. That's using the Social Security Administration's own projections, which historically have been overly optimistic.

So why don't we do it? Why not take the privatization pill and terminate this unwanted pregnancy? Even the Advisory Council on Social Security, which is a statutory body required by law to convene every four years, agreed that some form of privatization was necessary when it issued its last report in 1996. But you know Washington. It's 2000—four years later. Nothing's changed, except that we're four years closer to disaster.

Privatization is necessary to create a system that works, that actually gives you back a fair return on the money you put in. And it would allow us to take better care of those whose lifelong investment isn't enough to carry them through old age—but in a more direct way, by establishing a supplementary fund that is paid from the income tax. At the end of the day, a privatization plan like the one I describe will mean paying a lot less than we pay now, accomplishing a lot more good than we do now, and doing both in a way that is generationally fair, fiscally sound, socially responsible, and, finally, honest.

As for the debt, the lottery is a great way to begin to deal with the monster. In 1997, state lotteries took in $34 billion and net returns averaged between 30 and 35 percent. New York and New Jersey were higher, bringing in 41 percent of the gross to their state coffers. Not bad. A federal lottery could generate twice that, if not more. Who knows given the multiplier effect that would occur as the jackpot got larger and larger. And although a national lottery would pull a little away from state lotteries, the goal is worthy of it.

A national lottery would have the largest jackpot of any lottery in the world, making some people so rich they wouldn't know what to do. But it also would be the most responsible, beneficial, and justified lottery in America. Gambling to save future generations—what could be a better reason to gamble? It also would be a weird kind of fiscal atonement for all those Americans who tolerated the debt buildup and voted for the politicians who did it. DEBTBALL: THE NATIONAL LOTTERY. A lottery to make Powerball seem like chicken feed. But more important, a lottery with a moral purpose: to rescue the economic future of the next generation.

To people who say a lottery is immoral, I say nothing is as immoral as a $6 trillion debt that is growing annually. Not as immoral as a multi-trillion-dollar retirement system that is underfinanced, fundamentally fraudulent, and heading for certain collapse on the backs of future generations. Not as immoral as lying about the state of our national fiscal future, ignoring the warning signs, and waiting for the disaster before taking action.

Our massive debt and crippled Social Security system, and our nation's refusal to deal honestly with these problems, say more about America as we enter the twenty-first century than almost anything else. They show how entrenched we are in the old ways of doing things and how afraid we are to risk the bad we have today for the good we might get tomorrow.

The national debt and the crumbling Social Security system are the products of the past—relics of the twentieth century. They are reminders of how we have already failed, not of how we might yet succeed. And as long as we hold on to them, we hold on to not only what they are in practical terms, fiscal catastrophes, but also to what they represent spiritually, the moral forfeiture of a higher social good and the loss of any real national ideals. Ending the silence, putting a stop to the national denial, would be a salve to our national psyche. It would allow us to stop living a lie, to own the mistakes of the past, and to prepare more honestly for the future. It would allow us to move on. Let's stop pretending about this.

- We do not have a budget surplus; we have a $6 trillion debt.
- We do not have a Social Security Trust Fund surplus; we have an unfunded liability running in the trillions of dollars, and we already have spent what limited and temporary trust fund reserves we did have saved.
- We cannot afford to wait until some undetermined date in the future to deal with these fiscal crises; every day wasted makes a massive crisis more likely. Despite the rising stock market and Washington's rosy election year economic forecasts, we need to take comprehensive and radical action now.
- These problems are not too large or complex to address; there are solutions. It is the political will and moral courage that is lacking.

At the end of the day, Social Security and the national debt are generational issues. For better or worse they define my generation and are the dividing line between the Baby Boomers and everyone who comes after. More than any single indicator they are what set us apart. Like AIDS or computers, they will reshape the world as we know it. They will influence us, defining our social and political priorities, framing how we look at the world and what we learn to think of as possible, and dictating the future course of American society.

If we tackle these generational inequities head on, we will restore not only fiscal stability but also moral accountability in government, and we will lay the foundation for a whole world of social and economic opportunities. If we continue to avoid these "crisis" issues, putting off for as long as we can, the inevitable day of reckoning nonetheless will come. But we will be unprepared to meet it, and we will pay a price that no economist can predict. We will do more than plummet millions into poverty. We will do more than trigger a worldwide depression. We will murder the American dream. That is not a legacy I want to be remembered for.

When I was eleven years old, I kicked a field goal on the goalie in a game of asphalt soccer. She was mad that I had scored, so she lied and said I missed. It was so obvious that it was a joke. Unfortunately for me, one of her teammates was a three-time flunky who should have been in eighth grade, was eight inches taller than me, and had a crush on her. He told me to get on my knees, apologize, and beg her forgiveness. I got on my knees. But I wouldn't say what he wanted. He put his big hand on my head and pulled me by the hair. "If you don't apologize I'll kick all your teeth in."

I'll never forget the next moment. I was afraid and ashamed at the same time. I wished I had never gotten down on my knees in the first place, because then maybe I could have run away or maybe just gotten punched. Now all I could see was his big steel-toed boots. Yeah, I apologized, said I hadn't made the goal, and begged his and her eternal forgiveness, and for the next hour I was happy. I had saved my teeth. But ever since, I have wished I hadn't. I avoided the pain and lots of dental work, but I lost something so much more important—my self-esteem, my integrity, and my inner power. At eleven years old on a grassless asphalt playground in the heart of Milwaukee I lost something it would take years to regain: my faith in myself.

All of us have been cowards at some point in our lives. Most of us, myself included, more than once, whether it involves bowing down to a bully or failing to take a stand for something we believe in. And what I've learned is that the more often I cop out, the easier it gets. Yet each time I act out of fear, each time I don't do the right thing, I lose a little more of who I am and of what I could become. I lose a little more of my best self. That is not the kind of a person I want to be or the kind of a society I want to live in. It is not the attitude with which I want to lead my life or the standard from which I want my nation to operate. I don't want to live like a coward. I already was one. The alternative is so much better.

It was early 1993. Ross Perot had just become the first independent presidential candidate to win 20 percent of the popular vote, running as a 1990's populist. Jon and I met with him high up in the Dallas headquarters of his new company. Perot had campaigned on the platform of fiscal accountability and had even taken the Lead . . . or Leave pledge in the third televised presidential debate. The election was over, but our work was just beginning, and we had come to ask Perot for a large contribution to help support the next phase of our national accountability campaign. Perot heard our pitch, looked at our nonprofit business plan, and then generously offered us a $5 million bankroll—but there was a catch.

Essentially, Perot would help us only if he could own us, by co-opting Lead . . . or Leave in all but name, merging it into United We Stand, his newly founded political movement, and using us tour organization Lead . . . or Leave for his own future personal political purposes. Jon and I were outraged. "Mr. Perot, Lead . . . or Leave is not for sale," I said. "If you're going to give us support, make it an amount you can give with no strings attached." Perot looked at us and smiled. "I thought you boys had principles. And I'm sorry I can't help you."

We were stunned. Here was a guy who had run for the presidency on our issue. He had warned that the runaway debt would destroy the fiscal solvency of the country, and he had castigated Americans for their apathy, saying that what was needed was real citizen-led action. Now here we were, two guys doing it, and succeeding more than anyone had thought possible six months before—and Perot was refusing to help us because he couldn't take us over. Jon calmly but persistently tried to negotiate, again making the case for why supporting Lead . . . or Leave was so vital to what Perot claimed to want for America. But Perot held firm. "A smart businessman doesn't give money to what he can't control," he finally shot back.

What a bastard, I thought. I started to speak and then bit my tongue. What was the point in pissing him off? We might need something from him in the future.

Then I remembered those steel boots.

"Mr. Perot," I said, "you run for the presidency on our issue, you preach to the whole country how the debt and the deficit is killing us and then call on people to get involved and do something about it. Well, Jon and I have dedicated a vital part of our lives to doing this—working seven days a week, reaching into our own pockets to finance the campaign, and standing up to some of the most powerful institutions in the country—and you turn down our request for help because you can't own our organization."

OK, I know I was mad, but what I did next came from a place beyond anger—it came from a place of truth.

"You know what?" I said loudly as I literally pounded my fist on the table. "In my book, Mr. Perot, you owe us money!"

The faces on the two lackeys on either side of Perot had gone white. His temper was infamous, and he didn't like to be crossed. Jon looked over at me with a kind of knowing smile on his face, shrugged his shoulders, and leaned back to watch the fireworks. I braced for the explosion. Perot starred at me in disbelief. Then he leaned back in his chair and broke out laughing. He made a $40,000 donation on the spot and picked up the phone to call the then-chairman of Disney, Frank Wells, to ask him to help us out as well.

Perot changed because Jon and I had been unwilling to back down. We had gotten to him in the first place because we were willing to take risks: We'd pushed him to take the Lead . . . or Leave pledge and then refused to be turned down for a meeting with him. Once in the room, I had found the courage to say the truth rather than back down out of fear. It was an experience that changed me and lent me strength many times over the next two years of co-comman-deering a national political organization. Here was a power-ful man, a billionaire empire builder who had an ego the size of Texas and a temper like a tornado. A guy who got so mad at then–President Jimmy Carter over the fate of the Iranian hostages that he organized his own rescue mission complete with marine commandos. And I had just basically ordered him to donate to our organization.

Believe me, as I thought about it afterward, I wasn't sure what had come over me. But I'll always be glad I did it. Had I bowed my head and walked out, not only wouldn't we have gotten any money out of Ross Perot, but once again I would have swallowed my convictions in order to stay on the good side of a potentially powerful supporter. Once again I would have gotten on my knees to save my teeth, to appease a bully, to avoid the pain of standing up for what I knew was right and true.

It's why Washington's political elite won't tell you the truth about Social Security and the debt, won't take the necessary actions to solve these potential crises before they happen—because they don't want to piss off the powerful senior citizen lobbies or risk losing your vote. And it's why most of us have failed to look more closely at the problems and then to demand the kind of actions that, no matter how hard to accept today, would save us from fiscal catastrophe tomorrow. We are afraid. So we get on our knees and repeat the lies. And for today we save our teeth. But one day, somewhere around 2011, we will have to stop lying to ourselves and deal with the consequences of what we have avoided for so long. We will have to confront the truth about the national debt and the collapsing Social Security system. And we'll be lucky if all we lose is our teeth. Because by then, on top of the havoc that our denial and avoidance will wreak on our nation, we will—all of us—have to look collectively in the eyes of our children and our grandchildren and tell them we're sorry for destroying their future.

No doubt we will rationalize the whole thing, telling them we never thought the situation would be this bad, the consequences so grave. That we heard the warnings but didn't believe them. And that even if we had, it probably already would have been too late. But deep down all of us will know the truth. We were just too afraid to do anything about it. We heard the warnings and ignored them. We had time but waited. It was easier that way. I can't live with that. Can you?

8.

Judgment Day 4:15

TERRI WAS A BARTENDER AT a popular bar in San Francisco. Every night a mix of foreigners, locals, and students packed the small downtown bar, drinking, smoking, and running up tabs. Terri took care of them all. "I have a connection with people. I really do," she told me. "People warm up to me immediately no matter who they are. Customers often just buy a beer and give me twenty. They could be a grumpy person. They could hate life. But they tend to relate to me." Maybe it's her look—a curly blonde with big breasts. Maybe it's that she's worked at the bar for four years and has built up a clientele. Maybe it's that she has a great memory. Terri will remember your name, face, and what you drink, even if she's only met you once. Whatever it is, it worked. Terri averaged $500 to $600 a night in tips, most of which she didn't report.

Terri worked five nights a week, reporting forty hours at $7.00 an hour, for $280 a week. She also reported to the IRS 8 percent of her sales as tips. Last year Terri reported $38,000 ($14,000 in salary and $24,000 in tips). In reality, she made $97,000, $59,000 of it in unreported tips.

Like many people who cheat on their taxes, Terri considers herself a person with a strong sense of right and wrong. But asked whether she felt bad about cheating the government out of so much money, she replied dramatically, "Oh God, no! Maybe I'm rationalizing. But I don't feel that they do anything for me. I think I deserve the money. I earned it." Likewise, when asked about others, she couldn't think of a single person she knew in the bar business who didn't underreport. "Anyone I know in the service industry only gives what they're required."

Heather is a stripper—well, she calls it dancing. She dances in all-nude nightclub in downtown Washington, half a mile from the White House. She is paid a hefty sum of $5.95 an hour from a greedy Middle Eastern nightclub owner to take off her clothes and spread her legs in front of a room of leering men. They, on the other hand, pay her between $400 and $1,000 a night in tips for the privilege to watch, all of which goes unreported.

Heather works between five and six eight-hours shifts a week and reports only the wage income ($250 to $300 a week), which she files as a self-employed "dancer." The approximately $10,000 to $14,000 a month in tips goes in her pocket. In addition, Heather takes legitimate deductions against her income—for costumes (what little of them she wears), spiked heels, manicures, bikini waxing, and transportation, among other "job-related" expenses.

Despite the popular conception that dancers are victims, trapped in an abusive environment, Heather just points to her tip stash and smiles. She sees nude dancing as relatively short term and believes in the end it will enable her to get the things in life she wants. "Already it's enabled me to go to school, buy a house, and pay for my mother to live with me." Besides, she reasons that at the end of the day she'd rather sell her body than her mind, she thinks most of the thousands of DC lawyers, a number of whom she's had the pleasure to meet while on stage.

Terri and Heather are hardly unique. And it's not just bartenders and strippers. Almost everyone I know cheats on their taxes.

Two things about Americans and taxes seem historically and eternally true: First, we hate them—we always have and we always will. It's a safe assumption to say that the vast majority of us, even those who are the most scrupulously honest and strong supporters of government, dislike taxes. Let's face it, the IRS is like the Grim Reaper. It's up there with child molesters and parking enforcement personnel.

Second, most of us, no matter who we are, what we do, or how we lead the rest of our lives, try in some way to avoid paying taxes. Call it whatever you like: cheating, cutting corners, getting even. Justify it and rationalize it however you want. But admit it—we do it. We hate paying taxes, and most of us will do whatever we can not to. Like death, taxes have become inevitable, and few of us are Zen enough to resist trying in some way to avoid Judgment Day. At least with taxes, some of us succeed.

Christine is a first-generation Greek American from Chicago. Her family was part of a small community of immigrants who bonded together to carve out a life in America. Her parents, like those of her friends, wanted to give their kids something better than what they had—and they worked hard, scrimped saved—and cheated on taxes to make it possible.

Christine's dad owns a small family diner. Even as a kid, she knew that the family income was somewhat increased by tax evasion. It was a small setup—low tech—with all the documentation running through a single register that rang up receipts. When a person brought up the check, Dad sometimes rang up the check, sometimes not. The amount of the register receipts was what got reported. The extra cash went to immediate family needs and long-term income generation.

Christine and her family never talked directly about the family's tax cheating, but even as a little girl she was aware that it was going on. She attributes the widespread practice and the corresponding silent acceptance largely to unwritten rules in the Greek community. "They open a restaurant. Yeah, they probably cheat on their taxes. That's just how it is," she says.

Lyndsey was a ballet dancer. In 1989, when she was eighteen years old, she joined the Pennsylvania Ballet Company as an apprentice. When the company toured, Lyndsey received a $36 daily per diem (just under $2,000 for the year). She didn't report this per diem. In addition, Lyndsey worked as a waitress on the weeks she wasn't traveling. She made an hourly wage of $2.01 (yes, really one cent), paid under the table, plus tips. Tips were about $50 a night, for about $200 a week.

In 1989 Lyndsey made about $6,000 waitressing, none of it reported. Added to her per diem, she underreported about $8,000. Does she feel bad? Hardly. "It's such a small amount of money," she says. "Why does the IRS need to know?"

Jill had a skin care business, doing facials and massage in Los Angeles. She wrote off everything, including skin care supplies, equipment, training, and lots of meals. Jill admits to exaggerating what some expenditures were and to writing off a few too many lunches where she was supposedly entertaining clients. Also, she kept no receipts. She even wrote off a trip to Mexico. "Don't ask me how I justified that," she adds. Eventually the pressure built. She got audited, and the IRS, irritated perhaps at the degree of exaggeration and the lack of receipts, basically disallowed all but the most basic and obvious expenses. Jill couldn't pay the resulting back taxes and had to declare bankruptcy.

Jill said that she didn't feel guilty about cheating on her taxes but felt bad about getting caught. "I did feel bad that I had to declare bankruptcy. I felt like a big loser. Joining the ranks of all those slimy people who get our taxes raised." She also learned her lesson. When asked about doing it again, her answer was an unequivocal no. "It's just not worth it. I have enough legitimate receipts. As a single parent, I get a big deduction for my son." Besides," she says, "I'm just too paranoid."

*   *   *

Lou was a junior advertising executive in Chicago when he decided to go to business school at Harvard. Hoping to benefit from the loophole that allows deductions for ongoing education and training when in your same field of business, Lou rationalized that his current job made him a form of advertising consultant, which was contained within the larger category of marketing consultant, which was contained within the larger category of management consultant, the profession he claimed he was going to go into after business school. "I started as a management consultant and will go back to being one," he said. "So as I see it, I deserve the deduction."

Talk about twisted reasoning. But determined to avoid the tax man, Lou wrote off his first year of business school—tuition, books, a computer, supplies, even rent. He filed with a supplementary statement explaining his rationale and plans to take the deduction against future losses. But Lou knew he would never be a management consultant, even when he filed for the deduction in 1995. "When I filed my taxes I had already accepted to law school," he admits. "I knew then I wasn't going to be a consultant."

Despite this knowledge, and three years of law school, Lou intends to hold on to the deduction and use it in the future. When I suggested that his deduction, both then and now, violated the spirit if not the letter, of the law, Lou held firm. "It's all about loopholes," he rationalized. "That's the way the system is designed. If you can position yourself so you can slide through one of the holes, then you're fine."

Ludwig and Kay Schaeffer were opera singers. While in graduate school, they met on the set of *Madame Butterfly* in which they were the male and female leads. They fell in love and got married. After getting their degrees, the Schaeffers moved to

Michigan, where Ludwig became dean of music at a state university. In 1970 the couple decided to go to New York on an opera excursion and, although neither was performing any longer, deducted the whole trip: plane, hotel, tickets, meals. Ludwig and Kay continued this practice from 1970 to 1977, traveling several times a year to different cities in order to see operas. In 1977 the Schaeffers received a letter from the IRS, informing them that they had noticed a series of unusual deductions on their 1977 tax return.

The IRS audited—and the Shaeffers got shafted. Professional expenses were OK, said the IRS, but they were really incensed by the trips. Ludwig and Kay had to payback $10,000 including interest and penalties for all the trip expenses between 1970 and 1977. The sum was so much for them (remember, this was 1977) that they had to cancel a planned three-week family trip to London. Life is hard, isn't it?

Anyway, the Schaeffers were sufficiently chastised—and scared—to stop the practice for twenty years. Then, in 1997, Ludwig and Kay started again. In 1998 they went to New York six times, taking the maximum possible deductions on travel, tickets, and meals and accommodations, all nicely itemized on a Schedule A. Thinking it might bolster their position, they attached a supplementary sheet explaining why each opera they see is one that will never be performed again, so it is a matter of critical professional advancement that they see it. "My colleagues do it every year and I've been scared because of my bad experience," says Ludwig. "You know, I got to thinking, and the IRS is wrong. These are valid professional expenses."

*   *   *

Most people avoid taxes—even to the point of cheating—at least once in their lifetimes, if not more often. We bend the rules, twist the logic, and put the money in our pockets. After all, it's so easy to justify. In fact, it's become not only acceptable to cheat on your taxes, but you're kind of a fool if you don't. Everyone else is doing it, and the whole system is so complicated and unfair anyway. Besides, we all know that the rich get away with murder when it comes to taxes. So why shouldn't we? No matter what the government or the papers or the lawyers tell you, the truth is that the rich are not paying the same share of their income in taxes as you are.

In 1993 Stanley Druckenmiller, a megamillionaire investment fund manager in New York, summed up the attitude and the behavior of most of the rich and powerful in America. When Clinton pushed through his famous first-term tax hike, Stanley responded by adding additional tax attorneys. I don't care what I spend, he told me, I'm not going to give the government any more of my money. He paid a fortune more in legal fees, but at the end of the day his marginal tax burden remained about the same. The lawyers got rich. Stanley got richer. The IRS got almost nothing. But you know what, I couldn't blame him. I'd do the same thing, wouldn't you? I hate the IRS. I hate taxes. I resent how much of my income they scarf up, so relentlessly, so cavalierly.

Taxes in America remain embedded in our national psyche much as they began over 200 years ago with the Stamp Acts and the tea taxes—as a symbol of the unbridled and terrifying power of government, in direct conflict with our notions of personal liberty and a trigger point for hostility toward government and those who administer and collect its revenues. And therein lies the trouble with taxes.

Americans pay nearly 3 trillion a year in taxes, 60 percent more than in 1990. Between 1955 and 1997 the percentage of a median two-income family's earnings that went to state and local taxes combined grew from 7.45 to 11.5 percent, according to the nonprofit Tax Foundation. Federal, state, and local taxes claimed 37.6 percent of the income of a median two-income family ($54,910) in 1997, up from 35.5 percent in 1996. In terms of inflation-adjusted dollars, the $22,521 total tax burden that a median dual-earner family experienced in 1998 was the highest ever.

Think of it this way: The average person has to work until mid-May to pay off her the tax burden. That's almost half a year dedicated just to taxes. Flush it down the toilet. You'll never get it. If you're the average person, you'll spend two hours and fifty minutes of each working day to pay your taxes—two-thirds of it to pay federal taxes, and the other third for state and local taxes. That's more than the amount of time you'll spend working to pay for housing and household items, food, tobacco, and clothing combined. Knock a little off if you don't smoke. According to the Tax Foundation, federal, state, and local governments will collect an average of $26,434 in taxes for every household and an average of $9,881 for every resident. Again, Washington takes the biggest chunk, almost 70 percent. In 1999 federal taxes represented 20 percent of gross domestic product (GDP), the highest peacetime percentage in American history.

In 1993 a Harris poll found that 68 percent of Americans were at their breaking point in terms of the amount of taxes they paid. A Roper Starch Worldwide poll in 1996 found that 66 percent of Americans were dissatisfied, angry, or "boiling mad" about the amount of taxes they paid. It's not surprising. We're paying taxes through the nose. Per capita we're paying almost 20 percent more than we were a decade ago, and there's no end in sight. Well, at least for most of us.

When it comes to taxes, not all men are created equal. The American tax regime, despite the egalitarian nature of the Constitution and national identity on which it is built, is highly income and class sensitive. It rewards those with more income, intelligence, and power. It seems that the more you have to spend, the more you can take advantage of various loopholes in the law—and that the loopholes themselves cater for the most part to higher-income earners.

It's as if there is a several-tiered taxing structure. At the top are the superrich. Whether earned or inherited, they have the resources to avoid, evade, and outright cheat with a minimum likelihood of getting caught and an even smaller probability of having to pay much if they do get caught. For these people, cheating makes sense, both financially and emotionally. If they caught, they hire a good lawyer and maybe suffer a little loss. Emotionally it feels good to know that they are doing their best to keep Uncle Sam away from the family jewels.

At the bottom of the system, subject sometimes to no tax and even eligible for significant credits, are the poor. They are the charitable interest of the tax regime—those without enough to help themselves. Most people see the poor as the group that drains the system, eating up the money that the rest of us pay in. When it comes to hostility around taxes, the poor (and government bureaucrats), not the rich, get most of our wrath. Maybe because with the rich, while we begrudge their good luck, we envy their ability to avoid what *we* all hate.

The we, of course, is the proverbial middle class—the vast majority of Americans who, like me, think we pay too much, get too little, and have no real power against the abusive arbitrary governmental machine called the Internal Revenue Service. It is us, the bulk of the government's revenue base, who are the most disenfranchised and the most ready to support some kind of radical change in the nature of U.S. taxation. If asked, most people will say that they pay too much in taxes. Given the threshold income necessary to live successfully and comfortably in America, many in the middle class really do.

Not everyone is caught in the tax trap. Some people, like Stanley Druckenmiller, figure out how to shield millions of dollars from the IRS, offset expenses that the rest of us routinely pay for out of our own pockets, and, in some cases, ensure that even after death the value of their labors will stay out of Uncle Sam's greedy clutch.

I know someone, for example, who has set up what is called a dynasty trust. The difference between the dynasty trust and the "average" trust is that the dynasty trust is set up in perpetuity, with each new generation of the family becoming beneficiaries. In this way, the trust will never be subject to an estate tax—even after the settlers (the parents) and the initial beneficiaries (the children) die. Then, to make absolutely certain that Uncle Sam gets absolutely as little of his money as possible, upon his death, this man's substantial stock ownership of his company goes to his family foundation and the dynasty trust, leaving only about 3 to 4 percent of his extensive net worth to be inherited—and thus subject to tax—by his children.

All perfectly legal and, if you ask me, justified.

Others, like Terri the Bartender, are able to hide the vast majority of their income from the IRS by a simple deception—and one that almost certainly will go unnoticed. Still others find loopholes and work them until they fit inside, often getting away with large deductions that fit within the letter of the law, even though they violate its spirit. Others, usually those not smart enough to do it the right way, get screwed.

Theodore emigrated to the United States from Poland in the early 1990s. His older brother came to the States before him, and got a job working as a doorman for Donald Trump. Theodore arrived two years later and, with his brother's help, landed a job as a manager of a buildings owned by Donald's father, Trump Sr.

One of the jobs of the super in most New York City buildings is to keep a list of people waiting to move into better apartments. Hoping to move up on the list, it is not uncommon for people to bribe the super, paying anywhere from $400 to $500 for a bump nearer the top. Between four and ten people a year offered Theodore these payments, which he took and didn't report. In addition, Theodore often did repairs for tenants, which they paid him for in cash, plus he received Christmas presents. None of this was reported. Theodore also was responsible for the twenty-four-hour doorman; sometimes when the regulars couldn't make it, he'd get illegal immigrants and pay them out of his own pocket, but often a little less than what the management company actually paid him to pay the doormen. The practices continued for four years, with Theodore illegally pocketing about $20,000 a year on top of his reported $23,000 salary.

Unfortunately for Theodore, he got caught. Probably because of the payoffs and the IRS's more severe approach to underreporting than overdeducting, Theodore was charged with a felony. In the end he got a three-year prison sentence, suspended with community service, plus six years interest and penalty. His total due came to almost $120,000, 50 percent more than the approximately $80,000 he underreported over four years. As a lawyer/accountant friend of mine said, "He was caught in the net. When you're caught in the net, that's what happens." Perhaps what is saddest about Theodore is that he, unlike so many people who do much worse, got punished so severely for something that to most people I doesn't seem that bad. What's more, Theodore came from a country where his actions were not only widespread but perfectly acceptable.

True, Theodore took bribes, but they were no different from the maitre d' taking a twenty to give you a better table. Besides, any accountant will tell you about all kinds of false deductions—whether it's the people who say they dropped off $1,000 worth of clothing at the Salvation Army (but didn't get a receipt) to those who pay their medical bills, don't report that they were reimbursed by their insurance company, and then deduct the expense. And while the IRS may treat these over deductions as less severe than underreporting, in some ways I find them more offensive. After all, they involve active knowing falsification—a deceptive act of commission—not just hiding what you made—more a passive act of omission.

For better or for worse, we are on the whole a nation of tax cheats. And I suspect that most Americans (if not all) in one way or another, in letter or spirit, at some point in their lives cheat on their taxes. People justify their cheating on lots of levels, from claiming not to realize it was illegal to arguing that they probably didn't deduct something the year before that they could have. (I call this lifetime tax accounting: "If I consider what I paid the IRS over all these years that I *didn't* owe them . . .") But underlying all the rationales and reasons we might give, the driving force for our tax avoidance is as American as apple pie: a general dislike of the state taking away our hard-earned money (as if they were the king's tax collectors coming to get tithes) and a corresponding distrust of how the money, once *taken* from us, will get used. As a friend said to me, "If I thought they were going to use my money on education, feeding hungry children, the environment—even infrastructure—that would be different. Instead, my money is being wasted by some bureaucrat who never worked a day in his life. Besides," he added, "any money I don't give them I feel I am putting to better use than they are."

The current system is designed kind of like a flexible web. Unlike, say, a spaghetti strainer with set holes that don't change, it's more like a net that you can stretch out, squeeze, contort. This flexible and weblike nature of the system causes people to break the law, by encouraging them to try to get through the holes. The web catches some people, trapping them like flies for a spider's dinner, but that's generally only those who are either too big to avoid being noticed or those who are just plain stupid or unlucky. It also catches those who don't think in a sufficiently deceptive or criminal way but who nonetheless—and often for completely valid and understandable reasons—break the law in avoiding taxes. What kind of a way is that to finance our government?

All of which leads me to an obvious and hardly new idea: We need radical tax reform. Whatever the statistical findings of equity and distributional balance, few people in America see the tax system as fair. And even fewer think it is effective. A nation with a revenue system that doesn't have the faith or support of the majority of its citizens is too much like the tyrannies of old—tyrannies that America expressly rejected—for my tastes.

So what's the answer?

SOLUTION #8

- **America should eliminate the current complex income tax structure and adopt a single-rate flat tax.**

Right now we have five marginal tax rates and so many loopholes, deductions, exceptions, and shelters that you have to be a tax accountant to make sense of it. The IRS website has 569 tax forms. The IRS needs 62 million lines of computer code to manage the current tax code. There were over 11,000 tax code subsection changes between 1981 and 1997, and the 1997 budget act alone created 285 new sections and added 820 new pages to the tax code.

A flat tax would change all that. A single rate, 17 to 20 percent. No deductions. No loopholes. No exceptions. You'd get a tax form from the IRS (no bigger than a postcard), add up your various incomes (wages, salaries, and pensions), subtract your personal allowances, and pay a flat rate on what's left. To ensure that those at lower incomes don't get hurt, we continue to have generous personal exemptions—so say we exclude the first $30,000 to $35,000 of income for a family of four, and $13,000 to $14,000 for a single person with no dependents. Meaning that if you make less than that in a given year, you don't pay a dime of taxes.

Interest, dividends, and capital gains would not be subject to tax—solving the current problem of double taxation, which happens now when the government first taxes what you earn and then taxes the interest you earn on whatever you save from that money, or when it taxes businesses on what they earn and then taxes the shareholders when they get dividends. Under a flat tax, there would be only one-time taxation. Businesses would be subject to the same tax—on all receipts, less cash wages and any goods, services, or other materials purchased for use in business as well as all capital equipment investments.

It's so simple, obvious, and fair that it seems ridiculous that we haven't already done it. So why haven't we? I'll tell you why. Because taxes are big business in Washington. The Federal Election Commission found that between 1995 and 1996, the thirty-nine members of the House Ways and Means Committee, the primary House tax bill–writing committee, received a total of $14 million in contributions from various political action committees, while the Senate Finance Committee's twenty members got $26.5 million.

That's reelection money, and that money is the main reason they're going to tell us that a flat tax won't work, that it won't be fair, and that somehow the complex, confusing, and indecipherable to all but a tax lawyer or accountant system with five marginal rates, hundreds of loopsholes, pages of instructions, and massive tax forms is better, fairer, and more sensible than a simple, easy-to-understand, across-the-board, one-rate-for-all, put it on a postcard with a stamp and mail it in flat tax.

Once we have a flat tax in place, to make sure Congress doesn't monkey around too much and put it back the way it is now, we also would need to require a mandatory supermajority vote (three-fifths) in both houses of Congress to make any changes—raising or lowering tax rates, adding or subtracting allowances, or adding any loopholes.

Critics of the flat tax will argue that the government will lose revenues; that it will hurt the poor, help the rich, fail to stimulate savings and investment, and be unfair to the middle class. I say they're just afraid of change. All income groups will benefit from a flat tax, with the greatest benefit going to those in the lowest income group. The rich will end up somewhere in the middle, benefited, but not as much as the rest of us. The government will likely get more money, not less, as businesses and people make more economically rational choices, free of the false incentives that now lead them to misallocate resources in order to avoid taxes. And the nearly $130 billion the private sector now spends on compliance can be put to more productive uses.

If you think about it, how can a flat tax be unfair? Take Bill Gates and you. Let's say the flat rate is 17 percent, which is what was proposed by Congressmen Dick Armey and Richard Shelby in 1998. Now let's assume Bill Gates personally makes $10 billion this year. He pays 17 percent of that in taxes—$1.7 billion, with no loopholes like he has available to him now, only whatever personal exemptions we all get. You pay 17 percent too, whether you make $25,000, $75,000, or $500,000, again with personal exemptions for you and any dependents. Same for the poorest person in America. On a scale of one to ten, with ten being fair and one being a rip-off, how fair does that sound to you? Forgive me if I'm missing something, but wouldn't most people rate it about a ten? A multibillionaire like Bill Gates pays 17 percent on what he earns. You and I pay 17 percent on what we earn. Same percentage for all of us, without exception.

A flat tax seems so completely fair that I can't understand how anyone can argue against it. And most amazingly, I actually can understand it. Which is saying a lot, because I studied tax law for half a year with one of the best tax professors in the country and I still don't fully understand how it all works. So I know that if I don't get it, a whole lot of other people don't either. And it seems to me that our tax system, probably the heaviest financial burden in every one of our lives, should be accessible, clear, and comprehensible to each of us.

In addition to being fair and easy for all of us to under-stand, a flat tax would have administrative and efficiency benefits. My God, think of how much time and money we all spend paying taxes, avoiding them, or, in the case of the gov-ernment, collecting them. A flat tax would increase disposal income for every single income class, with the biggest in-crease going to those making less than $13,000—the people who really need it the most. It also would trigger economic growth. The current federal tax system, which taxes people at rates that vary from 15 percent to almost 40 percent, is a big disincentive to economic growth and a huge incentive to spending money and time to hide, bury, or remove income. A flat tax changes all that, it rewards those who the work the hardest but doesn't penalize those who don't. It would put everyone on an even playing field, while still making sure the rich pay more and the poorest pay nothing.

But even more important, a flat tax would have national psychic benefits. Aside from the cost/benefit analysis both for citizens and the government, its inherent simplicity would go a long way to making people feel they can understand the tax system and, in so understanding, judge its fairness. Under a flat tax, essentially we would move from a case-by-case, or kind of totality of the circumstances, approach to taxation to a bright-line approach. Everyone (with very limited excep-tions for the poor) would pay the same amount. No more stretching the net. There would be no loopholes, no way to hide your income—in this lifetime or any other—and no class, education, or income bias. If nothing else, a tax system that people understand and see as fair will go a long way in reducing class tensions and beginning the restoration of our national faith in government and in those empowered to spend our money for the public benefit.

Real tax reform is more than a fiscal issue. It's not just

about our pocketbooks, it's about the way we view our government and our relationship to it. It deals with the most basic elements of liberty and the issue of what happens to the fruits of your labor or the gifts of your ancestors. When you stop to think about it, taxes, the world's most boring subject, actually have been the source of much of the world's political and social unrest.

A tax revolt gave birth to the United States. Outrage toward the taxing authority of Britain, its willingness to tax people without representation and its use of various taxes to politically penalize and economically bilk the colonists, led not only to the Boston Tea Party but ultimately fueled the tempers that triggered a revolutionary war. Today there will be no war over taxes, there will be no revolution in the streets; but that doesn't mean that taxes are any less relevant to the state of our democracy or to the fate of our nation—to the social, economic and political well-being of our people and of the landscape we will shape for generations to come.

The current income tax system has served its purpose but is now outmoded. It's a product of its times—the twentieth century—and was a benefit to the era in which it was born. Like the current Social Security system or the current prison system, it no longer serves us or promises to advance us. It's a liability, a chain around our necks, a symbol of negativity and hostility. Changing the way we tax ourselves will do more than save us all some time and money. It will begin to rebuild a bridge of trust between Washington and the American people and to open our hearts to the vast social challenges that require our attention, our government's resources, and ultimately our faith in and commitment to that government. If we fail to reform what we have, eventually we will destroy it. If we continue to allow an unfair tax system to fester, it will poison the entire well of government, and give those who hate all government the power to destroy the possibilities that a good and fair government could help us create.

Tax reform is not an academic issue. It can be the wellspring of a millennial politics, the launch pad for a new era of national renewal, civic participation, and social progress. Taxes gave birth to our nation. A new national tax regime can become a vehicle that empowers us and inspires us, creating a system that is fair, just and equal to all. For the first time in decades we won't all trudge toward April 15 with dread. It can help all of us feel more willing to participate and make it easier for us all to believe that the government of our nation is not a negative necessity but a positive hope.

Thomas Paine once wrote that all government is bad but some is necessary. He was wrong twice. A bad government is never necessary and a good government is not impossible, just rare. Lincoln dreamed of a government of the people, by the people, for the people. We can have it if we want it.

9.

Brain Surgery?

DID YOU VOTE IN THE last election?

I didn't. Not because I didn't think my vote would matter. Not because I didn't care. Not because I was apathetic and sick of politics, although any of those would be reason enough. I didn't vote because I had failed to register in time. I'd recently moved, and although I knew I had to reregister, I didn't know by when. By the time I tried it was too late. So I decided to vote absentee. Then I didn't know where to get the form. By the time I got it, I had only a day left to send it in. I misplaced the form that night and left home without it the next morning. By the time I realized my mistake it was too late.

At first I felt like an idiot. Then I thought about it. I wanted to vote. I intended to vote. I tried to vote. Now, if it was difficult for me—someone who wanted to do it, who was well informed, and who is a regular voter—how much harder and less likely would it be for someone who is more apathetic, less informed, and not a past voter?

Did I kill myself trying? No. But why should I have to? Daily life is sufficiently busy and complicated as it is. Why should voting require so much effort? Although I vow not to let the registration snafu happen again, with the current system and my nomadic lifestyle, it probably will. And not just to me. Every time you move, every time you switch residences, even in the same state, you have to register again. And all too often something goes wrong. It happens all the time. Maybe it's even happened to you,

Even if you do manage to get and stay registered, voting itself seems to require an unnecessary amount of work for something that we want to encourage. First there's finding and getting to the appointed polling place—which is usually a local school that you've never been to or heard of or some other obscure and rather depressing-looking public building. Then you have to make sure you get there during the appointed hours (which no one ever seems to know exactly). Once in, you have to wait in line—staring at your watch because you have to be somewhere in fifteen minutes—only to discover that there's some problem with your name. Some states require a voter registration card. Others a driver's license. Some both. Some neither. Some need proof of residence. Others just a signature. God help you if you move too much. Finally you get to do the deed. Now, maybe this is just my pet peeve, but what is up with those ridiculous voting booths. Have they changed at all in the last fifty years? Could they be any less user friendly or more old-fashioned? I feel like I'm going into a Porta Potty to vote.

Voting is the most basic and fundamental activity in a

democracy. So why is so backward, complicated, and low tech? Why is it so hard to do? Why can you vote in only a limited number of public places, and only on the first Tuesday after a Monday in November? In fact, why is the entire political process-from registering and voting, to the rules and structures we use to elect people-so poorly fitted to the society we actually live in? **The 9th of my commonsense solutions would change that: A string of reforms that would make the American political process simpler, fairer, and more accessible.**

MAKING VOTING EASIER

Something is really wrong when less than half of us vote. Some of us don't vote because we don't think it's worth it, don't think it matters, or just don't care. That's a separate problem. For many, however, it's not just our indifference that stands in the way. We have made voting a civic duty, but we haven't made it something that's easy for everyone to do.

Registering and voting should not be an ordeal, an effort, something that requires a lot of time, thought, and energy. It shouldn't be hard to do. It should be hard not to. I was at the White House signing in 1993 of the Motor Voter Act, a bill that expanded voter registration to enable registration with car licenses. The president, flanked by a bipartisan coalition of members of Congress, called it a vital first step. He was right. The problem is that there was never a second step.

- **We should make voter registration automatic upon turning eighteen and make voting more user friendly by increasing the number of ways, places, and days for voting.**

Why not allow voting in more places, both public and private? Why not have polling booths at all college campuses with over 200 students, at shopping malls, and at churches? What about on-line registration and voting? With the Internet so ubiquitous and encryption technology so advanced, there is little reason other than fear to not move toward an on-line electoral process. We could do it gradually, but we're doing everything else on-line, so why not vote?

Why is the election held on only one day instead of over a weekend, giving us two or three days to vote, and not all of them workdays? That way everyone could vote—even those people who are really busy, have crazy stressful jobs, are out of town for a day, or just plain forget.

The truth is, the first Tuesday after a Monday in November was chosen because America was an agrarian society and the writers of the Constitution wanted to avoid harvest time. Then, since it would take more than a day to get to the polls, they made it a Tuesday so as not to interfere with church, and the first Tuesday after a Monday to avoid All Saints Day, a big religious holiday. But like good soldiers, we still have it on that day-the first Tuesday after a Monday, on November Why not pick a day that works better for Americans today rather than for those who have been dead for nearly two centuries?

As for registration—the government doesn't seem to have a problem finding me for my car registration (and that nice fat annual registration tax). They always seem to track me down for any overdue parking tickets, even if I've moved six times. I know the IRS can find me. So can the Selective Service. So why is it so hard to keep me registered to vote?

In fact, why isn't it automatic? Like getting a Social Security number. You're born, the government gives you a Social Security number. So why not the same for voting? You turn eighteen, you get a voter ID number. You get a little voter ID card, and you're automatically registered in a national voter registry, with an 800 number to update your current address easily should you move into a different voting district. Am I missing something? It seems so simple and obvious that it makes me think that the only reason it's not automatic and continuous is that someone with a lot more power than me doesn't want it to be that easy for me to vote.

One way to do it is to assign everyone a number, automatically upon turning eighteen, that stays with you for the rest of your life and requires no reregistration, even if you move. Why not our Social Security numbers, since no two people have the same one? When you show up to vote, you give them the number. Once it's entered into the system, verified with a driver's license, passport, or equivalent picture ID, and authorized with your signature (which the polling place person checks against your driver's license or passport), you can vote. You are automatically registered as a voter in the district that corresponds with your state driver's license or state ID card.

Once your voting ID enters the system, another with the same number can't enter. The national databank verifies the data, deletes obvious fakes, and looks for any duplicates. If it finds them, voter fraud analysts employed by the government and working for the Treasury Department trace the ID and figure out from signatures, addresses, and Social Security numbers who the real person is. I'm not an expert on this stuff, and maybe there's a better way, but if I can come up with something this logical, I think our country's finest in Washington could come up with a way to do this that works.

It's not brain surgery. We're not going to sever a vital organ if we make a little mistake. I know there'd be some technical problems with automatic and mandatory voter registration, expanded polling places, and multiday voting. We could work them out. We've tackled much harder and more complicated problems and done just fine.

The reason registration and voting are so archaic and complicated isn't because they have to be. It isn't because there is no easier or more inclusive way to do them. It's because there's a powerful group of people with a vested interest in the status quo. It's because this is the way we've always done it and not enough of us ask if there's a better way. It's also because when it comes to our participation in politics, the majority of the people who make the laws, the majority of the 535 members of Congress and the president, like things pretty close to the way they are. They don't *want* all of us to vote.

It's not a conspiracy or anything like that, just the realities of the American electoral process. If all of us were registered, if it was almost effortless to vote—if it was hard *not* to vote—then so many more of us would. Just like that. And just like that, there would be trouble for the incumbent class of politicians, all of whom, Democrats and Republicans, benefit from a selectively limited voter turnout and registration. It's the simple economic realities of election campaigning. Incumbents from both parties spend a lot of time and money figuring out how to please various important constituencies, how to raise money from them, and how to win their votes in future elections. The more voters, the more work to get reelected. More constituencies to satisfy. More money to raise. More special interests to please.

Even those who claim they want easier voter registration probably say that only because they think that a lot of those who would register would be voters for their party. Neither party wants automatic, universal registration—just cost effective access to voters likely to line upon their side of the partisan divide. If it was easy for everyone to vote and if almost everyone did, think how much more work it would be for incumbents.

First of all, how could they please everyone? They would have to make tough choices, not easily calculated to benefit their reelections, because they'd be facing a much more diverse, divided, and fickle voter base. Second, the whole reelection strategy would be messed up. How could they target all the necessary groups with all the necessary ads and messages? It would be nearly impossible. My God, they'd have to do things that were for the good of the whole, not for a particular constituency that they want to win votes from. They'd have to be leaders. And a lot of them, a whole lot of them, no matter what they said and did, would not get reelected. At a minimum, simplified registration and expanded voting opportunities would be a big disincentive for people to make a career out of politics. In fact, the people who would benefit would be the rest of us, who would now have to make a real effort not to vote.

The sheer act of simplifying and facilitating the registration and voting process would increase the vote more than most of us realize. And that would be even before we started to see the benefits of increased participation—and participated even more.

It's sort of like having a money-back guarantee. When you buy something from a store like Eddie Bauer, if you don't like it you bring it back. Every so often someone brings back something he wore 150 times and suddenly realized he didn't like. The store gives that person back his money. But for most of us, that some guarantee allows us to go ahead and make the purchase even if we're not sure we want to keep it. Usually we're happy with it, so we do keep it and even shop there again. That's why the store has the guarantee—because it works, both for it and for us.

Well, automatic registration and simplified voting procedures would be a little bit of a money-back guarantee on the political process. Washington would give us the chance to see what happens when we all vote—and I think we'd be surprised by the results. Widespread participation would lead to better candidates, a more informed public, and greater integrity in the national political process.

Modernizing and expanding the voting franchise, by ensuring universal, automatic registration and liberalizing the actual voting process, is the first step to increase public participation in our democracy. Making it hard not to vote would mean that a lot more of us would vote a lot more often. That would be good. But procedural changes, as important as they are, won't by themselves be enough to make us all participate—and to make that participation matter.

A FAIRER, SIMPLER WAY TO ELECT THE PRESIDENT

America's national political process is an anachronism—complex, unfair, hard to participate in, and way out of date. When it comes to politics, we're still living in the dark ages, with archaic rules, procedures, and institutions, from parti san primaries and national nominating conventions to the granddaddy of eighteenth century politics, the Electoral College. We've got a bunch of elitist, antique institutions governing the election of the president in the most advanced and supposedly democratic society in the world.

The four-year presidential election is a huge, laborious, and expensive process that few of us understand and less than half of us participate in. It's controlled by two parties that differ little from one another, divide the riches of elected office between themselves, and, with few exceptions, keep alternative voices and views out of power. The whole process is a joke. Why do we have months and months of costly and time-consuming primaries, delegates, partisan nominating conventions, and an Electoral College? Why not a national direct primary—or even no primaries and just a single direct election of the president? No conventions. No delegates in queer hats. No more nineteenth-century political buffoonery.

Here's how it works now. Every four years, the Democrats and Republicans hold a series of state by state primaries to pick a candidate for president. The first caucus is in Iowa in mid-February, followed by the first primary in New Hampshire about a week later. The primaries and caucuses continue until the summer, when the nominating conventions are held, and the Democratic and Republican candidates are formally chosen. I say formally, because what voters actually are doing in the primaries is electing the delegates for the candidate of their choice. The official nomination then goes to the candidate with the most delegates in a pro-forma convention held during the summer. They go through a vote, but it's a joke, because the choice has already been made, months before, and the delegates in the primaries are bound by law to vote for the candidate they represent.

If it sounds ridiculous and complicated, that's because it is. You see, before there were primaries, the delegates used to be chosen in those infamous smoke-filled rooms by party bosses. The state-by-state primaries originally were devised as a way to give voters (well, at least rank-and-file members of the political parties) more say in selecting the party's candidate. Although the primary process succeeded initially at limiting the distortion of political bosses, today they have led to a different kind of distortion in the political process.

Ever since Jimmy Carter won the presidency by building a strategy around winning the Iowa caucuses, candidates have learned that winning the earlier primaries and caucuses—particularly New Hampshire and Iowa, even though those states have a relatively small number of voters—can be key to winning the nomination. Winning Iowa and New Hampshire alone can determine whether a candidate has a shot at the nomination, despite the fact that these states have the thirtieth and forty-first smallest populations of the fifty states. Talk about a disproportionate influence. But frontloading of primaries means candidates are effectively chosen well before the actually nominating conventions, and usually before many or most states have held primaries. Bob Dole really had won the 1996 nomination by March 5, after only nineteen states had held primaries. In 1980 Jimmy Carter and Ronald Reagan both had their nominations locked up by March 20, before half or more of the states had held their primaries. In fact, a candidate hasn't actually been chosen at a convention since 1952. So much for the value of participation.

In response to the disproportionate impact of going first, an increasing number of states have begun to shift their primaries earlier, to try to have more influence in the selection process. In 1996 the Democrats had thirty-three primaries in March and the Republicans twenty-seven. In this year's election, more than twenty states will have their primaries during an eight-day period in early March. It could mean that almost three-quarters of the delegates are selected before the middle of March. And New Hampshire, determined to remain the first primary in the nation, is thinking of moving its primary to November—a full year ahead of the election. All this for a pro-forma nomination that doesn't take place until the summer and for a general election that is almost half a year away.

The whole trend further distorts the already badly distorted political process and leads to all the wrong results; it encourages candidates to spend disproportionate amounts of time and money on very small states and makes for longer campaigns, which cost more money, which has to be raised faster and earlier. All of this makes for an increasingly higher hurdle for less well-known candidates. To be a viable candidate in this election, you probably needed to have nearly $20 million raised by the first of 2000, just to make it through the primaries.

Then there's the national election. Same basic idea as the primaries. Delegates from each state—so-called electors—represent the candidates. Whichever candidate gets the most votes in a state wins that state, and all the Electoral College votes and electors, attached to it. The number of electoral votes differs from state to state and equals the number of members of the House of Representatives in that state (which is based loosely on population) plus two additional electoral votes, one for each member of the Senate. Whichever candidate wins the most electoral votes wins the election, regardless of how the popular vote comes out.

That's the problem. We are not actually directly electing the President of the United States. Just as in the primaries, we're electing the electors, or delegates, who then cast their votes for the president. Whoever wins the majority of individual votes in any given state gets all the electoral votes of that state, regardless of whether that person wins that state by one vote or by 10 million votes.

As a result, someone actually could win a majority of the

popular vote nationwide (by winning big majorities of the voters in a lot of states and then losing closely in several states with large Electoral College votes) and still lose the Electoral College, and therefore the presidency. It happened already, in 1888, when Benjamin Harrison won the presidency over Grover Cleveland, even though Cleveland won the popular vote. And eventually it will happen again, if more of us vote, and when there are more independent candidates in the process.

The Electoral College was set up for a different time and in response to very different concerns. A direct election was considered and rejected. Most likely this was not the founders of our country fear a popular vote but because that weren't sure how to have an informed one, with everyone spread out along the Atlantic seaboard and with the limited communication and transportation systems of the 18th century. On top of that—and here's the real joke—they distrusted political parties and thought campaigning was undignified, so they wanted a mechanism that would avoid both. As a result, they settled on the indirect election process of the Electoral College. Whatever their reasons, the framers of the Constitution set it up so that there would not be a direct election of the president; rather, each state would choose, in a manner the individual states saw fit, a small group of people to select the president. The electors were supposed to cast a vote for the candidate of their choice based on merit, without regard to party affiliation.

Over the years the whole process has changed, supposedly to better reflect our times, but one thing remains the same. We don't actually elect the president directly. Although we have no intention of letting a small group of people actually select the president, we still have a system in place that technically allows a limited number of delegates—or electors—chose the president, based on the majority of votes cast in the state. And that means that someone can become president without winning the popular vote or even a majority of those who vote.

Today almost all states have direct election of the "electors" (Maine and Nebraska are the exceptions), and the way it works is that the candidate who wins the simply majority of the popular vote in a state (that means a majority by one) gets all the electoral votes in that state. But the fact is when you vote for president you actually are voting for an elector who has pledged to support the candidate of your choice, and that person conceivably could—and, on occasion, someone has, seven times in this century and as recently as 1988—cast a vote for someone other than the person the majority voted for.

There are a number of other problems with the way we elect the president. For starters, the Electoral College system overrepresents rural states, since they get the same two extra votes for the number of senators that the big states get. As a result, in 1988 the seven states with the least population carried the same voting strength in terms of Electoral College votes as Florida, with a voting population three times as large. That's democratic.

The current system also depresses voter turnout. Because a state gets the same number of electoral votes regardless of turnout, there's no incentive for turning out more voters. In fact, there may even be a disincentive to have more voters if you are a major-party candidate, since with fewer voters a minority of voters can determine the outcome of a given state's vote, something that wouldn't be possible with a direct election, one-person, one-vote, you-must-win-a-majority-to-be-president approach.

Finally, the current system doesn't require that you win a

majority of the voters to win the election. It's already happened fifteen times, including both of President Clinton's
electoral victories, and with Nixon in 1968 and Kennedy in
1960. These guys all won with less than 50 percent of the
total popular vote—meaning that a minority of those who
actually voted voted for the person who won. Something is
just not right with that.

The whole setup is archaic and deceptive. Most people
think we have a direct election or something close to it. So
why do we keep in place a system that was designed for an
indirect election—one that was intended to allow a very
small number of people to make a choice on the public's
behalf? That's not what we do today, elect a handful of people to choose for us, so let's get rid of the vehicle—the Electoral College—that was set up for that purpose and put in
place a system that reflects the way we think and make decisions in a modern democratic society.

- **We should eliminate state-by-state primaries,
  nominating conventions and delegates, and the
  Electoral College and instead have a single, direct
  national election for president.**

A single big national election in November. A direct vote.
Whoever gets a majority of our votes wins. No more state-by-
state primaries that give lopsided weight to a tiny state like
New Hampshire or allow a candidate to win the nomination
after less than half the states have held primaries.

No more fifty-four votes if you win California, three if
you win Montana or Vermont. Just a pure one-person, one-
vote add them all up and the person with a majority wins. In
a modern democracy, it's nuts to have a system where it's
possible that the person who wins the most votes could lose

the election; or where a person who doesn't win a majority of the popular vote can become president; or one in which we vote for electors rather than the candidates themselves.

In the event that no one gets a majority, then there's a runoff. If we're worried about too many candidates, we can set a bar that ensures random loose cannons don't get on the ballot—something like having to have a certain number of signatures by October to qualify. Or we can have a single national primary in July to determine the top five candidates, regardless of party, who would then be on the ballot in November. The point is to eliminate the long, costly, state-by-state partisan primary process that makes the presidential election two years long, lopsided, and unrepresentative, and that ultimately favors the two big parties and the people with the most institutional political power behind them rather than the candidates who might make the best president.

Replacing the Electoral College with a direct election makes total sense. With a direct election, if everyone in California turns out to vote and no one in New York does, California voters will have a greater say in who is president. That's how it should be, giving people an incentive to vote—and making each vote really count rather than the current system in which a simple majority in a state captures all the Electoral College votes for that state. Right now you could turn out 100 percent of the voters in a state and win 100 percent of those votes, and you'd still only get the same number of electoral votes as if you turned out 10 percent and got 51 percent of the vote. That puts a premium on getting just enough votes to win.

Under the current Electoral College indirect vote system, it's almost impossible to win if you don't win some combination of the five to eight states with huge Electoral College votes: California (54), New York (33), Texas (32), Florida

(25), Pennsylvania (23), Illinois (22), Ohio (21), and Michigan (18); and it's impossible to win if you don't win at least one of the eleven states with the most Electoral College votes. That's right, even if you win all thirty-nine other states. In fact, if your opponent wins just a simple majority of the voters in the eleven states with the most Electoral College votes (51 percent in each state), you would lose even if every single person in all the other thirty-nine states voted for you. Something is not right about that.

With a more direct approach, if you turned out every voter in New York, California, Texas, and Florida and won the vast majority of those votes, you might win even though you lost majorities narrowly in twenty other states. And vice versa. And that's how it should be. Whoever wins the most direct votes—not Electoral College votes—from across the nation wins the election. Fair is fair.

Making the shift away from the Electoral College and state-by-state partisan primaries would make campaigns for president shorter and less expensive and give third-party candidates a better chance at winning. And it would have a vital symbolic value as well. By making the whole presidential election process more understandable, simple, and in sync with how we live and think, it will make politics more relevant. In contrast, by keeping the system so complex and arbitrary, even if the result is often the same, we keep politics removed from our daily lives and our practical realties.

Real Campaign Finance Reform

Campaign financing is another major problem with the fairness and accessibility of the political system. But it may not be for the reasons you think. For starters, if you're a dyed-in-the-wool Democrat, don't kid yourself. Although Democrats have done well at projecting an image of being in favor of reform, the reason we don't have campaign finance reform is not because the Republicans don't want it. Both Democrats and Republicans oppose real reform and advocate only those changes they think would make it easier for their own party to make electoral gains. Neither side can take the high ground, and they both use the issue shamelessly to appear committed to changes they have no intention of making.

Second, and this is the big thing, the real problem with our current campaign finance system is not that there are insufficient controls on money. It's that there are too many controls already, and none of them does any good. In fact, just as with taxes, the current rules enable the rich to get elected. The current campaign finance laws allow the people in power (of either party) to stay in power and keep out the little guys with less money, less power, and less access to the big money.

You can thank the Supreme Court for making the whole thing such a mess. In 1976 the Court, in a case called *Buckley v. Valeo*, addressed the constitutionality of a new series of campaign finance laws that Congress had passed in the wake of the Watergate scandal. The Court ruled that you could put all the money you wanted in your own campaign (a political free speech argument) or in the campaign of your immediate family or your spouse (family is a direct link) but that you could only give a limited amount to someone else.

Now, think about it. That means Ross Perot can run for office and spend $1 billion if he wants. He also can put that money up for Ross, Jr., or for his wife. But I can't go to Bill Gates and ask him for the money to run against Ross, Sr., Jr., or the Mrs. Why not? I have to go out to millions of people and raise $1,000 or less while Ross, Jr., can just use Dad's money. That doesn't seem fair to me, since it makes it easier for the rich to run than for the average Joe.

The current approach is inconsistent and ineffective, favoring the rich and those already in power. It's got to be all or nothing. Either you can't give more than a certain amount, even to yourself, or you should be able to get as much as you want from anyone. To say you can't spend an unlimited amount of your own money does seem unfair. So let's lift the arbitrary wall that keeps someone like me from competing with a billionaire.

- **Instead of the arbitrary and convoluted current system of campaign finance laws, we should eliminate all restrictions to campaign financing and require full disclosure, making a level playing field for all candidates.**

The Supreme Court's warped reasoning for the current limits on contributions to anyone who is not a family member comes from a fear that if I could go to Bill Gates and get $1 million he would control me. I'd be owned and therefore not making independent decisions, which the Court seems naively to believe doesn't happen under the current system of financing in which there are contribution limits. People will be no more or less owned because they get the money from one, ten, or ten thousand people. Power corrupts, and, to that extent, everyone is vulnerable once they get it. The good thing about a no-limits system with full disclosure is that it will make it easier for a wider range of people to get in to start with, an effect that actually will offset the incumbency corruption factor.

Besides, there are so many ways for incumbents to get

around the current limits, from funneling money through official party organizations like the Democratic and Republican National committees (the main political arms of the two parties, which have no limits on what they can give to a candidate or on what an individual can contribute to them), to obtaining large donations from industry groups, special interest political action committees (PACs) and labor unions—that we really couldn't make the system any worse, more unfair, or more susceptible to abuse. Special interest, PAC, and political party contributions influence and control votes in a systematic and institutional way that few individuals, even wealthy ones, can match.

Lifting the current limitation-based approach would enable people without a lot of money or without party backing to get the money to run, something that is almost impossible right now. Under the current $1,000-per-person limit, if you aren't rich, you need to have a huge base to from which to fund-raise or a political party to work on your behalf. That tends to limit who runs and ultimately to limit the range of ideas and the diversity of interests that the political process represents. It also reinforces the two-party system, keeping marginal parties and candidates out.

Beyond the fairness and efficiency benefits, a no-limits system would be easier to understand and harder to abuse. Right now the campaign finance laws are so complicated, obscure, and convoluted that only campaign lawyers and political consultants understand them. Guess who that benefits? I've %ien the system up close during the 1996 campaign when I was a member of the president's National Youth Advisory Board, and during the 1992 and 1994 elections from the vantage point of a watchdog group like Lead . . . or Leave. Terry McAuliffe, the president's campaign finance chairman in 1996, was formerly the co-chair of Lead . . . or Leave's

National Advisory Board along with former Republican Congresswoman Susan Molinari. Jon and I were friends with the director of finance at the Democratic National Committee. We knew countless fund-raisers and campaign consultants from both parties.

Did I ever see anyone directly violate a campaign finance law? No. People weren't that careless or stupid. Did it happen, and did I know about it? Absolutely. It happened and still does—all the time, by both parties. Everyone in Washington knows that. You think the president didn't know he was basically renting out the Lincoln bedroom when he said "bring in the big donors"? Or asking for money to benefit his reelection at those coffees in the White House that you saw the videotapes of? Of course he did. He's the consummate politician. That's obvious. Do you really think he didn't know where that money was going? Or Al Gore with the Buddhist monks? Or the China connection?

The reality of Washington is that the people in power will use any and every loophole they can to get around the rules. The current approach-with a complex structure of limits (try reading through the federal campaign finance law. It's like trying to read *Ulysses*), different classifications of cash contributions (for example, there's hard money, which are contributions used to *directly* aid a candidate, and soft money, which are contributions that are used only to *indirectly* aid a candidate), and bifurcated standards for different types of candidates-is overcomplex, unfair to those not in power, and too easy to abuse if you are in power. The only people the limits really limit are the very people we ought to be helping—the less-powerful, less-party-affiliated candidates who don't happen to be multimillionaires. The Supreme Court thought it was creating a consistent standard, but as usual it followed an academic and intellectual logic, completely devoid of any practical analysis based on what really happens in Washington.

Besides, winning an election isn't just about being seen (something that money can buy you). It's ultimately about making the best case and making sure people hear it (something that money also can help you do, but that is almost impossible to do without money). We're not a bunch of idiots. If Ross Perot put up the money for some fascist crackpot to run, no matter how much he spent on ads, we'd see through it—or elect the person because we wanted a fascist in office.

If, on the other hand, you have a bunch of really good ideas, chances are that not many people are going to know about them under the current system. And until they hear about you and your ideas, they aren't going to be able to give you money. That would change if you could convince a Perot or a Gates or a Barbra Streisand or some collection of rich and famous people to finance your initial efforts. Then millions of people would get the chance to know who you are and to hear your ideas. Then they could decide not only whether to vote for you but whether to help you financially— something that can almost never happen now since it's so hard for anyone but the rich and powerful to get the critical mass to be heard and seen by a majority of Americans.

In the long run, a no-limits approach would enable a broader base of financial support for a wider range of candidates. It would facilitate more political dialogue and a more liberal political process. It's just like any other product. You can't produce and sell it on a large or national scale without a lot of capital. So unless you're independently wealthy or have rich and generous parents, you depend on getting the money from others—investors and venture capitalists.

True, they often take a little equity position, or try to. But it's a good trade-off. Otherwise, only the rich would have businesses. They would make all our products and monopolize all the markets. Which is exactly the way it was in the early 1900s with the railroad barons and the industrial tycoons. Thank God we don't have contribution limits in the commercial marketplace; if we did, we wouldn't have the growth, creativity, and stunning achievements that have characterized American businesses in this century.

That's the real burn of the current system. It's structured, both in terms of the election process and the financing limitations, to keep out anyone who doesn't have the backing of one of the two major parties or millions of dollars of personal or family wealth. Maybe some of the Founding Fathers wanted to exclude commoners from high office, but I don't think we do. So let's make it a more open and accessible system all the way around. As for the campaign finance laws, somewhere along the way we got it stuck in our heads that free speech means being able to spend whatever you want on yourself and your views but not necessarily on someone else. It's just not true, any more than the notion that you ought to have the freedom to say whatever you want, whenever you want. Free speech is hindered, not aided, by our current lineage-limited finance laws. A more open approach, with unrestricted access to money for *all* people and full disclosure, would facilitate speech and create more diversity in the political process, not the other way around.

Again, it's about getting clear what we want rather than holding to what we have just because we've always done it that way. I want whatever enables the most people, from the most diverse backgrounds, to be able to run and win with the least institutional backing and the least personal wealth. A "no-limits" approach actually would open the process to "average" citizens. You could give to whomever you want as much as you want—with one big caveat: full disclosure. It's all public. You would know exactly who gave me how much and when. I'm not saying you shouldn't run and win if you are rich and powerful. Just that not being rich and powerful shouldn't be a bar to keep others out.

Being affiliated with one of the two major parties does allow some people to beat the money rap, but the parties come with their own strings attached, strings that are not helping American democracy fly. Both parties break the law constantly. They raise millions of dollars as "soft" money (which has no contribution limits but can be used only to indirectly promote a candidate—things such as endorsing an issue, a platform, or a political party) and then shift it to "hard" money uses, effectively promoting candidates with it. (Money raised as "hard" money is subject to contribution limitations, but can be used for whatever purpose you want, including advertising for a candidate. Because of the limits, however, it's harder to raise.) Sometimes the shift is blatant, and probably illegal—that's most likely the story of Al Gore and the Buddhist monks. There's just an assumption that no one will find out and that everyone does it—which is probably true.

Even more frequent—and while not always a violation of the letter of the law, always a violation of the law's spirit—is a campaign finance sleight-of-hand in which candidates and contributors fudge what they consider *direct assistance* to a candidate, or assistance that is intended to directly promote an election effort. That's what happened in 1996 when the Democrats ran ads financed through "soft money" contributions against the Republican-sponsored bill to slow the growth in Medicaid. The ads ostensibly were issue oriented but made it clear that Clinton and most Democrats opposed the bill and that the Republicans who supported it were against old people.

Now, aside from the fact that the ads themselves were disingenuous, inaccurate, hypocritical, and shortsighted (Medicare is part of the generational entitlement nightmare we are going to face and slowing its growth is the only way to keep it from exploding), they were not "issue advocacy" ads as the Democratic Party pretended. What they really were intended to do was to directly help the president and specific Democratic candidates—something you're allowed to do only with "hard money," which has strict contribution limits attached, and which as I pointed out before is much harder to raise. The Sound unnecessarily complicated? It is.

The distinction between hard and soft money, direct and indirect election support, is arbitrary, usually impossible to define, and, in practice, unworkable. Everyone inside the Beltway (except the nine out-of-touch members of the Supreme Court) knows it. The distinction is hard to enforce and works to the advantage of all incumbents—which might explain why, despite all their public bellyaching, Congress never simplifies or erases it. Although both parties want a bigger slice of the total electoral pie, they still do better when it's divided between two plates rather than among three or four—which is what would happen if campaign finance laws were really fired.

So let's eliminate this unworkable distinction, stop trying to force a round peg into a square hole, and accept that the best way to ensure fairness is to keep the system as simple and open as possible—which for starters means eliminating all contribution limits, ending the distinction between different kinds of support, and requiring full disclosure of all contributions and expenditures.

Revamping the current electoral process to make it simpler, fairer, and more accessible is critical to reinvigorating our democracy. All of the reforms I've mentioned would do that. That's step one. But why not make participation itself more direct? We live in an era of instant electronic and satellite communications, where a newspaper is too slow to deliver the news, where the half-life of a computer chip is four months. We vote with our dollars in the commercial marketplace on a daily basis. Yet we get to vote on how our leaders are governing us only every two and four years. Why not give ourselves a little more control?

SOLUTION #10

- **We should move toward having a limited direct democracy by creating a biannual national referendum on a limited number of national issues.**

I'm talking about hands-on decision making, with voters voting on key issues instead of politicians. Think about it. Wouldn't you like to have a more direct say in key issues that involve all of us, have a certain amount of control over the government we send to Washington? Let's give ourselves back some of the power. The shift is already in motion through public opinion polls, but it's completely unstructured and nonbinding. The politicians poll us and then do what they think the majority of us want. We all know that's true. Bill Clinton probably hasn't made a decision in eight years that hasn't been the result of a poll. That's basically how successful politicians in both parties make decisions today.

It's a multimillion-dollar political business. They poll for ads. They poll for positions on key votes. Jesus, they polled on whether to proceed with impeachment hearings and bombing Serbia. When they tell you they aren't polling, then you should worry, because at that point they are spinning spin, and that's scary. The problem with so much polling—other than that it really flies in the face of effective leadership—is that it is not necessarily an accurate gauge of what the public wants. Pollsters ask 500 people a question and then say that's what 200 million people think.

Who are those 500 people? Do they reflect your life and your views? Besides, the questions themselves are so arbitary. Change a word and you get a different answer. Polling might be okay for testing movie endings, but I don't want my political leaders deciding whether to go to war based on that kind of survey. Besides, if that's how they want to lead, I'd rather just have a direct say myself. Eliminate the middleman. Cut out the fat.

Representative government is a good idea, but in practice it's become something of a joke. Our leaders rarely lead. They rarely act on what they think is best regardless of public support or opposition. We all know that. So let's call a spade a spade and take control. They want public guidance, they'll get it—without the option of saying no. Instead of a bunch of random polls with Congress and the president picking and choosing what voice other than their own to follow, we have mandatory national votes on key items that would be included on the ballot at election time. Kind of like the referendum or proposition process many states now have, except that, at least initially, we wouldn't include citizen initiatives—although we could move toward that.

For starters, and to get us and them used to the process, we could limit direct voting to a handful of foundational considerations: tax rates, how to use any budget surpluses, limits on deficit spending. We could do more or less, but the basic idea would be the same. We, the voters, set the limits. They, our "representatives," work within them. Kind of like when a board of directors gives upper management a set of guidelines or when your boss gives you a budget.

We could make it a biannual national referendum, or do it every four years at the presidential election and just include the issues on the ballot. We could begin by using the current ballot process and eventually move toward an on-line or more electronic approach. For example, we could issue every American a Smart Card—basically an intelligent ATM card with a pin code—and let people vote with that card at kiosks located everywhere, from the 7-Eleven to the bank or the post office. Or even at home, if your computer met a national voter encryption standard and had a Smart Card reader.

Giving voters a more hands-on voice in big, across-the-board issues would serve to get us more involved, giving us the power and the responsibility to control the process. I know there are skeptics out there who think the American people can't handle it—and a lot of those skeptics are the people in government. But I believe in us. We would rise to the occasion. Besides, I just don't see the people in office now doing such a great job that we have all that much to lose.

Mandatory and universal registration, extended voting times, eliminating state primaries, and having a direct election for president, a no-limits approach to campaign finance, and national referendums all will help move American democracy to the next level, making it reflect the world we live in rather than lagging behind it. At the same time, ensuring fairness, restoring simplicity, and creating more opportunity for average citizens to participate in the political process will go a long way to getting us off our butts and into the mix. But a part of the task falls just to us and us alone. It is outside of systemic changes, procedural improvements, and even radical political reforms. It's beyond programs and policies—social-economic, social-economic, or political. It's in the heart and soul of us.

There will be no fundamental change. There will be no new politics. There will be no new order in Washington, no constitutional convention, no eliminating poverty, reforming our tax system, turning the clock backward on crime, putting in place an infrastructure to save the next generation. There will be none of it, as long as most of us remain uninvolved in our national political process—literally and symbolically grounded, sitting on the sidelines of our democracy and watching the game like a spectator. No amount of tinkering with the system can change the part of us that doesn't care. And at the end of the day, when all is said and done, that alone is the biggest and most fundamental change we need to make.

It's not just about voting. It's not just about being informed. Anyone can do that. Going through the motions might be easier and less meaningful than not going through them. It's not about issues or ideologies, Democrats or Republicans. It's not about abortion or family values, welfare or laissez-faire. It's not about immigrants or illegal aliens, bilingual education or Western Civ. It's about commitment. Commitment to the underlying ideal that is America. Commitment to this nation, to this people—all of us, whatever our origins, whatever our class. It's about deciding to care, no matter what; deciding to reconnect, no matter how. Do you really care what happens to this country? And if you do, do you care enough to do something about it?

10.

Last Call

IT WAS 1992. BILL CLINTON had just been elected president, promising a new era of politics for a new generation. It was a message that had resounded with younger voters, millions of whom had helped push Clinton into office. And this was their party. The MTV Ball. It was the hottest ticket of the inaugural.

The ballroom at the Washington Convention Center was packed with celebrities, rock stars, political insiders, and big-money contributors. A victory celebration for some, I saw it as a great opportunity to enlist support for the cause. The election was over, but as far as I was concerned the real battle had just begun. One by one Jon and I were making the rounds through the crowds introducing ourselves to people and giving them the skinny on Lead . . . or Leave.

"Mr. Nicholson, I'm Rob Nelson. I don't want to take a lot of your time, but we're working on a really important issue and your help in the future would make a big difference. It's a group called Lead . . . or Leave. We're trying to reach out to younger voters—you know, build on this election and keep them involved—and we need all the help we can get. I just wanted to introduce myself and see if maybe the next time we were in L.A. we could meet with your publicist to talk about whether you might get involved."

Nicholson looked at me and then at the tuxedo-clad escort at his side. "Who the fuck is this? Who is this guy?" His voice was loud now. "Someone get this guy out of my face." I was stunned. It was just about the last reaction I ever expected to get.

"What's your problem?" I responded. "I was asking you to get involved in a really good cause. You can just say no. You don't have to be such a jerk."

He swung around toward his little black-tie entourage. Now he was yelling. "Will someone get this asshole out of my face? Hey, is anybody listening to me? Get this guy away from me."

People behind me started cheering me on. "Don't take that from him," I heard somebody say. "Way to stand up to him," said another. Instantly his entourage surrounded big Jack, shielding him, protecting him from reality.

"Sorry, Mr. Nicholson. It won't happen again," said one of his attendees. "Please, give Mr. Nicholson his space." And then he was gone. Bunch of ass-kissers, I thought. But the memory lingered. His rejection felt like a punch in the face. I wanted Jack Nicholson's attention for a minute, and he freaked out. Why?

Then it hit me. I had broken his cocoon. I had asked him to care. Jack Nicholson isn't that different emotionally from the rest of us, just a lot more powerful. He is one of the few, one of the lucky who will always be OK, someone who can have whatever he wants and, for the rest of his life, keep the world and its problems at bay. And he is going to. He isn't going to use his celebrity to do good but instead to benefit himself. Sideline seats at Lakers' games and the best table at in any restaurant in America. As for everyone else, as Marie Antoinette said: "Let them eat cake."

It wasn't the last time I'd discover the aversion and avoidance from a celebrity. In fact, I found it pretty common. Late one night over a beer on the set of the movie *Tombstone*, Kurt Russell told me that he thought what Lead . . . or Leave was doing was a good thing, but when pressed to do something more active to support it, he took the I-don't-get-this-stuff approach. I'm not the political one, he said. My wife, Goldie, is. Talk to her. I'm just an actor. To be fair, Jack Nicholson and Kurt Russell are just like the rest of us but with well-known names and extra-large lives. Just like Christian Slater, they might appear able to do more, but in reality they probably feel just as disempowered as everyone else. So they disassociate. To some extent, it's what almost all of us do.

Most people I've met, from White House staffers to college students, from investment bankers and multimillionaires to artists and writers, hairstylists and doctors, all have the same reaction as Kurt Russell. "I'm not political." It's become our national mantra. Talk to the hand. I'm not listening. It allows us to wash our hands of the mess, step aside from the chaos, and ignore the disaster we have created. We seem universally to agree that all politics are bad and that almost all people in politics are bad, their motives impure and their ideas limited. And that *they* are the problem.

All this might be true. The problem is that we are they.

We see politics as something separate from us, independent of our lives, our personal experiences—an irrelevant side game that we watch with boredom or amusement but almost never with any personal connection. But the dysfunction in our politics reflects us and reflects on us. There's really no separation. And the disaster we want to ignore is a 500-ton freight train heading right for our lives. We can look the other way, we can close our eyes, but that won't stop the train from barreling over us.

I remember one night, a few months before we officially closed Lead . . . or Leave. I was alone in the offices of our national headquarters. They were small but funky, taking up the third floor of a 100-year-old mansion in Dupont Circle. A dozen Apple computers lined the walls, forming the perimeter of the office space. A huge table of phones in the middle of the room made up the phone bank that was used to call thousands of people across the country. A giant map of the United States hung on one wall—target districts and Lead . . . or Leave chapters highlighted with bright pins. Half-full paper cups of coffee and empty cigarette packs lay scattered; caffeine and nicotine, two telltale signs of frenzied political activity.

I turned off the lights and dropped to the floor in the middle of the giant space we called our War Room. I looked around and considered what we had done. A national political organization built from scratch. Several million dollars raised from people across the country. Thousands of members. Affiliates in every state. We'd had an impact, I told myself. We'd reached millions with our message. We'd helped register thousands of voters. We'd put a critical generational debate on the map. We definitely had had an impact.

But had we? What was different? Had anything really changed? It was 1995. All the enthusiasm of those first Clinton years were gone. A new Republican majority held power in Congress, seemingly more full of hatred and intolerance than of love and acceptance. The Contract for America seemed to be driven by a fear and hostility toward government, and Washington felt darker than I remembered. No one, not even the winners, appeared all that happy. It seemed we had become our worst selves. Governed by intolerance and fear. Loathing the very process that had made us into the nation we were.

I looked up at a picture of me and Jon on the cover of *U.S. News & World Report* from a year and a half earlier. THE TWENTYSOMETHING REBELLION: HOW IT WILL CHANGE AMERICA read the headline. I knew right then. I knew in my head what I head already known in my heart. I knew that we had lost the battle. We were not going to change America. It was going to change us. Tears filled my eyes. I tried to hold back my emotions, but it was useless. I dropped my head in my lap and cried.

I felt sorry for myself, sorry for the dedicated people who had given of themselves for our cause, sorry for all those who had believed in the ideals I had preached so relentlessly. No group of people had worked so hard as the Lead . . . or Leave team. I'd seen it firsthand. No group of people believed so strongly. I'd felt it everyday. And now I knew we were going to lose. And it didn't feel like there was anything at all that I could do about it. I sat there for half an hour, just sobbing. Then I got up, locked the door, and went home. It would be several years before I realized the full extent of what I had experienced and just how painfully and pathetically right I was.

America is at ground zero. Our democracy has bottomed out. We can ignore it, deny it, shift the blame, avoid the responsibility, but none of that changes the fact. Our democracy is on autopilot. We're given up command and we're all just along for the ride. Political participation in any meaningful sense is almost nil. It's politics ultra-light. Sure, some of us vote, but it's a ritualistic act at this point. We know our votes don't really mean anything. We're not changing much, and, for the most part, we're not even trying to anymore. Our indifference and our apathy toward politics and to the great social, economic, and political challenges facing our nation have poisoned the well of public life and left us with a vacuum of leadership and a black hole where there once was a vibrant national discourse. When it comes to politics and the national interest, we are bereft of new ideas, afraid of new approaches, and largely uninterested in the whole affair. We duck the challenges, dodge the tough questions, and put off until tomorrow whatever we can. We expect little from our leaders and even less from ourselves. Entering the first wave of a new millennium, we have never been more locked into the status quo.

Why are we so convinced that things can't be different? Why are we so afraid to try? It's as if we've all become so used to the way things are that we stop even considering new approaches. What's the benefit? We're not winning the war with the current battle plan. So we can either ignore what is happening, which is what most of us do now, or we can try something different. We can grab onto the American ideal with all we have, refuse to quit, refuse to settle, refuse to sit on the sidelines any longer. All it takes is enough of us to say yes. There's really no situation we can't change if we're willing to do whatever it takes, no problem we can't overcome if enough of us are willing to commit to finding a solution—whatever that solution is, however unconventional it is.

The point is this: Some critical problems are not being solved by what we are now doing. The ideas and proposals in this book offer new possibility. I think they will work. If you don't, then help me find others that will. Don't just throw up your hands, turn your head, walk away, and say it's not your problem. We need to deal with the enormous social, economic, and political challenges that confront twenty-first-century America, challenges that my generation and those that follow will have to live with.

We need to deal with a national leadership that is stagnant and incumbent laden. We need to deal with a Constitution that is out of date. We need to deal with a criminal justice system that is broken, archaic, and failing over the long term to deter crime or rehabilitate criminals. We need to deal with the painful reality that we are losing yet another generation of young Americans to poverty, ignorance, and crime, and with the very real possibility that the collapsing Social Security system, trillions of dollars of unfunded liabilities, and a $6 trillion debt will create a fiscal catastrophe in the next quarter century if not corrected now. We need to deal with a tax system that is unfair, ineffective, and morally counterproductive, and with an electoral process that is elitist, unfair, anachronistic, and complex, built for the eighteenth century and not well suited for the world we live in. Perhaps most seriously, we need to deal with the fact that our democracy is broken, and that as long as the majority of us sit on the sidelines, we cannot continue to function as a democracy. We need to deal with these realities and find solutions before it's too late. We need to deal. We *have* to deal!

While we're at it, we could do something else as well. We could take politics in America to the next level and return to the roots of our democracy, to the metaphysical underpinnings of what moved the nation forward in the first place. We could begin again the search for a national ideal, for a driving spiritual force to sustain us, to take us into and through this next millennium. We could put the heart and soul back into our national political process, rekindling our faith in our ideals and our power to realize them.

A couple years ago I spent some time with Richard Goodwin, speechwriter to and close friend of Robert Kennedy. (Goodwin's the guy Rob Morrow played in the movie *Quiz Show*. He told me this story: During the 1968 campaign, Bobby Kennedy told him one night that he realized either he was going to get elected and do the things he was talking about or someone was going to kill him. Well, we all know what happened, but here's the point. Bobby Kennedy may have started out as the trust fund kid of a ruthless and manipulative powermonger with less-than-pure ideals, but, by the time of his death, those who knew him well say Bobby Kennedy had changed. He had started to see the challenges facing America in a new light and realized the potential both of what he could accomplish as president and of what we could as a nation do if we were committed. He realized that the dream was only a dream until we made it real.

One idea can make a difference. There's no magic formula. It's about taking hold of the idea and refusing to let it go. No matter what. What we accomplish and what we don't accomplish is a direct result of what we commit to do. No one is going to single-handedly turn this country around; no one is going to end poverty, wipe out crime, or bring truth and justice to the planet. It isn't that easy. But, collectively, we can have an impact. One by one, each of us can do our part to create a shift in consciousness that will enable the changes we need to happen. That's how real change occurs. Because, when enough of us act individually, the whole system will react accordingly. Likewise, nothing is going to happen, nothing meaningful is going to change, if we all sit on our hands and wait for someone else to go first.

This whole country is the result of a simple idea—that a people can realize their true potential if granted individual liberty, self-government, equality, and the opportunity to pursue their happiness. Our forefathers laid the groundwork and subsequent generations took it from there. Some of it has come easily; some has taken us two centuries to get clear on. We still have a ways to go on fully realizing these tenets. But what an amazing thing: Driven by the spirit of an ideal, the generations before us made America into the most powerful and opportunity-rich nation on earth. So why are we stopping now? Why throw in the towel on democracy when we are five yards from the end zone? Never in history has there been such an opportunity for realizing the true potential of the American ideal.

Martin Luther King, Jr., dreamed of a colorblind society, of full equality between blacks and whites. He dreamed of a day when all men of whatever color could live together in peace and prosperity. He dreamed his dream at a time when blacks were second-class citizens; when there were "whites only" water fountains, rest rooms, and restaurants; when schools were segregated, blacks sat in the back of the bus, and Michael Jordan would have been painting a billboard rather than being on it. He dreamed of a colorblind society at a time when most people thought it couldn't come true. Although King's dream hasn't been fully realized, we're so much closer than we ever would have been if he hadn't had that dream, hadn't believed it was possible, and hadn't asked others to share it with him. King didn't accept the America that was. He believed in the America that could be.

I believe in the America that could be—an America where there are no poor, no prisons, no inner cities, no crack babies, no undereducated children, no longer a Grand Canyon between the rich and the poor. I believe in that America.

I believe in an America that is one nation united instead of several divided in conflict, a nation where we are all engaged, a nation that has rediscovered its ideals, a nation not of the least common denominator but of the highest shared ideal. I believe in that America. I believe in the America that can be more than it is today, can do more than it has done, and with the birth of a new millennium will celebrate a government that truly is of the people, by the people, and for the people. I believe in that America. It is an America of hope, promise, and prosperity for all people, regardless of color, class, gender, sexual orientation, income, and religion. It is an America that will allow future generations to look back on us and on our era with gratitude and inspiration instead of with shame and disappointment. I believe in that America. It is the America I want to live in. It is the America that I believe could be.

Of course it is unrealistic. So was flying across the Atlantic. Or walking on the moon. Or reaching *Titanic*. So was curing polio or stopping Hitler, or ending slavery, or test tube babies and cloning life, or skyscrapers, the Hoover Dam, prosthetic limbs and artificial hearts, or instantaneous communication, breaking the sound barrier, and splitting an atom. So was a 3.59-minute mile, or seventy home runs, or anything and everything that you've ever thought, said, or been told couldn't be done.

No matter what happens, no matter how many people tell me I am wrong, I will never stop believing in this America. It is not the America we are today, but it is the America we one day can and will become. It is not practical, predictable, or even probable. But it is possible. It is a dream, a hope, an ideal—and dreams, hopes, and ideals make the impossible possible, transform what could be into what is, and give us the power to move beyond what no longer belongs.

Why do we accept that some people will always be poor?

Why do we accept that criminals can't be rehabilitated? Why do we accept that our politicians will be skunks, that politics will be dirty, that violence will be the norm, that race will always be a divider? I know that wishing it doesn't make it so, but accepting it does. Nothing can happen if we don't first allow it to. Why are we so committed to what is instead of what could be? Why not set the bar high and miss rather than set it low and make it? Where does that get us? We proved that there could be a vast middle class. What about proving that there can be no lower one? We proved that criminals can be contained. What about proving that they can be changed? We proved that our system of government could last 200-plus years with only minor changes. What about proving that it can withstand some rather major ones?

Something is holding us back. We've buried our idealism, and it's going to take a lot of time and a lot of work and a lot of faith to get it back. It won't be quick. Maybe that's why we wait. The longer we wait, however, the harder it gets. The more accustomed we become to the way things are, the less we see the need, the possibility, and the promise of something different. The ability to change grows more difficult and transformation eludes us, until one day it's just too late.

THANKSGIVING 1988

I'd come back from Washington to spend the holiday with my family in Wisconsin, and were all sitting on the couch in the living room watching the movie *Witness*. As the credits started to roll, I got up to rewind the video. The movie's powerful ending had moved me, so I suggested to my dad that we watch the last scene again. He smiled and nodded. I turned back to the TV, transfixed by the final emotional images of the film. As the credits started to roll again, I turned back toward Dad. He lay hunched forward in his chair, eyes rolled up in his head, green bile foaming from his mouth. I stared at him in horror. A Christian Scientist my whole life, I didn't know what was happening, but I knew it was bad.

I stared at my dying father. Not again, I thought. This can't be happening again. I looked at my mother and my little brother and sister. They sat there as helpless as I. I was no longer a guy in my twenties but a seven-year-old boy who watched his brother die in his father's arms all over again, and I wanted an adult—a savior, someone who could take control, make things right. I wished my older sister were there. Maybe she'd know what to do. I looked at my father again. Everything seemed dark. Please let this be a nightmare, I thought. Please let me wake up. But it wasn't a nightmare, and no matter how much I wished it would, I knew that it wasn't going to go away.

"I'm calling an ambulance," I shouted as I ran into the kitchen, grabbing the phone from the wall and dialing 911. "I need an ambulance," I managed to say to the woman who answered the phone. "My father has had an accident and—"

"This is information," the woman on the other end calmly informed me. "You need to call 911. Hang up and dial 911."

I couldn't believe my mistake. Slightly dyslexic, I've always mixed up numbers, but this was a terrible time to fuck it up. Or was it a subconscious choice? Maybe I was afraid to go against the grain, to defy the religion. I'll only know one thing for certain. It was a fatal mistake. I pressed the disconnect button and waited impatiently for a dial tone. It was probably no more than three seconds but it seemed like twenty.

My mother yelled to me, her voice shaking. "Please, Robert. Hang up the phone. Don't call an ambulance."

She paused. "That is not what your father would want."

I was confused. She was right about my father. Right about what he would want if he could ask for it. But what he wanted would kill him. Prayer didn't save my little brother, and it wasn't going to save my father either. It was now or never.

"No. Mom," I shouted back. "I *have* to call an ambulance."

I redialed—911 for sure this time. As the phone rang, I heard my father's voice—a hoarse, raspy gurgle that still gives me nightmares ten years later: "Rahberrt . . . dohhn't kkall."

The dispatcher answered the phone, I think, but I'm not sure. All I remember is my father's voice—that gurgle—desperate and determined. His last conscious effort. He didn't want an ambulance. He didn't want a doctor. He wanted to rely on prayer.

I hung up the phone and went back to the living room, the good son, willing to put aside my own doubts, my own convictions, and do nothing as my father's life careened off the tracks. We sat there all night praying—me, my mother, my brother and sister—beside my dying father, huddled, like lambs being led to the slaughter. We didn't even know whether it was safe to move him, so we left him in a hard-backed chair, wrapped in a blanket with a pillow beneath his neck.

I tried. I really did. I prayed with all my heart for God to help me. I prayed for Him or Her to hear me, to save my father, to prove my doubts wrong, to once and for all make the nightmare that had haunted me since my brother's death go away. But even as I prayed, I knew my prayers would go unanswered. God, if He existed, was not going to save my father. I was going to watch him die and I had hung up the phone and walked away from the one thing, the one chance, that might have saved his life.

Dad lived through the night, but barely, suffering permanent nerve and brain damage and the loss of most of his speech, the use of one side of his body, and the bulk of his mental reasoning. He became like a little child, and for the next year my father was a semivegetable, in touch with his emotions but in control of little else, trapped in his body with the mind of a child, until he died in his sleep one night.

For a brief moment during that year, my father started to recover—an interlude for which I will always be grateful. But it was short-lived, and with the next stroke he lost what little he had gained and more. The last months of his life were spent futilely trying to communicate with those around him and pathetically struggling to relearn the basic physical and mental skills he had lost. He seemed confused a lot of the time and ashamed of his condition. He still seemed able to express emotion and would laugh or cry often. He clung to my mother, and to one possession, his beat-up old Timex watch. He would stare at it for hours, as if he were waiting for the end to come. Finally, and thankfully, it did.

I felt some relief when my father finally died. At last I could stop seeing him tortured and helpless. At last he could stop crying to my mother about what a burden he felt like. Still, there was a heavy guilt, as if his death were the result of a failure on my part. On one hand, I felt like a traitor—that my lack of faith was part of the reason my father never recovered. What if my faith had been stronger? I wondered. Would that have saved him? On the other hand, I was ashamed that I hadn't found the courage that first night to rise above my past and call for help. Instead, I had hesitated, slipping back to the mind-set of a desperate seven-year-old boy who had watched his brother die—and who, like that little boy, once again trusted and relied on something I knew would fail.

Still another part of me blamed my dad for his stubborn adherence to a set of doctrinaire beliefs. One day shortly before he died, I took him for a stroll in his wheelchair at the nursing home. As I was about to leave he took my hand and pulled me toward him. I looked at his withered hand. It was so frail it scared me. This was my father. Once a healthy, strong man, he had become an infant and an old man at the same time.

"I'm sorry," he said, forcing the words with difficulty from his mouth.

"For what?" I asked.

"Fffor . . . ffforr lleeet . . ."

Tears filled his eyes. His face contorted. The words wouldn't come. Then it hit me.

"For not seeing through this?" I asked, using Christian Science speak for having a religious healing.

A look of shame and anguish covered my father's face as he nodded. I choked back my own emotions. He was dying. I could see it myself, and I could see that he knew it.

"Dad, you didn't let me down," I lied as I pushed him back into the waiting area where a nurse met me.

I hugged my father good-bye and ran to my car. I turned on the radio as loud as I could and sat there and cried. It was the last time I saw Dad alive.

The image of that last day has never left me. Here was my dying father, upset that he hadn't demonstrated his faith and that as a result he thought he had cost me mine. Yet all I wished was that he had never clung so hard to his faith in the first place; that he had never indoctrinated me in it; and that he, me, and my whole family had found the courage to open our eyes and change our minds before it was too late. Had my father had that courage, it would have taught me so much more. By clinging so blindly to his faith, by being unwilling to change even in the face of overwhelming evidence that he should, he had only killed himself . . . and cast a shadow across my world. The most painful part, though, is that he did it all with so much love and so much misguided trust in the system that he had been taught to believe in. He was a gentle man, and a trusting one—and it had cost him dearly for his entire life.

I have forgiven my father for his choices, but I have never forgiven myself for hanging up the phone that day. I probably never will. No doubt, I was honoring my father's wish. It was his life, his choice. But I stood by and let it happen and lost him because of it. I could have taken a different course, but I didn't. I clung to that same blind faith. My father's death was the last straw and the end of my life as a Christian Scientist. Unfortunately, I too had waited too long. The damage was done.

Because I waited, because I was afraid to break the faith, because I clung to the convictions my parents taught me just as they clung to those taught them, I lost a father and a brother and years of my life. It was about being more comfortable with what was familiar to me than with what was right. It was about accepting what was known over what was best, about holding on to what was familiar rather than moving toward what was possible—even if that possibility offered the only hope of real salvation.

America today is doing much what I was doing then, holding on to blind faith—clinging to old ways, outmoded institutions and even failed doctrines—and it is holding us back. We are losing opportunities, people, and dreams. And we are losing precious, irreplaceable time. What are we waiting for a disaster? Is that what it will take? That's what it took to force me to look beyond what was familiar and to be willing to go to the next level, and I don't wish a national equivalent of my personal experiences on America. Not now. Not ever.

Maybe that's just how it is. We wait until it's too late, and then we try to fix the mess after the fact. If we want to wait for disaster, we're going to get it. It's just a matter of time until the social conflicts, economic inequities, and political apathy we have nurtured manifest themselves into a crisis— no matter how much the stock market is rising. It's a waste. There's a better way, a positive way. For once let's preempt the situation. Let's not wait for the crisis. Think of the difference it would make. Sure, we might fuck up. We might make a mess of the whole thing. So what? Staying the course when it's the wrong course isn't a better choice; it's a loser's choice—like the one I made with my father. It just prolongs the pain and puts off the inevitable day of reckoning. The alternative is so much more rewarding.

The hardest part is admitting the mess, acknowledging where we are. It's always easier to pretend we're not in the state we're really in—to just wait for everything to get so bad that we can't ignore it any longer and then hope something bigger than us intervenes. It's easier, but it's not smarter. It's like having unprotected sex and hoping you don't get pregnant. In the political sphere, that kind of gamble plants the seeds of fascism. Look at Huey Long, the flamboyant, authoritarian governor of Louisiana in the 1930s—who, had he not been assassinated, probably would have become president. Look at Hitler in Germany and Mussolini in Italy and Stalin in Russia. They all came at times of enormous chaos and promised stability and order—which they provided, making the trains run on time and the social strife go away, at the expense of millions of lives.

I'm not saying we'd ever have a gulag in America (although we did have concentration camps for the Japanese during World War II, which the Supreme Court somehow managed to uphold as constitutional, so anything's possible), but it's a slippery slope and we're already on it with our law and order, sweep the streets, lock 'em up, put more police on the streets. You don't think it could happen? Go watch *Bob Roberts*. Seriously, if we wait for the bad to get worse, sooner than we think we're not going to be able to control things without some kind of authoritarian type government regime. If we wait long enough, ignore the telltale underlying signs, it will happen.

Imagine this scenario. Throughout the next decade a massive underclass continues to drain America's economic prosperity and social stability. The gap between the rich and the poor, the haves and the have-nots, continues to widen. The seemingly perpetual but ultimately unsustainable stock market rise falters, and the pendulum swings back the other way, toward recession. Then, in 2012, Social Security collapses, triggering a national economic catastrophe and a worldwide recession, which in turn sets off a tidal wave of racial and class strife that explodes in cities across America. Meanwhile, widespread violence, deadly pollution, urban rot, moral decay, and political corruption continue to erode our spiritual and physical well-being, leaving us vulnerable, scared, and desperate. Technology continues to transform our society, revolutionizing many of the things we take for granted and creating an overwhelming pace of change and volume of information—creating the need for information buffers—or interfaces to limit what we see and know. The Bill Gateses and Larry Ellisons of the world now start controlling not only what type of operating system you use but also the information you receive. At first it's all done at your request, but that quickly becomes too much work. Soon we just buy it like we do Microsoft Windows now—except it comes packaged on our TVs. At the same time, all of your personal, criminal, financial, and medical data are on a Smart Card—a minicomputer on a credit card—which allows you access to your money or your records and allows the government access to you. With too much information and too little control, we want answers and someone we can trust to provide them. We want a leader. Who emerges? Some clean-cut, authoritarian, pseudoreligious type who makes conservative law-and-order New York City mayor Rudy Guiliani look like a liberal extremist. With easy control over the information networks, interfaces, and all our personal data, he organizes a massive national cleanup—kind of a cleansing, promising to return America to the good old days of economic prosperity, fiscal and social stability, moral order, and clean, safe streets. He'll clean up the mess—and we'll lose half our liberties in the process.

Extreme? Yes.

Likely? Hopefully not.

Possible? *Absolutely.*

It's arrogant and willful ignorance to think it couldn't happen here. It doesn't have to happen, but it's up to us. At the end of the day, this more than anything is America's millennial challenge. Can we find the strength and the courage to take control before we're too weak and too afraid to stay in control? Are we willing to get back in the driver's seat of our democracy and put this country back on course before Hal is in command and it's too late to turn the autopilot off?

America is in crisis. The crisis is economic, political, environmental, and spiritual. We feel the crisis in our own lives or see it in those around us. It affects our homes, our schools, our churches, and our communities. It is a crisis of action, purpose, and resolve. Deep down we all know that something is wrong in America—that our nation is off course, on the wrong track, in a funk. We can't exactly describe it, but we can feel it. America is in trouble, and those in power cannot or will not do what is necessary to rescue our nation. Neither, we think, can we. Lacking a national vision, a direction, a purpose, we sit frozen in place, watching our nation, our communities, and our lives fall apart. We know in our hearts what is wrong, but do not, we dare not, confront it. We are in denial.

Harsh? Maybe. But if you're honest, doesn't some part of you know it's true? Look around you. Look at what you haven't wanted to see. Listen to what you haven't wanted to hear. Look hard in the eyes of the next homeless person you see. There but for the grace of God is any one of us. Stop and visit an inner city high school. Would you send your kids there? Take a trip to your nearest prison. Can you even pretend that it is the best we can do? Do the math on Social Security and the national debt. Can we really justify putting off systemic changes any longer? Look at our national politics. Why do less than half of us vote? Why do we reelect and endorse leaders who have no integrity, lie to us daily, and shamelessly do whatever will keep them in office, regardless of whether it is good for the country or not? How is it that our standards have fallen so low? Why is that we have grown to hate, ignore, and consider irrelevant the single most powerful and important element of a free people, our democracy?

We can pretend it doesn't matter, but it does. Government by the people, for the people, and of the people is perishing from this earth—slowly, not the by force, not by tyranny, but by abdication—by the willing and consensual acts of a free people. And unless we wake up and do something about it, that freedom will disappear. We will lose it. Not today, not in this decade—but in this century, in my lifetime. More important, if we continue on our current path, we will continue to gut the essence of our country until there is nothing left but a shell—a soulless excuse for a nation, a fragment of a once-great ideal. Are you OK with that? Because we are, all of us, every single one of us, letting it happen. And it will take all of us, every single one of us, in some degree, in some way to do something to stop it. It's not too late. Not yet. But it will be. And when it is, then that's that. Then it's too late.

This book is a call to action. It is a call made in hope but also in urgency. It is a warning and a challenge—a plea to do something before it is too late. It is directed to everyone: young and old, white, black, Hispanic, Asian, rich and poor, powerful and powerless (for none of us is as powerless as we may feel), straight and gay, activists and apathists. It is a call to engage in the process of rebuilding America, to take responsibility for the solution rather than passing blame about the problem. It is a challenge to change. While America's crisis is extensive, it is not insoluble, and the solution, while hard—really hard—is not that complicated. It can be summed up in three steps:

1. Face the problem.
2. Take responsibility for the solution.
3. Make a commitment to action.

FACE THE PROBLEM

If each of us stopped hiding from the truth, stopped avoiding what is going on—if we tuned in, turned up the volume, and began to confront rather than avoid what is happening in

America—we would be able to begin to have a realistic dialogue about the solutions. No longer would we be content to let our political leaders lie to us, hiding or misrepresenting our national problems and promising junk-food solutions, things they know are either bad for the country in the long run or unachievable in the short run. By facing the problem, we would make ourselves ready to see the solution. By facing the truth about our national crisis, we would make it harder for our leaders to lie to us about the remedies. And by having the courage to look our problems in the face rather than to run from them, we would be giving ourselves the inner power to challenge them and overcome them.

TAKE RESPONSIBILITY FOR THE SOLUTION

It's easy to blame someone else for the problems we face as a nation; it also prevents us from focusing on the solutions. At this point it is irrelevant who is to blame—Republicans, Democrats; the rich elites or the welfare queens; management or labor unions; nineteenth-century southern slaveholders or the illegal aliens in California. At this point we need solutions. And until each of us accepts in our own lives some measure of responsibility for the solutions, we will never find them. We can't find a solution while we're all focused on assigning blame. And we won't be able to build a consensus for any possible solutions until enough of us feel invested in the outcome and take some responsibility for making it happen.

MAKE A COMMITMENT TO ACTION

At a minimum, making a commitment to action means we have to stop accepting the status quo. We need to ask more from our leaders and more from ourselves. We need to be willing to accept change in our institutions and to be part of the process of achieving it. We need to be willing to make some short-term sacrifices for some long-term gains—and begin to support policies and politicians who will invest today to help future generations rather than borrow from those generations to pay for today. Each of us can take part in making a better America, whatever shape that America takes.

We don't need more information or better leaders before we can act; and we are lying to ourselves if we think that we can be more effective later on, when we have more security or stability—or that we will get those things at all if we don't join the fight for a better society. America can't win if Americans won't play on the team. Conversely, if each of us gets on the playing field and commits to being part of the solution to our national crisis, we will find that solution and we will achieve it. It's not rocket science. It's just common sense.

It takes only a commitment to start. The rest is process. One day at a time. But it can't just be a few of us. It can't be a partial commitment. It can't be qualified, conditional, or indefinite. It's all or nothing. Fish or cut bait. Shit or get off the pot. Do or die. But if we go there, if we make the commitment, if we reach critical mass, then anything is possible.

In this book I've outlined ten radical reforms that I think would make a difference. All of them address critical problems and would help us make the transition into the next century with grace and power. They're not a comprehensive plan; there is no such thing when it comes to a national journey. But the ideas I've put out there do try to tackle a number of the biggest challenges we're now facing or going to face as a nation in the near future.

There are many possibilities. This book isn't an end but a beginning.

- Some of these proposals could be incorporated into the existing Republican and Democratic platforms, pushing the two main parties from their largely static and barely differentiated places.
- One or more of these proposals could be made part of a national voter pledge that candidates are asked to take in this election or in the 2004 election.
- If enough of us are determined, these ideas even could form the initial basis of a national political platform that a slate of independent candidates runs on for Congress and the White House.
- They could even be the launch pad for a third party, an independent party that promotes a third way: a progressive, postpartisan, populist reform to the current stuck-in-the-mud two-party way of thinking and acting. The Third Party, a sort of nondenominational approach to politics: everyone's welcome, no rigid ideological preconditions on membership, just an openness to new ideas and a faith in the American ideal and the possibilities it offers.

To recap, here are the ten big ideas that I propose throughout the book.

1. Throw everybody in national office out and start again.
2. Hold a Constitutional Convention. In addition to changes in some of the existing amendments— the First, Second, and Fourth—add some new ones, including a fundamental privacy right; an equality amendment; term limits for the Supreme Court, Congress, and the president; and a death penalty amendment.

3. Reform our current approach to crime and punishment by: (a) revamping our prisons to follow a military model; (b) eliminating prison terms for all nonviolent property offenses, replacing them with a system of restitution and community service; and (c) enacting a limited legalizing of drugs, with a federal rehab program to support the large addict population in America.

4. Privatize America's public school system and establish a National High School Exit Test.

5. Launch a Twenty-first–Century War on Poverty— a no-excuses national campaign to cut poverty by 50 percent in the next ten years and to ensure that all Americans (regardless of income) have food, shelter, and basic medical care.

6. Privatize Social Security, establishing mandatory retirement accounts and a gradual phase-out for everyone under fifty-five.

7. Pay off the national debt by establishing a national lottery.

8. Replace the current so-called progressive income tax with a flat tax of 17 percent (with the tax rate subject to a national referendum every two years).

9. Bring fairness, simplicity, and accessibility to the political process by making universal and automatic registration upon turning eighteen, extending voting to three days, eliminating the Electoral College, and adopting a no-limits approach to campaign finance that eliminates all restrictions on donations.

10. Create a limited direct democracy by having biannual referendums on major issues, beginning

with tax rates, use of budget surpluses, and deficit spending limits.

These are big changes. They go to the core of American life,
challenge some well-established, even if faulty, notions about
our society, and would radically change the way some of our
more traditional and sacred institutions operate. That alone
is going to make it hard for them to happen, no matter how
useful, timely, or even necessary they may be. Many people,
especially those in power, will oppose them. Some people
will say what I propose can't be done or that the problems I
want to address can't be solved. Others will say that my solutions are too extreme, that the problems aren't that bad, or
that the changes ask too much of us. There will be those who
challenge my credibility, my knowledge, and my integrity
and some who will simply dismiss me, saying that I have no
right to say what I'm saying. There will always be naysayers.
There will always be those too afraid to try. There will always
be those who will stop at nothing to keep things the way they
are. But they are not all of us.

Millions of people out there want the best for America
and would support a new way—a third way, something that
is between the politics of the right and the left, Democrats or
Republicans, liberal versus conservative framework that we
have grown accustomed to. The current system doesn't represent most of us very well or very often, and it doesn't represent some of us at all or ever. It works for a minority, and it
leaves a majority—a growing majority—disenfranchised, indifferent, and apathetic. So why not forge something new?
Why not make something that speaks to more of our interests, that better reflects the concerns and the realities of our
time? Why not modify the political system so that it repre-
sents more of us, more often, and more effectively rather

than continue with the this-is-how-we've-always-done-it-and-how-it's-meant-to-be approach to American life and democracy that dominates political consciousness in America?

It's the dawn of the twenty-first century. We can make America whatever we want it to be. We are not bound by the rules of our forefathers, by their ideologies, their shortcomings, or their expectations. What do *we* want? It's our nation now, not theirs. Is America everything you want it to be? Have we done the best we can? Is there nothing to improve on? If you think so, then sit back and have a cup of coffee—call it the Seventh Day and take a rest. But if you're not sure, if even some small part of you wants more, better, different, then hold on for that possibility. America isn't over. It's just beginning.

We're at mile twenty-first of our first marathon. We've only ever gone twenty in practice, and right now it feels like we are going to die. We want to quit. We don't think we can make it another five miles. We want to sit down. We want to walk. We wonder why we ever decided to run this goddamn race. But we don't sit down, we don't walk, we don't quit. This is what we trained for. This is what all the hard work was to lead up to. We remember what everyone who's ever run before said: It's in your head. It's the wall. You have to go through the wall. We don't know how to do that, but somewhere deep inside of us we know that we can. Others have done it before us; now's our time. We focus, we force our legs to keep going; we ignore the pain, close our eyes, and pass through the wall.

Afterword

Second Chances

I'LL NEVER FULLY UNDERSTAND HOW or why it happened. From the outside it looked like I had a twin brother.
One day I was on the cover of *U.S. News & World Report*,
going out to dinner with millionaires and movie stars, and
promoting my first book on *Good Morning America*, and the
next I was sitting in the back row of a classroom in northern
California with my hand in the air, waiting for the professor
to notice me—a bottom dweller in the most hierarchical and
tradition-bound institution in American education, law
school. I was broke, anonymous, living in a ratty room in
Palo Alto, and spending a lot of time looking at old pictures.

A year before, several hundred campuses had joined
Lead . . . or Leave's voter registration campaign, 150 student body presidents had attended a national conference in

Washington organized by Lead . . . or Leave, and I stood at a press conference on the Capitol steps surrounded by dozens of student activists, microphones, and TV cameras. I had spoken before rallies of thousands of kids at Virginia Tech and Florida State. I'd walked into the White House with *60 Minutes* cameras following me. I'd had Christian Slater and Val Kilmer take me to dinner, invite me onto the sets of their movies, and join the advisory board of my organization. I'd been a guest on *Nightline*, *The Today Show*, and *Crossfire*. Stories about me had been on all four national news networks, *60 Minutes*, *Time*, *Newsweek*, and the *New York Times*. I'd even done a full-page photo shoot for *Details Magazine* as one of twenty most promising young Americans. And now, not only did no one seem to notice or care who I was—but for the life of me, I couldn't even get arrested.

And then I did.

I was in the campus bookstore, exchanging a textbook for a different one. I couldn't believe how much textbooks were going to cost me. Money was an issue, as I hadn't made much doing Lead . . . or Leave, and law school at a private university, even with the assistance of loans, was going to be a crunch—not to mention the tens of thousands of dollars of debt it would create. I stared at the $50 price tag; it floored me. I had to buy so many of them. It seemed unfair. Then I did something really stupid. I put the book in my bag and walked out of the store. I'll never know for sure what I was thinking, why I was willing to risk so much for so little. I don't think I was thinking. I just did it.

Moments later a security guard stopped me. An hour later I was in police custody. I was taken to the county jail, where I was booked, stripped of my clothes and belongings, given a shower, asked to bend over for a drug check, sprayed with lice powder, handed a prison jumpsuit, a sandwich, a carton of milk, and then marched single file with armed guards and twenty other inmates to my cell block, where I was held for almost twenty-four hours.

As the electronic cell door slammed shut I felt like my whole life had just slammed shut. I looked over at my cellmate, thankfully a small, wiry guy.

"What's a guy like you doing here?" he asked. "Your first time, huh? Can always tell. What did you do?"

"You won't believe me," I said.

"You rape someone?"

"No."

"Drugs?"

No again.

"Hit a cop?" He looked baffled.

"I took a book," I replied. "I shoplifted a textbook from my university bookstore."

"You took a book and you're in jail." He was really stunned. "Man, you got some bad luck."

A day later I was out of jail, but—emotionally—the real imprisonment was just beginning. Legally, everything sorted itself out. I pled no contest to what's called an infraction, less even than a misdemeanor—the equivalent of getting a speeding ticket—and paid a $52 restitution fine. I did not get a criminal record; in fact, an infraction wasn't even something I had to report if I wanted to take the bar.

The real damage was on the inside, however, and was not so easily repaired. The horror of the experience, the humiliation, the forcefulness of the police response to such a small act, overwhelmed me, as did my relative helplessness in the whole situation. It really shattered my self-esteem. But more damaging even than that was what my own behavior made me feel. I had just done something that I would regret for the rest of my life. It was wrong, plain and simple. I knew that, but I could not take it back. I could not undo it. And no matter what, no matter how much time passed, I could not change that fact—and it felt like a moral deadweight around my neck.

A friend pointed out that the owners of the bookstore were being indicted on numerous felonies, including embezzling and misuse of the corporation's funds. What did my small indiscretion mean against that, she asked. But to me, two wrongs didn't make a right. Just because others did the same or worse didn't make my indiscretion any more justified. I knew better. There was no excuse and I wasn't going to try to find one. Instead, I punished myself in a way that no court could, denying myself the right to my dreams, gagging my ideals, and holding the event over my head constantly. It took most of the next three years to get over the daily demerits and the self-criticism I heaped on myself, and I'm still working at it.

I still sometimes want to go back to that day and undo it—start again, make different choices. I probably always will. But I know that I can't. Just like falling off the cliff in the Adirondacks, I can only let go and live in the moment. I can only embrace what is to come, whatever that is, knowing any meaningful possibility results from acceptance, not denial. I'm finally starting to see that and to find the higher lesson from the second big fall of my life.

When I fell off the cliff five years before, letting go had saved my life and launched me on the journey that would define the rest of it. When I slipped off my perch at Stanford, it seemed that I had just made a shipwreck of my life and that everything I ever dreamed of was over. It's taken me three years to find out that the two experiences were just opposite sides of the same coin. One gave me the strength to begin a journey—it prepared me to make a difference. In that sense, the very act of falling empowered me. The other was a hard slap in the face, forcing me to take stock of my life—to confront my weaknesses and to deal with my past. It forced me to make some big changes before it was really too late.

I've had to own a part of me that isn't very noble, a part of me that was weak and that could and did fail. I've had to look deeper into myself than I ever did before, to question how and why I've done things in the past, to challenge anew my values, beliefs, and preconceptions. What I've learned hasn't always been easy. Looking back at my time at the "top," I realize that I, too, often acted with a certain kind of arrogance, a feeling of invulnerability and indestructibility that earned me as many enemies as it did friends. It sometimes made me more brash than wise and in general less open to the changes that might have helped me avoid critical mistakes.

This was especially true with regard to the last year of Lead . . . or Leave. No doubt, we had run into legitimate and, at the time, seemingly insurmountable obstacles. Still, at the end of it all, I realized that I had gambled too much on things working out rather than making some difficult adjustments that might have enabled us to move past the barriers and transition the organization successfully into a new stage—one more fitting the environment of the post 1994 congressional elections.

I'm not saying it would have been easy. From the start we had a lot of people gunning to bring us down, and the more we succeeded in what I will always think was a very admirable mission, the more intense the opposition from all sides seemed to become. Every weakness we showed provoked new attacks. Every mistake we made was magnified by those who had something to gain from our demise. But my own carelessness and unwillingness to confront problems more honestly probably hastened the end, and certainly made it more painful.

At the time, the choices seemed reasonable enough. I feared that showing any weaknesses would undermine our credibility, so I often ignored or downplayed problems. Besides, I feared that if we admitted to making mistakes, it would just give our adversaries more ammunition to use against us—and to hurt the cause we were fighting for. And I feared that if we changed course too much, we would lose our way. So, too often I fought to hang on to things even when they weren't working.

In all these respects I was wrong. Showing weakness makes you vulnerable, but it also enables you to address the problem before it's too late. Admitting mistakes and refusing to live in denial, as difficult as it is, is the key to any kind of meaningful growth. And an openness to change and to new directions, as frightening and potentially disruptive as it can be, is the only way to make progress and to ensure survival. The surest way to kill anything is to prevent it from changing.

As painful as it was, falling down was probably the best thing that happened to me. Through it I am learning what I will need to know to get to the next level in my life. I'm learning what I'm truly capable of—and what I'm most deeply afraid of. I'm also discovering what I'm really made of. Failure is the ultimate test of character. How we respond to it, what we learn from it, whether we have the ability to get back up and try again—that's the measure of a man or a woman and the measure of a country. That's what defines the right stuff.

Just as I've done in my life, America has made some avoidable and costly mistakes. We've sat back on our laurels a little too often, resisted change, and sometimes been our own worst enemy. We haven't always done what we knew was right, and at other times we've done what we knew was wrong. But as I'm learning in my own experience, it's never too late to learn from the mistakes, make amends, and start again. It's never too late for a second chance. Not for me, not for you, not for America.

In Native American culture there's a ritual purification ceremony called a sweat lodge. Somewhat like a modern-day sauna but much more intense, the sweat lodge takes place in a sealed tepee in which participants meditate around a large pile of red-hot rocks while a medicine man throws water and herbs on the rocks and administers the ceremony. The "sweat" is a ritual act of purification—a symbolic cleansing ceremony to purge the body and soul of impurities and to reunite with the earth. Part physical ordeal and part spiritual journey, the "sweat" is also a way for members of the tribe to help clarify their own identities and to make amends with their community. I participated in a modern version of the sweat lodge several years ago. The medicine man was a well-known Native American actor named Floyd (Redcrow) Westerman. He played the old chief in *Dances With Wolves*.

Redcrow sat across from me in the circle, applying herbs and water to the red-hot rock pile in the center. The temperature in the tepee was so hot I thought I'd die. Acrid-herb-infused smoke filled the dark, closed space. The hot rocks fizzled with each new dose of water, the hot steam searing my skin. I wanted to get out, to crawl for the door of the tent, but I remained seated.

Redcrow looked at me and smiled knowingly. He spoke of forgiveness and asked everyone in the sweat to forgive someone. I gritted my teeth, grimaced, and hunched closer to the ground. I wasn't going to leave. I wasn't going to run. I was going to stay and find peace in the pain. More water. More heat. More pain. And there in that suffocating tent, my faced pushed down almost to the ground, I felt my heart lift. For one singular moment I felt above it all, outside of my body, removed from my personal experience. I felt free—at one with the universe. It was just a moment, and then the heat swept back over me searing my skin, burning at the tips of my ears, and parching my breath. I smiled. I wasn't going to leave. I wanted to die, but I wasn't going to leave. Seconds later the door to the tent opened. The sweat was over.

When I look back over my life, it is the unfinished conglomeration of so many diverse, even conflicting experiences. From growing up between a bar and a hippie commune on the East Side of Milwaukee to helping run a family farm and attending high school in rural Wisconsin. From watching both my brother and father die preventable deaths, to narrowly avoiding my own in a situation that should almost certainly have killed me. From creating a national political movement to landing in a jail cell in San Jose for shoplifting. From a mediocre public grade school with concrete playgrounds and bad teachers to Stanford Law School. Good and bad, they made me who I am today, and shape how I see and experience the world. They defined me, influenced me, framed me—as did being among the first of the post–baby boomers, one of those born in the border years between two eras that ten years ago Douglass Coupland named Generation X—and thereby experiencing the America that encapsulates the life of my generation.

I'm in my mid-thirties now. I have grown up in one millennium, and I will grow old in another. I had vinyl records in junior high, a manually operated TV and rotary dial phone, and the Internet was still a top-secret military invention of DARPA—the Defense Advanced Research Projects Agency. Today I have compact discs, DVD, a four-ounce cell phone that I carry around with my five-pound laptop computer and a remote control for my air conditioner. By the time I am an old man, all this will seem old-fashioned as well. My children will be born in a new millennium, they will grow up in a world radically different from the one I did. It will be a world more advanced, with more human promise, potential, and possibility than ever before in history. It is the world of today. How they fare, what they do or do not accomplish, has as much to do with what we do today as what they do tomorrow. It is the foundation we leave them that they will have to build upon. We can set arbitrary limits, we can say that some things aren't meant to be or always will be or just can't happen. Or we can let the future be the judge and give the generations that come after us the foundation to create a more perfect world. We have come so far in such a relatively short amount of time, but with technology, science, and knowledge what it is today, we can go so much further in so much less time. We won't solve all our problems overnight, and some we may never solve. We will never know if we don't try.

Starting over is difficult. I've had to do it a few times in my life, and it never gets easier. But the longer I waited, the harder it got. America has so much opportunity, so much promise, so much hope. It's not too late to begin again. We can't change what we've already done, but we can change what we do from now on. We can take whatever course we want. We have the ultimate power. We have the power to choose.

ABOUT THE AUTHOR

copy to come